American Negro Slavery

American Negro Slavery

A DOCUMENTARY HISTORY

Edited by

MICHAEL MULLIN

UNIVERSITY OF SOUTH CAROLINA PRESS
Columbia, South Carolina

AMERICAN NEGRO SLAVERY: A DOCUMENTARY HISTORY

Copyright © 1976 by Michael Mullin.

First HARPER TORCHBOOK edition published 1976

This edition published by the University of South.Carolina Press, Columbia, S.C., 1976, by arrangement with Harper Torchbooks, Harper and Row Publisher, Inc., New York, New York, from whom a paperback edition is available (HR/1806).

Manufactured in the United States of America

Library of Congress Cataloging in Publication Data

Mullin, Michael, 1938–
    American Negro slavery.

    Includes bibliographical references and index.
    1.   Slavery in the United States History—Sources.
2.   Negroes—History—To 1863—Sources.   I.   Title.
E441.M86   1976   301.44'93'0973   74–7606
ISBN 0–87249–339–3

For Jeannine and Michael

Contents

Acknowledgments

For leading me to documents in Part III, my thanks to Sidney Kaplan, Blake Touchstone, John Price and Margaret Fisher. For the opportunity to write this documentary history, and for editorial assistance, my gratitude to Stanley Elkins, Eric McKitrick, and to Martha, who did all the usual things wives do for their author-husbands.

American Negro Slavery

Introduction

Access to the minds of a bygone people may be made through an imaginative study of their most characteristic institutions.[1] To know the Roman forum, the Gothic cathedral, or the staple-producing plantation is to come to grips with the most cherished ideals and values of classical Rome, medieval France, or the American South.

Plantations and the societies they supported have been described in two ways. Latin Americanists writing about the European dynasties' New World colonies usually describe the plantation itself as a cultural entity—its peoples, organization, and attributes—before placing it in its social and political setting. U.S. historians, on the other hand, usually examine the plantation as an economic entity, and at a later stage of development—as part of a nation, not a colony—and so within the context of the rise of Southern nationalism and the coming of the Civil War. They have also characterized the antebellum South either as an essentially traditional or modern society, and concluded that the plantation was either a kind of feudal manor or a factory in the field. While these arguments emphasize the institution's political and economic impact on nineteenth-century society, they do not provide intimate views of the plantation itself.

But to be an effective guide to the sensibilities of our Southern ancestors white and black, and then to the world they made before the Civil War, the plantation initially should be studied internally and apart from its setting, and then comparatively and over a long period of time. These perspectives highlight the institution's parameters—regional variations in colonial settlement patterns, crops, and marketing practices—while illuminating its center—the relationships among the plantation's major components: organization, work routines, and the roles[2] of planter, overseer, and slave. Most important, this method (which provides a sense of how a historian goes about his craft) is inductive, and squeezes from the raw data the kinds of questions that lead to useful—and reliable—conceptualizations of the plantation and the South. (They are also questions that indicate ways a model may be modified with the infusion of new data and hypotheses: How did historical change of one component of the plantation influence the development of the others? and What were the most important relationships between institution and society?)

This strategy was the basis for selecting the documents; for making a sharp distinction between colonial and antebellum plantations; and for emphasizing plantation organization and the planter's role (an invaluable way of linking the institution to society · and to major historical developments) as they changed through time. This approach also shifted attention from the drama of sectional conflict to the humdrum reality of plantation routines and from the master class to those blacks and whites whose everyday, ordinary existences were massively and profoundly affected by the structures and rhythms of staple production.

Latin Americanists have been more sensitive to the historical, folk, and routine dimensions of plantation life than U.S. scholars. Caribbean area specialists (who are often anthropologists or historians inclined to reconstruct societies ethnographically) have taken a long and comparative view of features common to all plantation regions from the Chesapeake Bay to British Guiana, from the sixteenth through the nineteenth centuries. Sidney Mintz, an anthropologist, argues that in the context of post-Roman European history the plantation was an absolutely unprecedented social, economic, and political institution, which stemmed from the growing European demand for a wider range of foodstuffs and raw materials.[3] The large-scale production of these staples was only feasible in humid tropical and semitropical regions of open resources. Richard Sheridan, an economic historian who has spent a lifetime studying sugar and slavery in the Caribbean, has recently drawn together the indispensable elements of plantation America:

> The New World plantation represented a combination of African labour, European technology and management, Asiatic and American plants, European animal husbandry, and American soil and climate. . . . Animate sources of energy, such as plants, domesticated animals, and Negro slaves, were combined with inanimate energy

captured by windmills, water wheels, and sailing vessels. The plantation was truly an innovation in the Schumpeterian sense. It established new trade routes and shipping lanes, shifted millions of hoe cultivators from one side of the Atlantic to the other, determined the movement and direction of capital, induced the growth of temperate zone colonies to supply intermediate products, produced a class of *nouveau riche* planters and merchants, and became a prize in the contest for power and plenty among the mercantile nations of Europe.[4]

A hemispheric and colonial perspective dramatizes slavery's relentless development, while advancing the useful notion that plantations were a basic force for urbanization. After the Amerindian and later the white yeomanry were destroyed by the mid-seventeenth century, they were replaced by large plantations run by Negro slaves for a small and powerful planter elite (Barbados is the best and most familiar example of this process). Eventually, throughout the Americas in the eighteenth and nineteenth centuries, many big sugar (and some rice, cotton, coffee, and cocoa) plantations became factories in the field, and included processing operations and equipment ranging from crude tobacco-curing sheds to large sugar mills and distilleries. The large-scale, highly rationalized plantation, a remorseless engine of profit and change, transformed economies by creating backward linkages, that is, inducements to investments in such plantation inputs and transportation facilities as ships, farm implements, and slave provisions (clothing and food); and forward linkages, or inducements to investments in industries in the Mother Country that produced consumer goods for the factors who set up shop in plantation towns, ports, and processing and warehouse sectors.[5] In appropriating large areas in which the rural population (slaves or their descendants freed by revolution or emancipation) had to concentrate, in bringing improvements in transportation and communication, and in routinizing work practices and establishing company stores, the great Latin American plantation did "its powerful best to create a factory situation albeit a rural one."[6]

Unfortunately, these arguments have not been fully exploited by historians of the antebellum South, whose investigations of the nature of slavery and the sectional conflict may for convenience be divided into two interpretations. One view presents the Civil War as an inevitable conflict between two social systems, North and South, each with its own territorial base, and as a War for Southern Independence generated by a small, entrenched, and highly self-conscious ruling class, dedicated to the reactionary ideology that slavery was a positive good even though it was economically backward and unprofitable. The world these slaveholders made was essentially patriarchal and premodern ("semifeudal" or "seigneurial"), and based on plantations that reflected this ethos. They were not economically rational (that is, based on the most advanced methods for maximizing profit), because their most important function was noneconomic—enhancing the slaveholders' "aspirations to luxury, ease and accomplishment." Master-slave relationships were cast in the same mold: the typical master, a benevolent patriarch who shunned cruelty and system, dealt with his slaves paternalistically. The most persuasive spokesman for this argument is Eugene Genovese:

> . . . slavery gave the South a social system and a civilization . . . [that] increasingly grew away from the rest of the nation and from the rapidly developing sections of the world. . . .
> The premodern quality of the Southern world was imparted to it by its dominant slaveholding class. . . .
> The plantation society that had begun as an appendage of British capitalism ended as a powerful, largely autonomous civilization. . . . The essential element in this distinct civilization was the slaveholders' domination. . . .
> The planters commanded Southern politics and set the tone of social life. Theirs was an aristocratic, antibourgeois spirit. . . .
> The planter typically recoiled at the notions that profit should be the goal of life; that the approach to production and exchange should be internally rational and uncomplicated by social values; [and] that thrift and hard work should be the great virtues. . . .[7]

In brief, the plantation regime was economically retrogressive, antagonistic to the dynamic commercial and industrial economy of the North, and both reinforced and drew upon the elite's easygoing, leisured, and antibourgeois way of life.

The other major interpretation may be illustrated by Barrington Moore, Jr., who argued that the South was an integral—not an antagonistic—part of the North American economy, and an indispensable contributor to its rapid growth and transformation in the early nineteenth century. In his words,

Up until about 1830 it [cotton] was the most important cause
of the growth of manufacturing in this country. . . . From 1840 to
the time of the Civil War, Great Britain drew from the Southern
states four-fifths of all her cotton imports. Hence it is clear that the
plantation operated by slavery was no anachronistic excrescence on
industrial capitalism. It was an integral part of this system and one
of its prime motors in the world at large.[8]

The Civil War stemmed from a competitive relationship among
regional economies—the West as well as the North and South; but
it was a war between varieties of capitalism—agricultural versus
commercial capitalism. In this framework, the planter was basically an entrepreneur, his plantation a business that systematically
organized labor and capital to generate profits and political
power; and the normal relationship between slaves and their masters was that of labor and management. While the large majority
of slaveholders (who were never more than half of the white
population) owned fewer than three or four slaves, the great majority of bondsmen belonged to the rich. Planters who owned
more than thirty slaves, Kenneth Stampp notes, "were the ones
who achieved maximum efficiency, the most complex economic
organization, and the highest degree of specialization within their
labor forces."[9] Robert Fogel, among other econometricians, has
reinforced the work of Moore and Stampp. Arguing that the rate
of growth of the per capita income in the South exceeded the
national average, and that slavery was the growth stock of the
1850s, he concludes:

Thus when slaveowners invested in slaves, it was not because they
were doddering idiots wedded to an economically moribund institution. Nor was it because they were noblemen who were sacrificing
their personal economic interests to save the country from the
threat of barbarism. Perhaps slaveowners were nobly motivated. If
so, they were well rewarded for their nobility—with average rates
of return in the neighborhood of 10 or 12 per cent per annum. . . .
Perhaps the most startling of the new findings is the discovery that
Southern agriculture was nearly 40 per cent more efficient in the
utilization of its productive resources than was Northern agriculture.[10]

These conflicting views are based on two kinds of sources—
each with its own code words and concepts—pointing to different
realities of slavery. The first view of the plantation regime as pre-

modern and economically backward draws heavily on the writings of a very special segment of the slaveowning elite, those proslavery propagandists, the house intellectuals and politicians, who arrived late on the scene and who, if they were not usually completely separated from plantations and slaves, certainly viewed the system from the studies and verandas of the Great House. If truth is what emerges from a dialogue with our opposites, the apologists' opposites, audience, and message are especially informative. While defending slavery against the abolitionists, for European and nonslaveholding readers in both the North and the South, the proslavery writers were more intimately connected to national culture than they realized. "As industrial capitalism took more and more hold in the North," Moore writes, "articulate Southerners emphasized whatever aristocratic and preindustrial traits they could find in their own society: courtesy, grace, cultivation, the broad outlook versus the alleged money-grubbing outlook of the North." This message, part of a familiar intellectual tradition, was not uniquely Southern: "Such [antibourgeois] notions crop up everywhere as industrialization takes hold, even to some extent without industrialization. The spread of commercial agriculture in a precommercial society," Moore reminds us, "generates various forms of romantic nostalgia."[11]

But there is little "romantic nostalgia" in such antebellum plantation documents as ledgers, account books, daybooks, and farm books. Records of this kind,[12] which clearly support the second interpretation—antebellum slavery as agricultural capitalism—were created by men, working among slaves, for their own information and profit; and they provide a richer, more intimate, and reliable picture of the ordinary reality of slavery and plantations than a view based on the proslavery apologists. The scene inferred from the ledgers is corroborated by another major source—essays for an audience of planters and farmers (in agricultural journals) about the most desirable plantation conditions. Together, these documents are not ideological but are essentially about something much more tangible and immediate to the lives and livelihoods of whites and blacks, who were living slavery and not simply talking about it; namely, the most advanced methods possible for growing staples with slave labor.

But documents from an earlier period indicate that plantation organization was not always so businesslike; nor were relations between planter and slave so comparable to those between modern management and labor. Instead, the web of plantation relations before 1800 was shaped by entirely different circumstances —the planters' reactions to colonial status and "uncivilized" Africans.

Narrowing the focus initially to eighteenth-century sources restores a sense of slavery's development in time and helps resolve the conflicting views of North American plantations. Before Independence, the plantation, as a cog in an imperial apparatus controlled thousands of miles away in Great Britain, was the center of the rich planter's life and his way of achieving a degree of control and autonomy while coping with the psychological as well as the political and economic constraints of colonial status.[13] But following the Revolution and the creation of national sovereignty and an American economic system, large plantations were no longer all-consuming experiences for whites compensating for a sense of powerlessness inherent in colonial status, but rather business enterprises for owners who much of the time lived or traveled elsewhere.

This significant historical change in the plantation's function, critically important if we are to understand how the institution shaped the lives of blacks and whites, is conveyed in the following contemporary descriptions. Landon Carter, a rich Virginian of the Revolutionary generation, said his mansion, Sabine Hall, was "an excellent little Fortress . . . built on a Rock of Independency." Nearly a century later an anonymous contributor to a southern agricultural magazine wrote, "a plantation might be considered as a piece of machinery."[14]

These conflicting images—a fortress, conveying impressions of a rural, self-sufficient landed aristocracy, and a machine, evoking pictures of factories, standardized processes, and interchangeable parts—reflect faithfully the prevailing values and aspirations of their eras, and point to significant developments in plantation organization from the early 1700s to Emancipation and the end of the Civil War in the 1860s.

II

Slavery in the colonial era was not simply a prelude to ante-bellum slavery. In the eighteenth century, particularly, its unique-ness stemmed from processes that had passed from the scene by 1800: the first stirrings of an American nationalism—eventu-ally of revolutionary dimensions—that was shaped by the coming of age of the only landed aristocracy in America, and the accul-turation of Africans, who slowly became Negroes as they changed their Old World customs and adjusted to the cruel realities of plantation slavery. A view of these distinctive attributes, from one eighteenth-century slave society in which planters saw Africans as peasants and themselves as manor lords with a civilizing mission, is provided by a boastful letter from a wealthy tobacco planter to an English earl:

> ... Besides the advantage of a pure Air, we abound in all kinds of Provisions without expence (I mean we who have plantations). I have a large Family of my own. . . . Like one of the Patriarchs, I have my Flocks and my Herds, my Bond-men and Bond-women, and every Soart of Trade amongst my own Servants, so that I live in a kind of Independence on every one but Providence. However this Soart of Life is without expence, yet it is attended with a great deal of trouble. I must take care to keep all my people to their Duty, to set all the Springs in motion. . . . But then 'tis an amuse-ment in this silent Country and a continual exercise of our Patience and Economy.
>
> Another thing My Lord that recommends this Country very much—we sit securely under our vines and our fig trees without any danger to our property . . . [although] we have often needy Governors, and pilfering convicts sent among us.[15]

William Byrd's feudal images and paternalistic attitudes are de-ceptive. For in his or any other colonial setting, "sitting securely under vines and fig trees" was largely wishful thinking. Forced to deal with circumstances unknown to their nineteenth-century counterparts, Byrd and his countrymen talked about patriarchal independence, when in reality they were destined to be colonial planters and slaveowners in a mercantilist empire: as colonists they were obliged to recognize that authority for the most impor-tant decisions for their country originated outside its boundaries in England. As planters they had to submit to the Mother Country's control of manufactured goods, credit arrangements, and prices, and as slaveowners they exploited Africa as a cheap and consistent source of labor, only to realize gradually how thoroughly dependent they were on slaves.

Byrd's idyl was defined by space as well as time. In the midst of British officials and Africans at various stages of socialization, slaveowners pursued wealth and freedom in ways best suited to their local topographic, demographic, and urban conditions. In the tobacco colonies an extensive network of navigable rivers, a chronic absence of town life, and the gentry's ambition to be "independent on every one but Providence" scattered settlers far into the interior of the country, where they built the large and comparatively self-sufficient plantations that were the focus of their lives. Determined to be autonomous, tobacco planters encouraged cultural change among slaves, because their tanneries and blacksmith and carpentry shops required literate, skilled artisans. In Virginia, the oldest area of permanent settlement in British America, "living bravely" on autarkic, self-contained plantations maintained by black craftsmen was an old, resilient tradition stemming from the settlers' Elizabethan origins. In 1649 Captain Samuel Matthews' plantation was described in this way:

> He hath a fine house, and all things answerable to it; he sowes yeerly store of Hempe and Flax, and causes it to be spun; he keeps Weavers, and hath a Tan-house, causes Leather to be dressed, hath eight Shoemakers employed in their trade, hath forty Negroe servants, brings them up to Trades in this house; He yeerly sowes abundance of Wheat, Barley, etc. The Wheat he selleth at four shillings the bushell, Kills store of Beeves and sells them to victuall the ships when they come thither; hath abundance of Kine, a brave Dairy, Swine great store, and Poltery, . . . keeps a good house, lives bravely.[16]

Samuel Matthews was the product of what one historian has appropriately called "the world we have lost."[17] Colonial Virginia, whose values were set in Matthews' days of the early seventeenth century, was part of that world: a premodern society —small-scale, corporate, God-fearing and deferential—in which slaveowners were paternalistic and plantations were manors, "little Fortress[es] of Independency"—that is, once they came to be economically self-sufficient and diversified, as Africans (or usually their American-born children) were assimilated and trained as artisans. In these circumstances, then, the tobacco gentry's patriarchal model for plantation organization was clearly a reaction to a particular time and place.

In the rice-growing region of South Carolina, however, settled more than fifty years later by Barbadians and Englishmen of the Restoration Era, a different kind of river system, a much higher percentage of unacculturated and untrained Africans among all slaves, and one of the largest cities in colonial America produced different relationships between the land and its settlers.[18] The low-country planters, concentrated on a plain of sea islands and marsh that was extremely productive agriculturally but most unhealthy, grew only rice on specialized—not diversified—plantations, employed few black artisans, and spent much of their time in Charleston, the source of the urban goods and services that the Tidewater tobacco planters had to produce on their own plantations. Rice in fact made so much more money than tobacco (the weed's market declined severely after 1750, producing a string of bankruptcies and forcing planters into wheat and general farming) that by mid-century the low country had the highest per capita income in America, and probably the fastest growth rate in the world. By the 1750s a monoculture society had developed, and, in important ways, South Carolina was similar to British West Indian society: that is, a colony characterized by a well-defined urban export area (and a city rather than the plantation as the focus for white society and culture), great fortunes, and extensive planter absenteeism.

III

Further comparisons between rice and tobacco regions, as an indication of what antebellum plantations changed from, should be made from the slave's vantage point. A view from the bottom up accomplishes (as it should) much more than simply a reconstruction of the lives and settings of a neglected and historically silent people. Examining the reactions of Africans illuminates a process (if shorthand is admissible) in which a plantation society once small-scale, corporate, and colonial came to be populous, individualistic, and sovereign; and planters once inclined to be paternalistic fathers became impersonal businessmen.

In the colonial era, slave behavior was largely accounted for by the extent of planter absenteeism and by the slave's origin (birthplace), job, and degree of cultural change (as seen in the most plentiful and reliable sources on slaves, those describing resistance).[19] For our purposes, the relationships between acculturation levels and styles of resistance on the one hand and the planter's role on the other are most informative about comparisons between colonial and antebellum plantations.

Acculturation was the process in which native Africans, while learning English and ways whites would have them behave, changed their customs and became Negroes. This process was marked by three stages and often lasted more than a generation (especially in South Carolina). Native (or "outlandish") Africans, at the first level of socialization, seldom learned English well, nor did they lose the essentials of an African orientation. When forced into field labor, they were called "new Negroes," a second stage of acculturation; and, as they began the slow and sometimes demoralizing process of cultural change, their reactions were dramatically transformed into individualistic rather than collective patterns.

Philosophically as well as socially Africans were aliens, whose acts of rebellion often exposed novel preconceptions and expectations about relations with others and the way the world worked. As a communal and tribal folk, they saw slavery as a temporary misfortune, to be confronted cooperatively—and rejected totally. In the colonial period Africans were the only slaves reported as runaways in large groups who often traveled into the wilds, where they attempted to reestablish village life as they knew it before they were enslaved. But assimilated blacks (especially artisans), the third level of acculturation, typically resisted slavery alone, and in ways that were not nearly as threatening to whites. They ran off and often hired themselves out in cities, where in a labor-starved economy talented runaways (white servants as well as slaves) often achieved a modicum of freedom, which was impossible within the confines of the plantation.

The concept of cultural change dramatizes the historical dimension of slavery, while providing a more precise way of talking about slave behavior. But "acculturation" is a rather stilted, dormant word that does not begin to convey a sense of the tragic confrontation among races in colonial America. The epic European conquest, settlement, and importation of Africans (which brought nearly 200,000 slaves to the eighteenth-century mainland) set in motion massive—also intimate—encounters between blacks and whites that profoundly shaped our basic cultural modalities (sex, diet, domesticity, language, politics, and religion) in ways that are still only little understood.

Documents about Africans in South Carolina are most informative about the unique mood and feeling of colonial slavery. In the Carolina low country, slaves in organized, warlike groups often fled to the frontier or to the Spanish presidio at St. Augustine, Florida, or rebelled and fought back.

In September, 1739, Angolans, who were part of a large and poorly supervised road crew on the Stono River, led one of the largest slave uprisings ever in North America. Although Africans were usually as competent as Indians in surviving in the wilderness, they were occasionally confused by their isolation on the rice plantations, as well as their rapid movement from a west to an east coast, which distorted ways of making the world intelligible (by calculating direction and time). The Stono insurrectionists were no exception. After burning several plantations and killing scores of whites, Sunday night, September 9, their force grew rapidly from twenty to sixty, "some say a Hundred," by additions of "new Negroes." Monday morning they "burnt all before them without Opposition," swept south and west through the hamlet of Jacksonboro, and, later in the day, "thinking they were now victorious over the whole Province," they halted in a field, and set to "Dancing, Singing and beating Drums, to draw more Negroes to them." But the Africans had marched only ten miles to the Pon Pon River, where they were eventually surrounded, scattered, or shot. The rebellion ended after the murder of twenty-one whites and more than forty blacks, but two years later Settlement Indians were still presenting claims to the legislature for rebels whom they had tracked down and killed.[20]

These violent rituals of a society groping toward basic arrangements between races rarely occurred after 1750. Acculturation, which diffused black anger by making slaves less cooperative among themselves, proceeded rapidly. And by the end of the slave trade in 1807, "White over Black," already an intrinsic part of what it meant to be an American in the new nation, was also largely an uncontested reality.

The extent and quality of planter absenteeism—how slave-owners executed the role of master—was another major variable determining slave behavior. Absenteeism was not so much a question of whether or not an owner lived at home, but rather the degree to which the plantation was his base of operations, the way he oriented himself to the world, how much he came and went, and so the extent to which he was personally involved in its daily supervision. Slaveowners whose only home was the plantation, whose families lived among the artisans and household servants of the home quarter (all of whom in turn served as models of cultural change for "new Negroes"), were the real patriarchs in Southern history. Their knowledge of each slave, and willingness to intervene in the blacks' domestic lives, ensured both a faster rate of assimilation and degree of compliance than those whose slaves, supervised by overseers and black drivers, lived among their own.

Africans were in part the creatures of ecological parameters and the overriding objectives of plantation production, but acculturation was a two-way street. Slaves exerted significant influence of their own—and, at a crucial moment, when planters for the first time were helping define American ways while working out the best techniques for growing staples with slaves. In order to curb resistance (which in the colonial period was so often African—that is, persistent, organized, and dangerous), planters soon realized that they must either live at home, or provide a rationalized system of rules, routine, and command, a clearly perceived heirarchy of authority, as a substitute for their own constant surveillance, worrisome attention to detail, encouragement of cultural change by example, and paternalistic treatment of slaves. Eighteenth-century tobacco plantations and the larger antebellum enterprises best illustrate these two ways of organizing staple production for profit, status, and power. (And the situation in South Carolina is more confusing, but indicative of a transitional stage; sources on eighteenth-century rice cultivation, which are so sparse and thin, offer glimpses of the more progressive managerial styles that characterized large antebellum plantations.)

The patriarchal role—which did not survive the sea change from the colonial to the Early National period—was most highly refined in the Chesapeake Bay region. Tobacco patriarchs lived on their plantations and took their fatherly roles seriously, while habitually referring to their slaves as "my people," "my Bondmen," "the black members of my family." They saw slave rebelliousness as a transgression of the Fifth Commandment, "Honour thy Father and thy Mother," and assumed that both master and slave had certain rights and obligations: "I must again desire that you will keep Tommy strictly to his Duty & obedience"; "cruelty to the poor slaves is a thing I always Abhored. I would think myself happy could I keep them to there [sic] duty without being Obliged to correct them." Or "began this morning to enforce my resolution of correcting the drunkenes[s] in my family by an example on Nassau." Patriarchs also controlled the most important decision made for slaves—task allotment, placing them in the house, fields, or workshops. They doctored blacks who were ill and as a matter of course participated in their slaves' family lives, while moving new mates to the same quarter, placing a promising child in a workshop at a parent's request, and generally enforcing their moral codes on the Africans.[21]

But the tobacco planter's execution of these considerable responsibilities was seriously impaired by a failure to achieve real self-determination in the Empire, which in a declining tobacco market sharpened his need to be a competent father, one who saw plantation authority as absolute and indivisible. Masters used trusted slaves to report directly about activities on the satellite quarters, and insisted that overseers treat slaves as they would (that is, "benevolently"), while refusing to give them the means to make crops without "Driveing & Storming."[22] Consequently relations among tobacco planters, overseers, and slaves were typically chaotic, and overseers were especially vulnerable to the field slaves' petty rebelliousness.

Nonetheless the tobacco planter's presence was formidable. His direct supervision of slaves and routine channeled rebelliousness into reactions that were sporadic and noncooperative, into such low-keyed campaigns of sabotage as stealing, tool breaking, and truancy. As the slave population in the tobacco region became comparatively assimilated by midcentury, there were virtually none of those African uprisings that haunted the imaginations of rice planters to the end of the colonial era. In fact in Virginia, slaves at the other end of the acculturation scale, the relatively advantaged artisans, were the most troublesome, first as runaways (not simply "outlying" truants) and then as insurrectionists (who organized Gabriel Prosser's conspiracy in 1800). But in South Carolina planters concentrated their fear of black on Africans, singling out some tribesmen aboard slavers as more dangerous than others; while Virginians in the slave market were unconcerned about the "national character" of particular tribes, since Africans were expected to become Negroes as soon as possible.[23]

The few surviving documents about colonial rice plantations, where absenteeism was extensive and blacks remained African longer, present a different picture of the relationship between cultural change, rebelliousness, and performance of the role of planter. While examining ways of teaching Africans English so they could be more readily proselytized, a Charleston minister for the Society for the Propagation of the Gospel in Foreign Parts momentarily looked into the heart of a distinctive plantation culture. What he saw was

> a Nation within a Nation. In all Country Settlements, they [the slaves] live in contiguous Houses and often 2, 3 or 4 Famillys of them in One House. . . . They labour together and converse almost wholly among themselves.[24]

The nature of absenteeism that made this cultural autonomy possible is illuminated in the Josiah Smith Junior Letterbook (1770–1775), probably the only record of a colonial rice plantation surviving as more than a fragment.[25] Commuting between Charleston and Georgetown (the epicenter of rice cultivation until the 1870s), Smith pursued his own business interests while managing two plantations for George Austin (once a partner with Henry Laurens in the largest slave-trading company in North America), who lived in England. The tone of Smith's letters, and the patterns of authority and decision-making they reveal, were characteristically antebellum: the owner was nonresident, impersonal toward his slaves, and delegated authority rationally; his steward or manager visited the plantation to report on the nature of the market, and on major decisions concerning personnel, equipment, and buildings. Most important, overseers and black drivers (prevalent in antebellum records for large plantations, but in the colonial period mentioned only in South Carolina sources) were clearly in charge of daily activities. So the Josiah Smith Letterbook contrasts sharply with the documentation concerning the old-fashioned paternalism of Chesapeake Bay society.

But tobacco planters were businesslike in their own way. Their intimate knowledge of slaves and planting was essentially the "command experience" so often cited as the basis for their ascendancy at the national level during the Revolutionary and Early National periods. Living as fathers among their black and white families, they were hard-working manor lords, who spent hours a day in the saddle, riding about the only domain in which they enjoyed real power and independence, and scrutinizing overseers, slaves, livestock, and crops:

> Rode out this day. Corn except where the land is very stiff is coming up, and with a broad blade.
> Mill dam in tolerable good order but a little wanting to make things there very strong, and troughs to let the ponds from the runs into the canals run off into the meadow which is to be.
> Making tobacco hills. Potatoes came up, want weeding.
> Fork Corn not quite done in the Peach orchard. Therefore Cotton can't be planted there before next Monday, the old May day.
> Wheat looks tolerable, only a trespass from the Cowpen last Monday night.[26]

Landon Carter, one of the more scrupulous planters, even took to calculating the labor required, per plant per row, in an early time-and-motion study:

> I find it wondered at how any hand can tend 28,000 corn hills planted at any distance. But surely it cannot be reasonable to do so, when it is considered that at 2 feet and 7 an acre holds 3,111 corn hills and at 6 and 5 it holds only 1,452; for it is in such a case evident that at 7 and 2 the care contains more than double to what it does when planted at 6 and 5 by 202 hills. Allow then that at 6 and 5 ten thousand hills only are tended; it will amount to near 7 acres that are worked each hand. Now at 7 and 2, 7 acres will

contain 21,777 so that there only wants 6,223 to make up 28,000. Now that is Exactly 4 hill[s] short of 2 acres. So that the hand that tends 28,000 is only to tend 9 acres. And cannot a hand tend 9 acres of ground?[27]

Carter's entrepreneurial instincts were shared by his fellow planters throughout British America, but kept in check while they had to be colonial patriarchs and businessmen. His methods foreshadowed a more rationalized approach to plantation organization that changed the character of master-slave relationships on large antebellum plantations. As agriculture became increasingly commercialized, as pa.s of the profound changes set in motion or accelerated in the South by the Revolution, the management of slaves and plantations became less personal and more uniform and routine.

IV

This development took place against the backdrop of a familiar story—the winning of Independence, the political and economic crises of the 1780s, and under the aegis of the Federalist Party, the establishment of national government and an American economic system of centrally controlled commerce, banks, and currency.

Less well known is an "economic revolution in the South" (Lewis C. Gray), where a switch to wheat, general farming, and slave raising was only the most obvious indication of fundamental change.[28] Economic reorientation had been in motion since the nonimportation agreements. Following Independence, wartime saltworks, ropeworks, and shipyards, and textile, forge, and munitions manufactures (of which many had recruited and trained women, juveniles, and slaves in the 1770s) continued to generate urbanization, population growth, and expectations.[29] As usual, slaves were conspicuous participants in these developments, and their reactions are a useful way of evaluating the social impact of basic economic changes. In analyzing Gabriel Prosser's conspiracy, St. George Tucker in 1801 told the Virginia State legislature:

> There is often a progress in human affairs which may indeed be retarded, but which nothing can arrest. . . . Of such sort is the advancement of knowledge among the negroes of this country. . . .

Every year adds to the number of those who can read and write. . . .

In our infant country, . . . population and wealth increase with unexampled rapidity. . . . The growth and multiplication of our towns tend a thousand ways to enlighten and inform them. The very nature of our government, which lends us to recur perpetually to the discussion of natural rights, favors speculation and enquiry.[30]

Antebellum planters were also buffeted by the fierce currents Tucker described so well. They enjoyed the mixed blessings of national sovereignty and a market economy of specialized, interdependent sections bound together by the instruments of a "Transportation Revolution"—canals, paddleboats, and eventually railroads. They lived in a society which, in outlawing the slave trade and enfranchising nonlandholders, was less aristocratic and more democratic and egalitarian in tone than that of their forefathers. They also enjoyed greater space.[31]

In breaking out of colonial boundaries, including geographical ones from Delaware to Georgia, and plunging greedily into the deep South, from the Floridas to the arid lands of western Texas, antebellum pioneers and adventurers contributed to a new social order characterized by one foreign observer after another in essentially the same manner: fortunes and families were made and lost in the twinkling of an eye; the business cycle was like a cannon ball loose in the hold of a rolling ship, because in America rather suddenly enterprise had become a religion. And in the South as well as the North, it was worshiped passionately. America, Francis J. Grund, an English immigrant observed, was a vast workshop with a sign at its entrance: "No admission here, except on business."[32]

The boom-or-bust economy of the Jacksonian Era, like a freshly tapped keg of beer—bubbly, effervescent, and, on top, largely foam—checked the development of another relatively stable and coherent ruling class of slaveowners, while accelerating mobility in a new—an American—society that favored expectant capitalists whose careers contrasted sharply with the lives of the lordly barons of Westover and Sabine Hall, who had moved in a more stately, three-quarter time, in smaller, more elegant spaces filled with European art and music. The new leaders, like their hero Andrew Jackson, were "one-generation aristocrats," of "half-shod elegance"—suitable creatures of a comparatively raw and untried society possessing few of the traditions and refinements of the old colonial order.[33]

"It is imperative, indeed, to conceive it [the antebellum South] as having remained more or less fully in the frontier stage of a great part—maybe the greater part—of its history," wrote Wilbur J. Cash, who understood nineteenth-century planters as well as anyone. In his famous portrait of the rude origins that they never completely overcame, Cash directed attention to shrewd and useful criteria for evaluating a new elite's real nature and influence—longevity and stability (both geographical and structural). The colonial "gentleman," "accustomed to a comparatively aged and mellow world," was abruptly rejected by Cash as a candidate for antebellum leadership. "Like every aristocrat, he required above all things a fixed background, the sense of absolute security and repose which proceeds from an environment which moves in well-worn grooves." Instead, the new rich came from among "the strong, the pushing, the ambitious [of] the old coon-hunting population of the backcountry."[34]

Alexis de Tocqueville also understood the mysterious and potent connections between terrain, settlement patterns, and class structure. Moving his analysis of Jacksonian America from the more settled East to the new states of the West and South where democracy had reached its "utmost limits," he argued that here "society ha[d] no existence." "Founded offhand and as it were by chance, the inhabitants are but of yesterday" and the elite was "so completely disabled that we can scarcely assign to it any degree of influence."[35]

The transformation in the early nineteenth century of the social and political setting for American Negro slavery changed the planter's role and the mood of the documents he left about slavery. Planters were no longer colonists burdened by a need to make plantations self-sufficient and themselves patriarchs "independent on every one but Providence." Instead, masters could be masterful in a more rational and profitable manner by allowing the plantation to realize its potential, as an enterprise that concentrated most efficiently manpower, expertise, and capital in the production of staples. But as the large plantation changed from a way of life to a business, new and ominous techniques were developed for regulating and routinizing the lives of slaves.

Sensitive to the currents of the day, arbiters of the new agriculture and publishers of the popular farm journals demanded accountability and a systemization of production: "The plantation is a piece of machinery; to operate successfully, all of its parts should be uniform and exact, and the impelling force regular and steady." "No more beautiful picture of human society can be drawn than a well organized plantation. . . . A regular and systematic plan of operation on the plantation is greatly promotive of easy government. Have, therefore, all matters as far as possible reduced to a system."[36]

With the routinization of plantation operations came an even more important change: for antebellum slaves, most of whom lived on large plantations, slavery was no longer familial and domestic, but an impersonal and bureaucratic institution. The "management of Negroes" articles in southern agricultural journals, written by editors, travelers, planters, and overseers, encouraged slaveholders to devise more effective manipulative techniques: "make him [the slave] as comfortable at home as possible"; "treat your negro *well* and he will respond to it with fidelity and honesty; kind words, humane consideration, justness in discipline, unhesitating authority when required, forbearance towards venal offenses, arous[e] pride of character."[37]

Masters no longer aspired to be patriarchs but personnel managers, experts in motivational psychology: "[I] have found very little trouble in bringing them all under my system. . . . By exciting his pride I elevate the man." If slaves on Sundays insisted on dressing "in the ridiculous finery which they sometimes display, and which will often provoke a smile," they should not be mocked, because such dress as this "aids very materially in giving them self-respect."[38]

The new outlook encouraged a restructuring of the plantation community.[39] On many large units economic diversification by slave artisans (an important means of advancement for talented slaves) was all but abandoned. Aside from a household vegetable garden, a few pigs, and corn fields, big plantations produced staples and little else. Most slaves were "hands" reduced to field regimens under a clearly defined chain of command—overseers, suboverseers, drivers, and foremen; and each moment of the day was as accountable and organized as the actual weighing and recording of cotton sacks at dusk.

> Then begins another push, which continues until the whole crop is gathered and housed. During "picking time" . . . the hands are regularly roused, by a large bell or horn, about the first dawn of day, or earlier so that they are ready to enter the field as soon as there is sufficient light to distinguish the bolls. . . . The hands remain in the field until it is too dark to distinguish the cotton, having brought their meals with them. For the purpose of collecting the cotton, each hand is furnished with a large basket, and two coarse bags about the size of a pillow case, with a strong strap to suspend them from the neck or shoulders. The basket is left at the end of the row, and both bags taken along; when one bag is as full as it can well be crammed, it is laid down in the row, and the hand begins to fill the second in the same way. As soon as the second is full, he returns it to the basket, taking the other bag as he passes it, and empties both into the basket, treading it down well, to make it contain the whole day's work. The same process is repeated until night; when the basket is taken upon his head and carried to the scaffold-yard, to be weighed. There the overseer meets all hands at the scales, with the lamp, slate, and whip.[40]

As large plantations became factories-in-the-field, planters did all they could to make field workers contented charges. Antebellum counterparts of modern devices (piped-in Muzak in automobile assembly plants; lunch-hour group therapy sessions to iron out feelings of rebelliousness in large-scale Japanese industries) were all present: slave chapels with licensed ministers; nurseries for small children whose mothers worked in the fields; and games, contests, and rewards to encourage productivity and to make slavery fun. Planters large and small were quite frank about their motives for keeping slaves happy and presumably docile. But even "happiness" should be standardized: "Tattler" in the *Southern Cultivator* wrote: "When at work, I have no objection to their whistling or singing some lively tune, but no *drawling* tunes are allowed in the field, for their motions are almost certain to keep time with the music."[41]

The process of making the plantation "a perfect society" and the worker "comfortable at home" may have cost some slaves their individuality. If "Sambo" existed, that docile, passive creature of the plantation's infantilizing tendencies, he was a product of the largest late-antebellum plantations.[42] In the last years of slavery, rebelliousness changed, and may have decreased as a result of this tendency toward closure of the institution from all external and internal disruption: in the colonial period virtually every plantation record is filled with instances of boondoggling, feigned illnesses, truancy, and theft, but similar nineteenth-century records contain only rare accounts of rebellious slaves of any kind. When resistance did occur (usually on smaller, more loosely organized plantations) it was typically self-defeating, violent, and often deadly.

In transforming the familial and domestic character of colonial slavery, the wealthy antebellum planter created an alienating world for his slaves. Herbert Marcuse tells us that "free choice among a wide variety of goods and services does not signify freedom if these goods and services sustain social controls over a life of toil and fear—that is, if they sustain alienation."[43] Many slaves, reduced to mere numbers in account books and daybooks, were undoubtedly alienated—too enmeshed in a system with all of its small rewards to see ways out.

The new reality of plantation slavery revealed in the "management of Negroes" articles was faithfully replicated in the records of many large plantations. In comparison to colonial crop books and daybooks, entries for antebellum slaves were more abstract, uniform—and predictable:[44]

NAMES	MON	TUES	WED	THUR	FRI	SAT	SUN	TOTAL/ SICK
Richard	Roll logs	Ploughed	Hauled	Hauled	Ploughed	Chopped		
Emma	Cleaning up trash	Clear new ground	Clean up ground	Clean up ground	Scraped ditches	Shrubbing		
Big Henry	Pile and Burn	Shrubbing over Bayou	Burned	Burn	Cleaned new ground	Cleaned new ground		

and

> 1840. When a negro gets to be 50 years old his task must be reduced from 50 rows to 40. When a woman has a child her task must be 40 rows instead of 50. All the negroes under 20 years must have less than a full task, say from 17 to 20 years of age

about 45 rows. All of the age of 11, 12, and 13 years to work two to a task. They all go out at 10 years old and the first year must work with their mothers and both together make one task.[45]

The most astute and informative contemporary observer of antebellum plantation life, Frederick Law Olmsted, left this unforgettable picture of the field hands' stultifying world of work:

> They are constantly and steadily driven up to their work, and the stupid, plodding, machine-like manner in which they labor is painful to witness. This was especially the case with the hoe-gangs. One of them numbered nearly two hundred hands (for the force of two plantations was working together), moving across the field in parallel lines, with a considerable degree of precision. I repeatedly rode through the lines at a canter, with other horsemen, often coming upon them suddenly, without producing the smallest change or interruption in the dogged action of the laborers, or causing one of them to lift an eye from the ground.[46]

Planters' attitudes had changed about slaves and their duties and responsibilities toward them. Their new industrial consciousness allowed them to see themselves as estate managers rather than patriarchs, and to delegate to the slaves' supervisors the necessary authority to assure a smooth operation. As an effective substitute for their own constant presence on the plantation, planters established strict and comprehensive rules and regulations for overseers that dealt with all major components of the plantation operation—from the slaves' bedding, diet, and housing to the most intimate details of their religious, fraternal, and family lives. Managers and overseers kept detailed records of marriages, births and deaths, and physicians' visits; the quantities of clothing, supplies, and implements received from the planter; and quarterly inventories of stock, tools, and crops and daily accounts of cotton picked by each hand.

A quiet but significant advance in the technology of recordkeeping accompanied the rationalization of plantation organization. In place of cramped and hurried notes taken in the margins of blank sheets of hand-sized almanacs, reformers like Thomas Affleck of Mississippi published detailed printed ledger pages, which brought together in one place several of the miscellaneous records usually kept by staple producers. The colonial almanacs were "comic absurdities" when compared to the new comprehen-

sive ledgers, which Robert Williams argues were "essentially consistent with the intent and purpose of modern cost-accounting,
and followed the best and most advanced principles of efficient
administrative management."[47] The account books, for example,
considered the often neglected factors of capital depreciation,
labor costs, and social welfare. One of these new ledgers, which
allowed the planter to lay out a coherent plan for his operations
while providing him with a quick summary of his property and its
workings, was advertised in *De Bow's Review* in 1850:

3. PLANTATION ACCOUNTS

Thomas Affleck, of Mississippi, published, several years ago, a
Plantation Record and Account Book, of which Weld & Co., of
New Orleans, are now the agents and part proprietors. . . . There
are heads for inventories of stock, implements and tools; for daily
records of events on the plantation; for quarterly abstracts; of cotton picked each day, names of negroes picking, averages, &c.; of
articles furnished to the negroes during the year; of overseers' supplies; of birth and deaths on place; of physicians' visits and names
etc. of patients; of bales [of] cotton made; average weight and
sales; with full and ample directions to the planter in enabling him
to keep the accounts with greatest ease.

Price.—No. 1, for a plantation of forty hands, or under, $2.50.
No. 2, for a plantation of eighty hands, or under, $3.00. . . .

The planting community and the press have fully recognized the
simplicity and completeness of this work, and its perfect adaptation
to the end in view—that of affording to planters and their overseers
a plain and uniform book of blanks, embracing every record and
account necessary to be kept upon a plantation.[48]

Paradoxically, we associate capitalistic enterprise with "Yankee
ingenuity"; but trends toward a more strict routine and accountability were evident on southern plantations much earlier than in
northern mills. This is not surprising. Planters realized that they
had long controlled an indispensable factor for rationalizing such
enterprises as plantations: a disciplined labor force. Slaves not
only guaranteed built-in growth through their natural increase,
but in slavery there were no strikes, lockouts, or even endemic
turnovers of personnel. That planters enjoyed a slave's labor for a
lifetime in itself probably offset the profits lost by the slaves' non-
cooperativeness.

Southern agricultural enterpreneurs knew what they were doing economically. Drawing upon a much longer and more consistent tradition of large-scale enterprise, with a much more disciplined and more predictable labor force than their northern counterparts, they were able sooner to get down to fundamentals: producing staples efficiently. Ironically, the organizers of the partial and regional prewar industrial revolution in the northeast first had to contend with potentially the most disruptive issue in the country: the impact of a new, untried system of enterprise on small-scale agrarian society.[49] There is a separate reality to different kinds of historical records: the assumptions and values behind the antebellum plantation accounts and articles in agricultural magazines stand in sharp contrast to the homilies on chastity produced by northern textile mill owners and managers for their farm-girl operatives. Obviously, the culture of Industrial Man, which has a long history in our work-oriented society, had a distinctly southern bias in antebellum America. And it may now be profitable to follow the example of Caribbean area scholars by also construing the large nineteenth-century plantation as an urbanizing force creating not conservative, suspicious, frugal, and traditionalistic peasants, but landless, wage-earning, store-buying countrymen, who had nothing to sell but their labor.[50]

Exceptions to this frame of reference were the small planters, who were the real patriarchs and inheritors of the paternalism that pervaded colonial slave society. Clement Eaton, in *The Growth of Southern Civilization*, introduces a typical small slaveholder, James T. Burroughs, well known as the owner of Booker T. Washington. In this family, Burroughs and his sons worked all day in the fields beside their few prime hands, and everyone ate, slept, procreated, and died in the same small space.[51] The letters of Rachel O'Connor, who grew cotton with sixteen slaves on Bayou Sarah, West Feliciana Parish, Louisiana, and some of Olmsted's marvelous travel reports indicate clearly that old ways of slavery were very much alive in the antebellum era.[52] But these pockets of paternalism were usually located far from the routes to market —the navigable rivers, canals, and railroads. One senses that, had the Civil War not intervened, they would have been victims of an evolutionary process—reptiles in an age of mammals.

The antebellum South was not a semifeudal society dominated by a class of men defending an antibourgeois and unprofitable way of life. From the earliest times, however, the South had been locked into the most backward sector of Old World capitalistic imperialism, the New World plantation areas.[53] As tragic actors in this special niche, all Southerners, from the mightiest planter to the lowest slave, acquired a colonized mentality, fortified and refined by the interpersonal dynamics of the master-slave relationship. Even the application of the most advanced methods for maximizing profits from agriculture could not change that destiny. For this unhappy society civil war would be a painful but cathartic renewal.

V

But this is only half the story. Focusing on plantation organization is viewing history "from the top down" and reinforcing traditional interpretations that tell us more about masters than slaves. There is another way of looking at documents on American Negro slavery—one that insists on focusing on the slaves themselves, while recognizing that viewing history from the bottom up presents special problems in research and interpretation.[54]

One approach to the history of the inarticulate, those people who could not or were not inclined to write things down, is to realize that a few traditional sources, written from the elite's vantage point, may yield remarkable and relatively unbiased insights. Sometimes whites wrote valuable accounts about blacks in their families or among friends, worshiping, dancing, fighting, or otherwise saying or doing something outside their customary work roles (and also outside the white's stereotyped views of the way slaves should behave). On these occasions planters often recorded what they saw, rather than trying to explain what they did not understand.

Another approach to the problem of reconstructing the historical reality of underclasses is to recognize that they were often articulate in unusual ways, and speak indirectly in certain documents. The sources on plantations, the travelers' narratives, letters and essays in agricultural journals, are what Professor Daniel McCall (in *Africa in Time-Perspective: A Discussion of Historical Reconstruction from Unwritten Sources*) calls "narrative sources," written by authors who consciously intended to inform (or misinform) their readers. Documents of another kind are what the great French medievalist Marc Bloch called "witnesses in spite of themselves"—such bits and pieces of the historical record as plantation ledgers and daybooks, wills and estate inventories, court records and newspaper advertisements for runaway slaves. These sources are more appropriate than narrative sources for examining the lives of the inarticulate because they are seldom polemical, relatively free of elite bias (so apparent and unavoidable in most documents on slavery), and in the case of the fugitive advertisements, fairly objective.[55]

A third technique is to infer the values, motives, and aspirations of the inarticulate from their actual behavior or actions. The fugitive slave notices illustrate facets of these three approaches. By the time masters advertised, they had often received information from other slaves, townsmen, and officials who had dealt with the runaway. This information on the slave's behavior while on his own, forging passes, deceiving whites into believing he was on an errand or free, and hiring himself out in town, is relatively unbiased and extremely useful. Recognizing that this intelligence made advertisements more effective, owners inserted it presumably intact along with more explicit statements about the fugitive's most noticeable physical and psychological characteristics. The data on the runaway's activities also provide insights into slave personalities: the master's characterizations of a slave—as "brisk," "active," or "cunning"—may be correlated with what the runaway actually did while on his own. A fugitive's decision to resist, and his actions while free, forced the advertiser to recognize his slave's individuality—thus providing an unusual view of the elite from the vantage point of the inarticulate's actions. As the master sought to comprehend the runaway's real motives and whereabouts, he was forced to reexamine views of blacks as dependent children and other similar misconceptions about slaves and slavery. To know where a runaway was, or that he was participating in unheard-of activities, and yet to be unable to recapture him must have been a peculiarly frustrating experience for many a white (but an invaluable one for an alert researcher): "He ran from his overseer about 18 months ago and has passed for a free man ever since"; "there is a wench at Mr. Thomas Husk's between the Rappahannock and Potomac rivers who calls herself free Milla, who may probably be the same [slave as advertised]"; and "I advertised [Stepney Blue, who ran off with a free Negro woman] some time ago in this Paper, and have not yet been so fortunate as to get him, but have been informed that he has lately been employed by some Gentlemen in Fredericksburg as a Freeman."[56]

Historians of American Negro slavery have contributed to the difficulties encountered in understanding slaves and their culture. By examining slavery topically, concentrating on the last few years of its long existence, and using models based on advanced industrial societies, they have limited our understanding of the African cultural background and changes in slavery over a period of time, and obscured our view of the slaves themselves. Slavery has been recently characterized as one type of "total" institution or another (a prisoner-of-war or concentration camp, or maximum security prison). These sociological models sustain ahistorical treatments of slavery, promote misleading views of slaves as "Sambos," a "society of helpless dependents,"[57] and most important, imply that slavery was for slaves only, and simply another "institution" (like the churches or political parties) that gave the South its identity.

There is, however, a fundamentally different way of looking at the problem, one that concentrates on the slaves themselves and on their impact upon the total society. In 1946, Frank Tannenbaum, a man who saw slavery in this hemisphere from the vantage point of Latin America, argued that there were basically two ways of viewing a slave labor system: as merely an "institution," or as a system so pervasive that we may call the whole a "slave society." As slavery encompassed the South it changed profoundly all of its most important institutions: the family, law, religion, politics, and even diet and architecture.[58] "In any society where slavery has been institutionalized," Tannenbaum argued,

the issues between free and slave labor become infinitely variable, and it is often a question of where slavery ends and freedom begins. Stated in this way it is better to speak of a slave society rather than slavery, for the effects of the labor system—slave or free— permeate the entire social structure, and influence all of its ways. If we are to speak of slavery, we must do so in its larger setting, as a way of life for both the master and the slave, for both the economy and the culture, for both the family and the community.[59]

This documentary history, which may be titled "Rethinking Slavery from the Vantage Point of the Colonial Era," is part of a very personal quest for ways of comprehending the lives of the inarticulate, while in this case viewing slavery from one end of its long history to the other. Most of the documents focus on slaves and illustrate Frank Tannenbaum's conviction that in our American slave society, "nothing escaped, nothing, and no one."[60]

Berkeley
February 1974

NOTES

1. Ernie Isaacs, Eugene Genovese, Stanley Elkins, and Eric McKitrick made helpful suggestions (some of which I have followed). But I am responsible for the finished product, which is intended to be suggestive about several problems that can only be resolved by rigorous quantitative and comparative analysis. A shorter version of this essay was published in *Louisiana Studies*, 12 (Summer 1973): 398–422.

2. Two useful investigations of the applicability of the role theory to slavery are Stanley M. Elkins, *Slavery: A Problem in American Institutional and Intellectual Life* (Chicago, 1959), pt. 3, esp. pp. 123 ff; and Kenneth M. Stampp, "Rebels and Sambos: The Search for the Negro's Personality in Slavery," *The Journal of Southern History*, 37 (August 1971): 367–392.

3. Sidney W. Mintz, Foreword to Ramiro Guerra y Sánchez, *Sugar and Society in the Caribbean* (New Haven, Conn., 1964), p. xiv.

4. Richard B. Sheridan, "The Plantation Revolution and the Industrial Revolution, 1625–1775," *Caribbean Studies*, 9 (October 1969): 7. Cf. Sheridan, *The Development of the Plantations to 1750* (London and Barbados, 1970); Edward Brathwaite, *The Development of Creole Society in Jamaica, 1770–1820* (London, 1971), pt. 3; Sidney M. Greenfield, "Slavery and the Plantation in the New World: The Development and Diffusion of a Social Form," *Journal of Inter-American Studies*, 11 (January 1969): 44–57; Charles Wagley, "Plantation America: A Culture Sphere," in Vera Rubin, ed., *Caribbean Studies: A Symposium* (Seattle, 1960), pp. 3–13; Edgar T. Thompson, "The Plantation," in Thompson and Everett C. Hughes, eds., *Race: Individual and Collective Behavior* (New York, 1958), pp. 225–233; and Franklin W. Knight, *Slave Society in Cuba during the Nineteenth Century* (Madison, Wis., 1970), esp. ch. 4.

5. Sheridan, "The Plantation Revolution," pp. 7–8, 21 ff.

6. Mintz, citing Professor Henry Wallich in Guerra y Sánchez, *Sugar and Society*, p. xxxvii.

7. Eugene Genovese, *The Political Economy of Slavery* (New York, 1961), pp. 3, 15–16, 28.

8. Barrington Moore, Jr., *Social Origins of Dictatorship and Democracy: Lord and Peasant in the Making of the Modern World* (Boston, 1966), p. 116.

9. Kenneth M. Stampp, *The Peculiar Institution: Slavery in the Ante-Bellum South* (New York, 1956), p. 38, also pp. 41–42, 325; see too Lewis C. Gray, *History of Agriculture in the Southern United States to 1860*, 2 vols. (New York, 1941), 1:302.

10. Robert W. Fogel, "Historiography and Retrospective Econometrics," *History and Theory*, 9 (1970): 248.

11. Moore, *Social Origins of Dictatorship and Democracy*, pp. 122–123.

12. Plantation Record Book, 1853–65, Evans (Nathaniel, and Family) Papers; Plantation Record Book, 1859–66, Le Blanc Family Papers; Vital Register, 1832–62, McCutcheon (Samuel) Papers; Pre Aux Cleres Plantation Book, 1852–54; McCollam (Andrew and Ellen E.), 1847 Record; William J. Palfrey Plantation Diaries, 1852–59; the Comite Plantation Record Book, 1857, J. G. Kilbourne Papers, Louisiana State University Archives; Kollock Plantation Records, 1837–60; Manigault Plantation Records for Gowrie and Silk Hope, vols. 2–4; John Edwin Fripp Plantation Account Books; Arnold-Screven Papers, vol. 4, Plantation Journal, Southern Historical Collection, University of North Carolina Archives. See also Memorandum of Directions . . . 1846, Charles Crommelin Papers; and the James A. Tait Memorandum Book, 1831–40, Alabama State Archives.

13. These themes are developed more fully in my book *Flight and Rebellion: Slave Resistance in Eighteenth-Century Virginia* (New York, 1972), esp. chs. 1 and 2.

14. Landon Carter to the editors of the *Virginia Gazette* (Purdie and Dixon, editors), Fall, 1769, cited in Jack P. Greene, *Landon Carter: An Inquiry into the Personal Values and Social Imperatives of the Eighteenth-Century Gentry* (Charlottesville, Va., 1965), p. 26; "Management of Slaves," *The Southern Cultivator*, 4 (March 1846): 44.

15. William Byrd II to the Earl of Orrery, Westover, Virginia, July 5, 1726, *Virginia Magazine of History and Biography*, 32 (December 1924): 27.

16. Cited in Gray, *Agriculture in the Southern United States*, 1:453.

17. Peter Laslett, *The World We Have Lost* (London, 1965), passim.

18. This view of South Carolina is based on my own interpretation of the following sources in the South Carolina State Archives, Columbia: Records in the British Public Record Office Relating to South

Carolina, 1663–1782 ("Sainsbury Transcripts"), 36 vols. (particularly correspondence between officials in the colony and England relating to staples, slave trade, religion, and insurrections); manuscripts of the Society for the Propagation of the Gospel in Foreign Parts in South Carolina (Library of Congress transcripts); a quantitative study of all 664 estate inventories in the Charleston District Inventories R(2), 1753–1756, T, 1758–1761; and a sample of 600-odd fugitive slave notices; advertisements for slaves taken up and jailed as runaways in the Charleston workhouse; and plantation and land sale notices in the *South Carolina Gazette*, 1732–1775 (University of California at Berkeley microfilm collection). On the rice planters' great wealth, see M. Eugene Sirmans, *Colonial South Carolina: A Political History, 1663–1763* (Chapel Hill, N.C., 1966), p. 226.

19. This section is based on my *Flight and Rebellion*, ch. 2. Cf. Winthrop D. Jordan, *White over Black* (Chapel Hill, N.C., 1968), pt. 1; and George M. Fredrickson, "Why Blacks Were Left Out" (review of Jordan), *New York Review of Books*, 21 (February 7, 1974): 23–24.

20. *London Gentleman's Magazine*, n.s. 10 (1740): 127–129; Newton D. Mereness, ed., *Travels in the American Colonies* (New York, 1916), pp. 222–223; Governor William Bull to the Board of Trade, Charleston, October 5, 1739, South Carolina Records in the British Public Record Office ("Sainsbury Transcripts"), 20: 179–180.

21. George Pitt to Mr. Robert Prentis, Stratford-on-Avon, England, February 1, 1775, Prentis Family Papers, Alderman Library, University of Virginia; Charles Dabney to John Blair Jr., and Mary Ambler, April 1, 1769, Dabney Papers, Southern Historical Collection; Jack P. Greene, ed., *The Diary of Colonel Landon Carter of Sabine Hall, 1752–1778*, 2 vols. (Charlottesville, Va., 1966), 1: 363.

22. Cornelius Hall to John H. Norton, October 1791, Norton Papers, Colonial Williamsburg Research Center.

23. Elizabeth Donnan, "The Slave Trade into South Carolina before the Revolution," *American Historical Review*, 33 (July 1928): 816–817.

24. Rev. Alexander Garden to the Secretary, May 6, 1740, cited in Frank J. Klingberg, *An Appraisal of the Negro in Colonial South Carolina* (Washington, D.C., 1941), p. 106.

25. Southern Historical Collection photographic copy of the original ms. in the South Carolina Historical Society, Charleston. See also David R. Chesnutt, "South Carolina's Penetration of Georgia in the 1760's: Henry Laurens as a Case Study," *South Carolina Historical Magazine*, 73 (October 1972): 204, for Laurens' attempts to use a new style of agent-overseer system of management.

26. Greene, ed., *Diary of Landon Carter*, 2:1038.

27. Ibid., p. 679.

28. Gray, *Agriculture in the Southern United States*, 2:613 ff.

29. Mullin, *Flight and Rebellion*, ch. 4.

30. [St. George Tucker], *Letter to a Member of the General Assembly of Virginia on the Subject of the Late Conspiracy of the Slaves, with a Proposal for their Colonization* (Richmond, 1801), Virginia State Library microfilm.

31. This section is based on documents in Edwin C. Rozwenc, ed., *Ideology and Power in the Age of Jackson* (New York, 1964), esp. pp. vii–xxi, pts. 1 and 2; Edward Pessen, *Jacksonian America: Society, Personality and Politics* (Homewood, Ill., 1969), esp. chs. 2, 4–6; Douglass C. North, *The Economic Growth of the United States, 1790–1860* (New York, 1961); Marvin Fisher, *Workshops in the Wilderness* (New York, 1967); Douglas T. Miller, *The Birth of Modern America, 1820–1850* (New York, 1970); and Sigmund Diamond, "Values as an Obstacle to Economic Growth: The American Colonies," *Journal of Economic History*, 27 (December 1967): 561–575.

32. Cited in Richard Hofstadter, *The American Political Tradition* (New York, 1948), p. 57.

33. See Hofstadter's memorable characterizations of the antebellum nouveau riche, ibid., pp. 54–67.

34. Wilbur J. Cash, *The Mind of the South* (New York, 1941), pp. 12–20.

35. Alexis de Tocqueville, *Democracy in America*, ch. 3, "Social Conditions of the Anglo-Americans," trans. Henry Reeve, ed. Francis Bowen and Phillips Bradley, 2 vols. (New York, 1946), 1:53 ff.

36. *The Southern Cultivator*, 4 (March 1846): 44; "Management of Slaves," *De Bow's Review*, 18 (June 1855): 716, 718.

37. "Management of Slaves," *The Southern Cultivator*, 4 (March 1846): 44, "Treatment of Slaves—Mr. Guerry," *The Southern Cultivator*, 18 (August 1860): 258.

38. "Management of Negroes—Duties of Masters, &c.," *The Southern Cultivator*, 18 (June 1860): 177; "Overseers at the South," *De Bow's Review*, 21 (September 1856): 279.

39. On the structure of the Southern export and import markets and the degree of plantation self-sufficiency (importations of pork and corn, particularly), a good place to begin is Harold D. Woodman, ed., *Slavery and the Southern Economy: Sources and Readings* (New York, 1966); and an issue of *Agricultural History*, 44 (January 1970) devoted to "The Structure of the Cotton Economy of the Antebellum South," esp. Robert E. Gallman, "Self-Sufficiency in the Cotton Economy of the Antebellum South." See also James C. Bonnor, "Advancing Trends in Southern Agriculture, 1840–60," *Agricultural History*, 22 (October 1948); and Edwin A. Davis, *Plantation Life in the Florida Parishes of Louisiana, 1836–1846, as Reflected in the Diary of Bennet H. Barrow* (New York, 1943), esp. pp. 25–26, 28–29, 37–38.

40. J. H. Ingraham, cited in Charles S. Sydnor, *Slavery in Mississippi* (Baton Rouge, La., 1933, 1966), p. 13. Cf. Gray, *Agriculture in the Southern United States*, 1:553–554.

41. "Tattler," *Management of Negroes*," *Southern Cultivator*, 8 (November 1850): 163.

42. On Sambo, see Elkins, *Slavery*, p. 82; and Stampp, "Rebels and Sambos," pp. 367–392.

43. Herbert Marcuse, *One-Dimensional Man: Studies in the Ideology of Advanced Industrial Society* (Boston, 1964), pp. 7–8.

44. Record Book, 1859–1866 (entries for February 25–March 2), Le Blanc Family Papers, Louisiana State University Archives. Italics indicate handwritten entries.

45. James A. Tait, Memorandum Book, 1831–1840, Alabama State Archives.

46. Frederick Law Olmsted, *A Journey in the Back Country* (New York, 1863), pp. 81–82.

47. Robert Williams, "Thomas Affleck: Missionary to the Planter, the Farmer, and the Gardener," *Agricultural History*, 31 (July 1957): 46.

48. *De Bow's Review*, 8 (January 1850): 98.

49. Charles L. Sanford, ed., *In Quest of America, 1810–1824* (New York, 1964), pp. xxi, 351; Foster Rhea Dulles, *Labor in America*, rev. ed. (New York, 1960), pp. 74–75; and Herbert G. Gutman, "Work, Culture, and Society in Industrializing America, 1815–1919," *American Historical Review*, 78 (June 1973): 531–588, esp. 540–541, 550–554.

50. Cf. Mintz in Guerra y Sánchez, *Sugar and Society*, p. xxxvii.

51. Clement Eaton, *A History of the Old South*, 2nd ed. (New York, 1966), p. 235; also, a Small Planter, "Management of Negroes," *De Bow's Review*, 11 (October 1851): 371.

52. Weeks (David, and Family) Papers, Louisiana State University Archives, esp. Rachel's letters to Mary Weeks, January 11, 1830, June 4, 1832, and September 4, 1840; and to her brother, November 20, 1833, April 25, 1834, and July 30, 1836.

53. Stanley J. Stein and Barbara H. Stein, eds., *The Colonial Heritage of Latin America: Essays on Economic Dependence in Perspective* (New York, 1970); and Caio Prado, *The Colonial Background of Modern Brazil* (Berkeley, Calif., 1967).

54. For nonelite history "from the bottom up," see the writings of Jesse Lemisch, esp. "The American Revolution Seen from the Bottom Up," in Barton J. Bernstein, ed., *Towards a New Past: Dissenting Essays in American History* (New York, 1968), pp. 3–45; and "Listening to the 'Inarticulate': William Widger's Dream and the Loyalties of American Revolutionary Seamen in British Prisons," *Journal of Social History*, 3 (Fall 1969): 1–29.

55. Marc Bloch, cited in Daniel F. McCall, *Africa in Time-Perspec-*

tive: A Discussion of Historical Reconstruction from Unwritten Sources (New York, 1969), p. 19.

56. *Virginia Gazette* (Rind, ed.), September 22, 1774, John Harrison, Jr., subscriber; ibid. (Purdie and Dixon, eds.), November 10, 1774, Postscript, Nathan Yancy, subscriber.

57. Elkins, *Slavery*, pp. 103–114; George M. Fredrickson and Christopher Lasch, "Resistance to Slavery," *Civil War History*, 13 (December 1967): 315–329.

58. Frank Tannenbaum, *Slave and Citizen: The Negro in the Americas* (New York, 1946), pp. 116–119.

59. Frank Tannenbaum, "A Note on the Economic Interpretation of History," *Political Science Quarterly*, 41 (June 1946): 248.

60. Tannenbaum, *Slave and Citizen*, p. 117.

I

The Colonial Era

A. Beginnings: Three Views of Africa and the Atlantic Slave Trade

THE TRAGIC STORY *of American Negro slavery begins in accounts of West Africa and the Atlantic slave trade. Indelible memories of the trade and of this vast region's spectacular variations in climate, terrain, and cultures survived the Middle Passage to shape lives and institutions in the Old World as well as the New. For Dr. Alexander Falconbridge, a surgeon for British slavers, and Olaudah Equiano, an Ibo tribesman who lived to buy his freedom and write about enslavement, Africa was a stark and compelling reality that profoundly influenced the very course of their lives. Both men ended long and productive careers in late eighteenth-century England, an old society girding itself for industrial greatness by changing its mind about slavery and losing its first empire. Both men also returned to Africa and the barbarities of the slave trade in their writings, which contributed to its abolition in the early nineteenth century.*

Another view of Africa—of a significantly different tone and set of images—is provided by Americans, two colonial businessmen who as slave dealers were responsible for the domestic end of the trade. Their comments over port and beef about "charming markets," slave prices, and their customers' credit indicate that for them slavery was part of the natural order of things. Here, on the slavers and wharves of Virginia and South Carolina, the scene has changed: we are among a young people, and at the beginning, not the end, of an era. While the writings of Equiano and Falconbridge convey a sense of the moral indignation, or bitter understanding, that often returns to haunt a people with ancient traditions and a venerable past, the comments of Robert "King" Carter and Henry Laurens reflect the ethos of a new society unhampered by misgivings about the evil of slavery and man's inhumanity to man.

1. A Victim's View

OLAUDAH EQUIANO *was an eleven-year-old Ibo boy in 1745 when he was taken from his country by English slavers. He was an unusual slave who survived, purchased his freedom, and at the end of his life wrote about his experiences in Barbados, Virginia, the Leeward Islands, New England, and London.*

Equiano's homeland, Benin province, Nigeria, was defined by the grassy upland savannahs of northern Nigeria and the northern reaches of the vast Congo basin's tropical forest. In this setting his countrymen (or people like them) lived in small, independent tribal states of a few villages each, held together by common traditions, ancestors, and ways of living. Enclosing these settlements was a deep, thick web of forest and cultivated trees, shade and herb gardens, secondary forest growth, and paths leading outward, beyond the inner area and home, to the communal fields and the wilderness. In all, this was a closed and insular world: brought to the banks of a great river by his black kidnappers, Equiano later recalled, "I was beyond measure astonished at this, as I have never before seen any water larger than a pond or rivulet."

Equiano also said a great deal about himself and the nature of his West African existence with the remark "We are almost a nation of dancers." Among his Ibo countrymen (and in tribal societies generally) art, religion, and daily life are one—fused in communal dances that make explicit the ancient myths and values that hold a people together. In Ibo land nearly everyone danced in religious dramas and celebrations that renewed and re-created the culture on a stage as wide as the society itself.

For this proud, resourceful, and primitive man it must have been strange to be forced into a white society where religious and artistic rituals had been demystified and detribalized to such an extent that they had lost their original meanings and functions, and were sanitized, moved indoors, and reenacted by professionals—ministers—before passive audiences. For West Africans, who had led fully ritualized existences, sustained by cultures that functioned on a corporate and traditional basis, the comparatively secular and individualized colonial American societies must have seemed odd and unnatural, as well as dangerous. The Interesting Narrative of Olaudah Equiano *helps re-create a world of black men who lived so much closer to death and violence, to nature and their gods, than did the Europeans who made them slaves and eventually Negroes.*

SOURCE: Olaudah Equiano, *The Interesting Narrative of Olaudah Equiano, or Gustavus Vasa, the African. Written by Himself,*

3d ed., 2 vols. (London, 1790), 1:8–9, 11–18, 21–22, 30, 31–32, 33, 36–37, 43.

CHAPTER I

. . . That part of Africa, known by the name of Guinea, to which the trade for slaves is carried on, extends along the coast above 3400 miles, from Senegal to Angola, and includes a variety of kingdoms. Of these the most considerable is the kingdom of Benin, both as to extent and wealth, the richness and cultivation of the soil, the power of its king, and the number and warlike disposition of the inhabitants. It is situated nearly under the line, and extends along the coast about 170 miles, but runs back into the interior part of Africa a distance hitherto, I believe, unexplored by any traveller; and seems only terminated at length by the empire of Abyssinia, near 1500 miles from its beginning. This kingdom is divided into many provinces or districts: in one of the most remote and fertile of which, I was born, in the year 1745, situated in a charming fruitful vale, named Essaka. The distance of this province from the capital of Benin and the sea coast must be very considerable: for I had never heard of white men or Europeans, nor of the sea; and our subjection to the king of Benin was little more than nominal; for every transaction of the government, as far as my slender observation extended, was conducted by the chief or elders of the place. The manners and government of a people who have little commerce with other countries, are generally very simple; and the history of what passes in one family or village, may serve as a specimen of the whole nation. My father was one of those elders or chiefs I have spoken of, and was styled Embrenche. . . .

Those Embrenche, or chief men, decided disputes, and punished crimes; for which purpose they always assembled together. The proceedings were generally short; and in most cases the law of retaliation prevailed. . . .

The men [however] do not preserve the same constancy to their wives which they expect from them; for they indulge in a plurality, though seldom in more than two. Their mode of marriage is thus: Both parties are usually betrothed when young by their parents (though I have known the males to betroth themselves).

On this occasion a feast is prepared, and the bride and bridegroom stand up in the midst of all their friends, who are assembled for the purpose, while he declares she is thenceforth to be looked upon as his wife, and that no person is to pay any address to her. This is also immediately proclaimed in the vicinity, on which the bride retires from the assembly. Some time after she is brought home to her husband, and then another feast is made to which the relations of both parties are invited: her parents then deliver her to the bridegroom, accompanied with a number of blessings; and at the same time they tie round her waist a cotton string, of the thickness of a goose-quill, which none but married women are permitted to wear; she is now considered as completely his wife; and at this time the dowry is given to the new married pair, which generally consists of portions of land, slaves, and cattle, household goods, and implements of husbandry. These are offered by the friends of both parties; besides which the parents of the bridegroom present gifts to those of the bride, whose property she is looked upon before marriage; but, after it, she is esteemed the sole property of the husband. The ceremony being now ended, the festival begins, which is celebrated with bonfires and loud acclamations of joy, accompanied with music and dancing.

We are almost a nation of dancers, musicians, and poets. Thus every great event, such as a triumphant return from battle, or other cause of public rejoicing, is celebrated in public dances, which are accompanied with songs and music suited to the occasion. . . .

We have many musical instruments, particularly drums of different kinds, a piece of music which resembles a guitar, and another much like a stickado. These last are chiefly used by betrothed virgins, who play on them on all grand festivals. . . .

Our manner of living is entirely plain; for as yet the natives are unacquainted with those refinements in cookery which debauch the taste: bullocks, goats, and poultry supply the greatest wealth of the country, and the chief articles of its commerce. The flesh is usually stewed in a pan; to make it savory we sometimes use also pepper, and other spices, and we have salt made of wood ashes. Our vegetables are mostly plantains, eadas, yams, beans, and Indian corn. The head of the family usually eats alone; his wives and slaves have also their separate tables. Before we taste food we always wash our hands: indeed our cleanliness on all occasions is extreme; but on this it is an indispensable ceremony. After washing, libation is made, by pouring out a small portion of the drink on the floor, and tossing a small quantity of the food in a certain place, for the spirits of departed relations, which the natives supposed to preside over their conduct, and guard them from evil. . . .

In our buildings we study convenience rather than ornament. Each master of a family has a large square piece of ground, surrounded with a moat or fence, or enclosed with a wall made of red earth tempered: which, when dry, is as hard as brick. Within this, are his houses to accommodate his family and slaves; which if numerous, frequently present the appearance of a village. In the middle, stands the principal building, appropriated to the sole use of the master, and consisting of two apartments; in one of which he sits in the day with his family, the other is left apart for the reception of his friends. He has besides these a distinct apartment in which he sleeps, together with his male children. On each side are the apartments of his wives, who have also their separate day and night houses. The habitations of the slaves and their families are distributed throughout the rest of the enclosure. These houses never exceed one story in height: they are always built of wood, or stakes driven into the ground, crossed with wattles, and neatly plastered within and without. The roof is thatched with reeds. Our day-houses are left open at the sides; but those in which we sleep are always covered, and plastered in the inside, with a composition mixed with cow-dung, to keep off the different insects which annoy us during the night. The walls and floors also of these are generally covered with mats. Our beds consist of a platform, raised three or four feet from the ground, on which are laid skins, and different parts of a spungy tree, called plantain. . . .

We have also markets, at which I have been frequently with my mother. These are sometimes visited by stout mahogany-colored men from the south-west of us: we call them *Oye-Eboe*, which term signifies red men living at a distance. They generally bring us fire-arms, gunpowder, hats, beads, and dried fish. . . . Sometimes indeed, we sold slaves to them, but they were only prisoners of war, or such among us as had been convicted of kidnapping, or adultery, and some other crimes, which we esteemed heinous. This practice of kidnapping induces me to think, that, notwithstanding all our strictness, their principal business among us was to trepan our people. I remember too, they carried great sacks along with them, which not long after, I had an opportunity of fatally seeing applied to that infamous purpose. . . .

Our tillage is exercised in a large plain or common, some hours-walk from our dwellings, and all the neighbors resort thither in a body. They use no beasts of husbandry; and their only instruments are hoes, axes, shovels, and beaks, or pointed iron, to dig with. . . .

As to religion, the natives believe that there is one Creator of all things, and that he lives in the sun, and is girded round with a belt that he may never eat or drink; but, according to some, he smokes a pipe, which is our own favorite luxury. They believe he governs events, especially our deaths or captivity; but, as for the doctrine of eternity, I do not remember to have ever heard of it: some, however, believe in the transmigration of souls in a certain degree. . . .

We compute the year, from the day on which the sun crosses the line, and on its setting that evening, there is a general shout throughout the land; at least, I can speak from my own knowledge, throughout our vicinity. . . .

CHAPTER II

I hope the reader will not think I have trespassed on his patience in introducing myself to him, with some account of the manners and customs of my country. They had been implanted in me with great care, and made an impression on my mind, which time could not erase, and which all the adversity and variety of fortune I have since experienced, served only to rivet and record; for, whether the love of one's own country be real or imaginary, or a lesson of reason, or an instinct of nature, I still look back with pleasure on the first scenes of my life, though that pleasure has been for the most part mingled with sorrow. . . .

One day, when all our people were gone out to their works as usual, and only I and my dear sister were left to mind the house, two men and a woman got over our walls, and in a moment seized us both, and, without giving us time to cry out, or make resistance, they stopped our mouths, and ran off with us into the nearest wood. Here they tied our hands, and continued to carry us as far as they could, till night came on, when we reached a small house, where the robbers halted for refreshment, and spent the night. . . . The next day proved a day of greater sorrow than I had yet experienced; for my sister and I were then separated, while we lay clasped in each other's arms. It was in vain that we besought them not to part us; she was torn from me, and immediately carried away, while I was left in a state of distraction not to be described. I cried and grieved continually; and for several days did not eat any thing but what they forced into my mouth. . . .

I was now carried to the left of the sun's rising, through many dreary wastes and dismal woods, amidst the hideous roarings of wild beasts. The people I was sold to used to carry me very often, when I was tired, either on their shoulders or on their backs. . . .

At last I came to the banks of a large river which was covered with canoes, in which the people appeared to live with their household utensils, and provisions of all kinds. I was beyond measure astonished at this, as I had never before seen any water larger than a pond or a rivulet: and my surprise was mingled with no small fear when I was put into one of these canoes, and we began to paddle and move along the river. . . .

The first object which saluted my eyes when I arrived on the coast, was the sea, and a slave ship, which was then riding at anchor, and waiting for its cargo. These filled me with astonishment, which was soon converted into terror, when I was carried on board. I was immediately handled, and tossed up to see if I were sound, by some of the crew; and I was now persuaded that I had gotten into a world of bad spirits, and that they were going to kill me. Their complexions, too, differing so much from ours, their long hair, and the language they spoke (which was very different from any I had ever heard) united to confirm me in this belief. Indeed, such were the horrors of my views and fears at the moment, that, if ten thousand worlds had been my own, I would have freely parted with them all to have exchanged my condition with that of the meanest slave in my own country. When I looked round the ship too, and saw a large furnace of copper boiling, and a multitude of black people of every description chained together, every one of their countenances expressing dejection and sorrow, I no longer doubted of my fate; and, quite overpowered with horror and anguish, I fell motionless on the deck and fainted.

2. A Humanitarian's View

FOR WHITES *the slave trade was a tedious and sometimes hazardous but highly profitable business. For blacks the trade was a living hell. Taken in wars that were usually little more than piratical raids, or simply kidnapped outright, they were marched to the beaches or carried there in great canoes. Awestruck by the roar of the ocean and the technological miracle of the great wind-and-sail-driven ships, the captives were also terrified by a belief that whites were cannibals. Segregated on the basis of sex, age, and health, then branded and loaded aboard the slavers, the Africans were chained and stowed between decks. During a tragic voyage of about 4,000 nautical miles that, depending on destination and season, took between three and six weeks, they were fed horse beans and yams, and were forced to dance on deck in fair weather to maintain health and discourage suicidal reactions.*

But this is simply narrative, the basis of "impressionistic history," and extremely insufficient as a measure of the trade's impact on African and American societies. Statistics, beginning to be organized by such scholars as Philip Curtin, will soon provide a more systematic view of the trade's demographic dimension. In all, approximately 12 to 15 million blacks were exported in the four centuries between about 1450 and 1850. For every two captured, generally one survived to be sold in the New World. Mortality at sea (which declined in the late eighteenth century and was often as high for white sailors as it was for blacks) ranged from 13 to 33 percent, and varied greatly according to the treatment of slaves aboard the ship, the route and length of the voyage, and most importantly, the disease environment of the export and import areas, with smallpox the greatest killer.

A typical mid-eighteenth-century slaver was the Brookes, according to Captain Parrey of the Royal Navy, who measured the boat for an "angry book" he wrote in 1788 that led to a House of Commons Report and the great debates on the slave trade. In the Brookes, each man had a space that was 6 feet long by 16 inches wide and 2 feet 7 inches high, and each woman, a space 5 feet 10 inches long and 16 inches wide. By law this vessel of 320 tons was permitted to carry 454 slaves, who in a famous picture appeared to be stacked like cords of wood or, as another testified, like books on a library shelf. Out of the holds of these grim ships poured the baubles of England's new industrial cities of the midlands—woolens, linens, bedsheets, and glass beads—as well as the weapons to keep the entire crazy game in motion: knives, cutlasses, muskets, and gunpowder. On the formidable shores of West Africa, black people were bought for about £10 in 1708 to £15 by mid-century, and sold in the American colonies for about two or three times that amount.

In the following document, Alexander Falconbridge, surgeon, reports

on a voyage he made from Bonny to the West Indies. Bonny, immedi-
ately south of the Niger delta, was a slave station in the Bight of Biafra,
the same area (present-day Nigeria) where Olaudah Equiano had been
sold about thirty years earlier.

SOURCE: Alexander Falconbridge, *An Account of the Slave Trade
on the Coast of Africa* (London, 1788), pp. 7, 12, 16–17, 19–22.

The slave ships generally lie near a mile below the town, in
Bonny River, in seven or eight fathom water. Sometimes fifteen
sail, English and French, but chiefly the former, meet here together. Soon after they cast anchor, the captains go on shore, to
make known their arrival, and to inquire into the state of the
trade. They likewise invite the kings of Bonny to come on board,
to whom, previous to breaking bulk, they usually make presents
(in that country termed *dashes*) which generally consist of pieces
of cloth, cotton, chintz, silk handkerchiefs, and other India goods,
and sometimes of brandy, wine, or beer.

When the ships have disposed of all their merchandise in the
purchase of negroes, and have laid in their stock of wood, water,
and yams, they prepare for sailing, by getting up the yards and
topmasts, reeving the running rigging, bending the sails, and by
taking down the temporary house. They then drop down the river,
to wait for a favourable opportunity to pass over the bar, which is
formed by a number of sand-banks lying across the mouth of the
river, with navigable channels between them. It is not uncommon
for ships to get upon the bar, and sometimes they are lost. . . .

The time during which the slave ships are absent from England
varies according to the destination of the voyage, and the number
of ships they happen to meet on the coast. To Bonny, or Old and
New Calabar, a voyage is usually performed in about ten months.
Those to the Windward and Gold Coasts are rather more uncertain, but in general from fifteen to eighteen months.

THE MANNER IN WHICH THE SLAVES ARE PROCURED

After permission has been obtained for *breaking trade*, as it is
termed, the captains go ashore, from time to time, to examine the
negroes that are exposed to sale, and to make their purchases. The
unhappy wretches thus disposed of are bought by the black traders

at fairs, which are held for that purpose, at the distance of upwards of two hundred miles from the sea coast; and these fairs are
said to be supplied from an interior part of the country. Many
negroes, upon being questioned relative to the places of their na-
tivity, have asserted that they have travelled during the revolution
of several moons (their usual method of calculating time) before
they have reached the places where they were purchased by the
black traders. At these fairs, which are held at uncertain periods,
but generally every six weeks, several thousands are frequently
exposed to sale, who had been collected from all parts of the
country for a very considerable distance round. While I was upon
the coast, during one of the voyages I made, the black traders
brought down, in different canoes, from twelve to fifteen hundred
negroes, which had been purchased at one fair. They consisted
chiefly of men and boys, the women seldom exceeding a third of
the whole number. From forty to two hundred negroes are generally purchased at a time by the black traders, according to the
opulence of the buyer; and consist of those of all ages, from a
month to sixty years and upwards. Scarce any age or situation is
deemed an exception, the price being proportionable. Women
sometimes form a part of them, who happen to be so far advanced
in their pregnancy, as to be delivered during their journey from
the fairs to the coast; and I have frequently seen instances of
deliveries on board ship. The slaves purchased at these fairs are
only for the supply of the markets at Bonny, and Old and New
Calabar. . . .

The preparations made at Bonny by the black traders, upon
setting out for the fairs which are held up the country, are very
considerable. From twenty to thirty canoes, capable of containing
thirty or forty negroes each, are assembled for this purpose; and
such goods put on board them as they expect will be wanted for
the purchase of the number of slaves they intend to buy. When
their loading is completed, they commence their voyage, with colours flying and musick playing; and in about ten or eleven days,
they generally return to Bonny with full cargoes. As soon as the
canoes arrive at the trader's landing-place, the purchased negroes
are cleaned, and oiled with palm oil; and on the following day
they are exposed for sale to the captains. . . .

TREATMENT OF THE SLAVES

As soon as the wretched Africans, purchased at the fairs, fall into the hands of the black traders, they experience an earnest of those dreadful sufferings which they are doomed in future to undergo. And there is not the least room to doubt, but that even before they can reach the fairs, great numbers perish from cruel usage, want of food, travelling through inhospitable deserts, etc. They are brought from the places where they are purchased to Bonny, &c. in canoes; at the bottom of which they lie, having their hands tied with a kind of willow twigs, and a strict watch is kept over them. Their usage in other respects, during the time of the passage, which generally lasts several days, is equally cruel. Their allowance of food is so scanty that it is barely sufficient to support nature. They are, besides, much exposed to the violent rains which frequently fall here, being covered only with mats that afford but a slight defence; and as there is usually water at the bottom of the canoes, from their leaking, they are scarcely ever dry.

Nor do these unhappy beings, after they become the property of the Europeans (from whom, as a more civilized people, more humanity might naturally be expected) find their situation in the least amended. Their treatment is no less rigorous. The men negroes, on being brought aboard the ship, are immediately fastened together, two and two, by hand-cuffs on their wrists, and by irons rivetted on their legs. They are then sent down between the decks, and placed in an apartment partitioned off for that purpose. The women likewise are placed in a separate apartment between decks, but without being ironed. And an adjoining room, on the same deck, is besides appointed for the boys. Thus are they all placed in different apartments.

But at the same time, they are frequently stowed so close as to admit of no other posture than lying on their sides. Neither will the height between decks, unless directly under the grating, permit them the indulgence of an erect posture; especially where there are platforms, which is generally the case. These platforms are a kind of shelf, about eight or nine feet in breadth, extending from the side of the ship towards the centre. They are placed nearly midway between the decks, at the distance of two or three feet from each deck. Upon these the negroes are stowed in the same manner as they are on the deck underneath.

In each of the apartments are placed three or four large buckets, of a conical form, being near two feet in diameter at the bottom, and only one foot at the top, and in depth about twenty-eight inches; to which, when necessary, the negroes have recourse. It often happens, that those who are placed at a distance from the buckets, in endeavouring to get to them, tumble over their companions, in consequence of their being shackled. These accidents, although unavoidable, are productive of continual quarrels, in which some of them are always bruised. In this distressed situation, unable to proceed, and prevented from getting to the tubs, they desist from the attempt; and, as the necessities of nature are not to be repelled, ease themselves as they lie. This becomes a fresh source of broils and disturbances, and tends to render the condition of the poor captive wretches still more uncomfortable. The nuisance arising from these circumstances is not unfrequently increased by the tubs being much too small for the purpose intended, and their being usually emptied but once every day. The rule for doing this, however, varies in different ships, according to the attention paid to the health and convenience of the slaves by the captain.

About eight o'clock in the morning the negroes are generally brought upon deck. Their irons being examined, a long chain, which is locked to a ring-bolt, fixed in the deck, is run through the rings of the shackles of the men, and then locked to another ring-bolt, fixed also in the deck. By this means fifty or sixty, and sometimes more, are fastened to one chain, in order to prevent them from rising, or endeavouring to escape. If the weather proves favourable, they are permitted to remain in that situation till four or five in the afternoon, when they are disengaged from the chain, and sent down.

The diet of the negroes, while on board, consists chiefly of horse-beans, boiled to the consistence of a pulp; of boiled yams and rice, and sometimes of a small quantity of beef or pork. The latter are frequently taken from the provisions laid in for the sailors. They sometimes make use of a sauce, composed of palm-oil, mixed with flour, water, and pepper, which the sailors call *slabber-sauce*.

Yams are the favourite food of the Eboe, or Bight negroes, and rice or corn, of those from the Gold and Windward Coasts; each preferring the produce of their native soil. . . .

They are commonly fed twice a day, about eight o'clock in the morning and four in the afternoon. In most ships they are only fed with their *own food* once a day. Their food is served up to them in tubs, about the size of a small water bucket. They are placed round these tubs in companies of ten to each tub, out of which they feed themselves with wooden spoons. These they soon lose, and when they are not allowed others, they feed themselves with their hands. In favourable weather they are fed upon deck, but in bad weather their food is given them below. . . .

Exercise being deemed necessary for the preservation of their health, they are sometimes obliged to dance, when the weather will permit their coming on deck. If they go about it reluctantly, or do not move with agility, they are flogged; a person standing by them all the time with a cat-o'-nine-tails in his hand for that purpose. Their musick, upon these occasions, consists of a drum, sometimes with only one head; and when that is worn out, they do not scruple to make use of the bottom of one of the tubs being described. The poor wretches are frequently compelled to sing also; but when they do so, their songs are generally, as may naturally be expected, melancholy lamentations of their exile from their native country. . . .

3. THE BUSINESSMAN'S VIEW

BEFORE 1700 *most slaves came to North America from the West Indies in small "parcels" of fifteen or twenty. However, by the early eighteenth century the largest and wealthiest slave societies in British North America, Virginia, and South Carolina were sufficiently developed to provide markets for large cargoes of two hundred or more slaves coming in directly from West Africa. This critical juncture was reached when the southern mainland colonies developed a full-scale plantation system—the production of staples for overseas markets, on larger and more efficient plantations (developed on the best soils and waterways at the expense of yeoman farms), worked by slaves for the benefit of a landed aristocracy. Once the plantation economy was in full swing, the great annual importations of Africans began to the Carolina low country (rice and indigo) and to the Chesapeake Bay region (to-*

bacco). Before the Revolution about 2,500 slaves yearly were imported to South Carolina, and about 1,500 yearly to Virginia. In 1708 about 40 percent of the 9,580 people in South Carolina were slaves; and by 1724 their numbers had increased to 32,000, or two thirds of a total population of 46,000. Virginia, settled more than fifty years earlier, had about 70,000 people by 1700, and nearly 138,000 in 1725. Throughout the eighteenth century slaves were seldom more than 40 percent of the population, although in South Carolina blacks comprised 60 percent of the population in the 1700s, and in the parishes around Charleston, where many whites lived who owned plantations, only one person in five was white.

The Carolinians' nervousness about what large numbers of blacks might do if Indians or Spaniards attacked the community may account for their careful attention to the ethnic and tribal characteristics of recently imported Africans. They preferred slaves from Senegambia (present-day Senegal and Gambia) and Bumbara and Malinke people, and they disliked short Africans. Their second choice was slaves from the Gold Coast (Ghana). Farther south in Nigeria were men like Olaudah Equiano, whom they avoided, arguing that Iboes were despondent and sometimes suicidal. While only 2.1 percent of all eighteenth-century South Carolina slaves were from this region, nearly 2 in 5 (or 40 percent) of Virginia's slaves were from Nigeria. Instead, Carolinians obtained 40 percent of their slaves from farther south, in Angola, while only 16 percent of Virginia's slaves came from that region.

SOURCES: Robert "King" Carter Letterbook and Diary, 1722–1727, Alderman Library microfilm, University of Virginia Archives; *The Papers of Henry Laurens*, ed. Philip M. Hamer and George C. Rogers, Jr. (Columbia, S.C., 1968–), 1:274–275, 2:83. Reprinted by permission of the University of South Carolina Press.

Robert "King" Carter to Isreal Pemberton
(Liverpool Merchant), Corotoman, Va., September 15, 1727

After Capt: Hayes in the Leopard had bin in York River to meet with Mr. Nelson who is gon for England and finding no Orders for him there he came into this River [Rappahannock] to me, upon Seeing the Strictness of your Orders I told him I could not meddle with his Slaves it being impossible in my Esteem at this season of the Year to bring them out, at your Premptory termes so I let him go, he immediately goes up the River to Colo. Tayloe w[ha]t their Agreement may be I dont yet know the Ship is gon up the Bay to Peturkson and Tayloe meets her there.

Our Govr: arrived into James River the 7th Inst: I went from home to wait upon him the 9th: the 11th the King was proclaimd I got home last night at one a Clock. Capt. Christian came about from York [River] into this River the 10th: is now in Corotoman and I am going aboard him. I shall do you the best Service I can in the Sale of the Slaves but I fear that will not be very good I doubt I must be forced to Stay for a great many bills till Aprill. . . .

19 May [1726].   Cool in the morning. Sent my Mare away. I went aboard Cap[tai]n Denton, Agreed to Sell his Negroes . . . at £20 per head I am to draw 10 Per Ct on the Sale for Commission to make good all debts in this manner if any of the Bills of Exc[hange] will not be p[ai]d the Protests are to be returned to me, I am to give new bills for the Principal, the Protests to be mine, he is to run in to Corotoman shore to lye for the Sale, I am to be at no manner of Charge, all to be Chargd to the Owner.

21 [*May*].   I began the sale. 32 went of[f] this day.

23 [*May*].   Sold . . . in all 56, 3 of them for Tob[acco]. Tho. Berry owes me £5, Simon Sallard [Carter's overseer] owes me £40. . . . I trust Gregory with a large Negro Girl he is to give me his Bond to pay me Sixteen Pounds Sterl[ing] with Interest till the money is paid. I trust to Tho. Carter for £24 Sterling, I am to Stop so much out of his Crop.

July 18 [1727].   I go aboard Capt. Denton, 4 Clock. Chose 8 men 7 wom[en] at £20 each, came ashoar at 12 in the Night, my sloop came from the Carter in the Night.

[*July*] *20.*   Sale of the Negros began, sold off 92 Slaves & 2 Children those that I had come ashore the 18th.

[*July*] *21.*   Sold off 15 Negros I made a present of a Girl to my God Son Jno. Wormley. . . .

Aug. 2.   Sold the broken back Negro to Jno Hudnal

[*Aug.*] *3.*   Sold two more Negros remains 3 sick Negros to Sell

Sept. 18.   Began the Sale of the Negroes, sold 28 this day. . . .

[*Sept.*] 19. Fine weather . . . got aboard at 12, Sold 6 n[ew] Negros this day came home a little before dark. . . .

[*Sept.*] 21. Continues very warm, I had a very [good?] Night, Slept from 4 to 7 got aboard the Negro ship abt 1 Clock, sold nine Negros & eat a leg & wing of a Chicken drank 6 glasses of wine, slept broken but eaisie.

Henry Laurens to Thomas Mears (Liverpool merchant),
Charleston, S.C., June 27, 1755

SIR:

. . . We fear your Snow the *Mears,* Capt. Allen, has mis'd a most charming Market with us. If what we have heard of her be true that she was very forward in her Slaving the beginning of March she must if well have reach'd the West Indias long before this. We had no opportunity of forwarding Letters to meet him at Barbadoes 'till a Week ago when we thought it too late. Some have been laying at St. Kitts for many months past in which we gave Capt Allen good encouragement to come down here if he could dispence with selling them on Credit as usual which if he was to come in so late in the Year as this would be nearly as expeditious as from the West Indias where for nine Cargoes out of ten they keep one fourth of the produce 12 months, delay your Ship 8 or 10 Weeks with them & most of the Bills they send you are payable 3 months after sight. We sold a Cargo from Angola three days ago, none on longer Credit than the Month of January. The bulk of the Men brought £280 & £270. Five of them £290. the Cargo avarages £33.17/ Sterling. If we had stood out for ready money are of opinion the Sales would not have run so high by 6 or £7 Sterling. We must stick to this modus to keep up our Sales. The Importer is extreamly well paid by laying 3 or 4 months out of their money. . . .

We have very good prospects of Crops this Year both of Rice & Indigo. By our computation shall make at least 500,000 lb. weight of the latter barring accidents. This spirits up our People to give good prices for Slaves, many having planted largely in expectation of buying new Negroes to give them a Lift in their Crops so that a Cargo or two more would just now do extreamly well but our People growl in the Gizard a good deal at paying more than

£260, this price they would be contented with which is equal to £37.2.10 Sterling. We wish you a successfull Voyage in the *Mears* wherever she sits down. . . .

Laurens to Gedney Clarke (Barbados), Charleston, S.C., January 31, 1756

. . . Permit us now to inform you what progress we have made in the Sale of your Slaves address'd to us which we have taken every measure in our power to put off to advantage but with poor success. Our People thought them a very indifferent parcell, that they were much too small a People for the business of this Country & on this Account many went away empty handed that would otherways have purchas'd. Another grand impediment to the Sale was a Parapenumonia breaking out in many parts of the Province & sweeping off great numbers of Negroes a little before the day of Sale which prevented a great many from attending & the success of a Sale much depends on the Numbers that attend. In short every thing contributed to induce us to think we must inevitably make a very poor Sale & what added greatly to it was that we could only bring into the Yard 105, the rest that remain'd alive were in a bad condition with the Flux, from which disorder there are dead to this time 13 & we are sorry to say several more in great danger. What we have sold at this day are 102. The Amount £21,291.10/ Currency. We have 14 more that are able to come aboard and 11 sick in the Hospital. Those which are well are a very dimunitive parcell of Mortalls, Children in size but at their full growth, so that upon the whole we fear you must make a very indifferent Voyage & what will add to it is that the major part of those sold are on Credit to January next. The monstrous prices given for a few Slaves in the month of October has produced all this Evil, brought down parcell after parcell from the West Indias incessantly all this Winter which has put it in the power of the Planter to play upon the Sellers their own Game.

B. The Eighteenth-Century Dynamic: Plantation Self-sufficiency and Cultural Change among Slaves

THE FATE *awaiting the African in America ultimately depended on his psyche and the character of the man to whom he was sold. But both were products of larger, more impersonal forces. Despite significant differences among plantation societies, colonial culture at its core was Christian, and whites were unified in part by the belief that Africans were black, lewd, dangerous, and suitable for little more than a godless, slavish existence. But a major goal for founding colonies was to Christianize "heathens"; in addition, pronounced differences in plantation organization from colony to colony also mitigated the settlers' xenophobia, while shaping the ways in which slaveholders chose to "save" their "savages."*

Christianizing Slaves in Colonial South Carolina and Virginia

IN THE CHESAPEAKE BAY REGION *(Maryland and Virginia), where whites outnumbered blacks almost two to one and where society was sufficiently settled and secure from Indian attacks, planters were relatively open about the controversial issue of Christianizing slaves. But in South Carolina—a frontier through most of the eighteenth century plagued by Indian wars, hurricanes, epidemics, Spaniards, and Caribbean pirates— slaves were seen as an "intestine enemy" made even more dangerous when converted to Christianity.*

Virginians, however, came to recognize the value of religious instruction for the Africans' American-born children. Literate blacks could be trained as artisans who would help provide the self-sufficiency and diversification great planters needed for their self-esteem and economic survival. But Carolinians saw educated blacks as bold, troublesome, and inclined to turn religious meetings into conspiracies and rebellion. In an attempt to change this belief, the Society for the Propagation of the Gospel in Foreign Parts sent Anglican ministers to the frontiers of the empire. In 1713 the S.P.G. ministers in South Carolina met in Charleston and "laid open their grievances" about the rice planters' hostility toward missionaries who worked among slaves. Meanwhile, in Tidewater Virginia, Hugh Jones, a tobacco planter and amateur historian, presented a rather different view on socializing blacks.

4. "A SLAVE GROWS WORSE BY BEING A CHRISTIAN"

SOURCE: South Carolina Society for the Propagation of the Gospel ministers to Mr. Gideon Johnston, March 4, 1713, Society for the Propagation of the Gospel Mss., Reel 2, 423 ff., South Carolina State Archives microfilm of Library of Congress transcripts.

The Conversion of Slaves, which is the Second Article is, considering the present Circumstance of things, scarcely possible. Tis true indeed that an odd slave here and there may be Converted when a Minister has Leisure and Opportunity for so doing, but this seldom happens. Nevertheless it must be said to Dr Le Jau's advantage that his Endeavours have been very great this Way, and not altogether unsuccessful tho' some unreasonable Malicious People can give him no thanks for his Service. . . . The Success must be little and inconsiderable in comparison of what might be expected because there are so many rubbs and impediments that lye in the Way:

1st. The Slaves have not time to be instructed by the ministers but on the Lord's Day; and then he has work enough from the White folk on his hands.

2ndly. The Plantations are so many and so remote and distant from one another that the slaves can't be well assembled together for their instruction; and if they could there would be a great deal of Hazard in the Experiment, because they would thereby have an opportunity of knowing their own Strength and Superiority in number, and perhaps may be tempted to recover their liberty tho' it were the Slaughter and destruction of the Whole Colony.

3rdly. The Masters of Slaves are generally of Opinion that a Slave grows worse by being a Christian; and therefore instead of instructing them in the principles of Christianity which is undoubtedly their Duty, they malign and traduce those that Attempt it. This I say is the Case of most Masters, however, I must not forget to do justice to Some, who have distinguished themselves by a contrary practice; and are very eminent for the care they take about their slaves in matters of religion.

4thly. The legislature does not countenance or encourage a

work of this importance as much as it should or could. The conversion of slaves is thought inconsistent with the planters' secular interest and advantage; and it is they that make up the bulk of our assembly. For beside the general notion that they have of their slaves being worse for being Christians, they know that if they would encourage their conversion, they must allow them some reasonable time for their Instruction; and this would consequently be a hindrance to their work and an abatement of the master's profit. And tho' this is not openly owned and avowed to be the true cause of that luke-warmness or rather unwillingness, they express on this occasion, yet I may venture to say 'tis so at the bottom. Nor can some of them forbear to speak out their minds, though they endeavour to justify and excuse themselves by pretending that the slaves (the negroes especially) are a wicked stubborn race of men, and can never be true converts, tho' to gull and deceive their masters they may put on an air and appearance of religion; and hence they conclude that it is not only a sensible loss to them, but likewise so much time and pains thrown away to no purpose.

5thly. There are many Planters who to free themselves from the trouble of feeding and cloathing their Slaves allow them one day in the week to clear ground, & plant for themselves as much as will cloath and Subsist them and their familys. In order to do this, some masters give their Slaves Saturdays, some half that day, & others Sunday only, which they Endeavour to Justify by saying, that if they were not obliged to work that day, they would be Employed in that which is much worse. 'Tis needless to shew the Weakness of this Excuse and therefore I will only observe, that those who have Saturdays given them seldom fail of working more or less on the Lords day too. . . .

Thus I have given a short account of those more obvious impediments that lie in the way to the slaves conversion nor indeed do I see any likelyhood, humanely speaking, how this necessary work, so shamefully and Scandalously neglected hitherto, can be carried on with any great hope of success if the Legislature does not promote and Encourage it by proper Laws to be enacted for that Purpose.

If any one should think that the Clergy can do this of themselves without the Government Countenance and the help of Itinerant

Catechists he is greatly mistaken: for with equal grief and truth I speak it, they have a worse generation of Infidels than those poor heathen Slaves to deal with; who tho' they are children in one respect have made themselves worse than dogs in another sence and are scarce worthy to feed upon the crums that fall from their fathers Table. The ignorance therefore of these poor Slaves in the principles of Christianity in a Christian Country and under a Christian Governm[en]t is not so much their fault as their unhappiness in falling into the hands of such ill Masters who not only neglect to instruct them but scoff at those that attempt it, and give them likewise Strange Ideas of Christianity from the Scandalous lives they lead.

5. They "Affect Our Language, Habits, and Customs"

Source: Hugh Jones, *The Present State of Virginia,* ed. Richard L. Morton (1724; Chapel Hill, N.C., 1956), pp. 37–38, 70–71. Reprinted by permission of The University Press of Virginia.

The Negroes live in small cottages called quarters, in about six in a gang, under the direction of an overseer or bailiff; who takes care that they tend such land as the owner allots and orders, upon which they raise hogs and cattle, and plant Indian corn (or maize) and tobacco for the use of their master; out of which the overseer has a dividend (or share) in proportion to the number of hands including himself; this with several privileges is his salary, and is an ample recompence for his pains, and encouragement of his industrious care, as to the labour, health, and provision of the Negroes.

The Negroes are very numerous, some gentlemen having hundreds of them of all sorts, to whom they bring great profit; for the sake of which they are obliged to keep them well, and not overwork, starve, or famish them, besides other inducements to favour them; which is done in a great degree, to such especially that are laborious, careful, and honest; though indeed some masters, careless of their own interest or reputation, are too cruel and negligent.

The Negroes are not only encreased by fresh supplies from Africa and the West India Islands, but also are very prolifick among themselves; and they that are born here talk good English, and affect our language, habits, and customs; and though they be naturally of a barbarous and cruel temper, yet are they kept under by severe discipline upon occasion, and by good laws are prevented from running away, injuring the English, or neglecting their business.

Their work (or chimerical hard slavery) is not very laborious; their greatest hardship consisting in that they and their posterity are not at their own liberty or disposal, but are the property of their owners; and when they are free, they know not how to provide so well for themselves generally; neither did they live so plentifully nor (many of them) so easily in their own country, where they are made slaves to one another, or taken captive by their enemies. . . .

Several of them are taught to be sawyers, carpenters, smiths, coopers, etc., and though for the most part they be none of the aptest or nicest; yet they are by nature cut out for hard labour and fatigue, and will perform tolerably well; though they fall much short of an Indian, that has learned and seen the same things; and those Negroes make the best servants, that have been slaves in their own country, for they that have been kings and great men there are generally lazy, haughty, and obstinate; whereas the others are sharper, better humoured, and more laborious. . . .

As for baptizing Indians and Negroes, several of the people disapprove of it; because they say it often makes them proud, and not so good servants: But these, and such objections, are easily refuted, if the persons be sensible, good, and understand English, and have been taught (or are willing to learn) the principles of Christianity, and if they be kept to the observance of it afterwards; for Christianity encourages and orders them to become more humble and better servants, and not worse, than when they were heathens.

But as for the children of Negroes and Indians, that are to live among Christians, undoubtedly they ought all to be baptized; since it is not out of the power of their masters to take care that they have a Christian education, learn their prayers and catechism, and go to church, and not accustom themselves to lie, swear and steal, though such (as the poorer sort in England) be not taught to read and write; which as yet has been found to be dangerous upon several political accounts, especially self-preservation.

The Plantation Ideal in Chesapeake Bay Society

WILLIAM BYRD II'S LETTER *to an English lord in 1726 is the outstanding statement of what tobacco aristocrats thought their society and careers ought to be. The document also provides additional insights into the acculturative process: while Hugh Jones described Africans as "barbarous and cruel," Byrd saw them as tractable laborers, and so speaks at a later stage of cultural change. Incorporated into the plantation setting at Westover, they had become "my own Servants," "my Bond-men and Bond-women."*

But the plantation system was not simply a way of assimilating a strange and sometimes threatening people, or solely a means of making money. It was also arranged to make colonial status more manageable. Tobacco aristocrats—initially as patriarchs but later as revolutionaries —were preoccupied with questions of independence and local autonomy. One solution was to become so wealthy that "freedom" could be achieved with money and perhaps a home in England (a solution to colonial status for West Indian sugar planters and some rice growers), but this avenue was closed for most tobacco growers. The market was not steady, nor were profits as great as those from sugar and rice. Thus wealthy Tidewater planters created their own miniature private empires, or so Byrd claimed in a boastful remark to the Earl of Orrery, saying that, "like one of the Patriarchs," he lived "in a kind of Independence on every one but Providence."

6. "WE WHO HAVE PLANTATIONS"

SOURCE: William Byrd II to the Earl of Orrery, Virginia, July 5, 1726, *Virginia Magazine of History and Biography*, 32 (December 1924): 26–28. Reprinted by permission of the publisher.

Besides the advantage of a pure air, we abound in all kinds of provisions without expence (I mean we who have plantations). I have a large family of my own, and my doors are open to every body, yet I have no bills to pay, and half-a-Crown will rest undisturbed in my pocket for many moons together. Like one of the patriarchs, I have my flocks and my herds, my bond-men and bond-women, and every soart of trade amongst my own servants, so that I live in a kind of independence on every one but Providence. However this soart of life is without expence, yet is attended with a great deal of trouble. I must take care to keep all my people to their duty, to set all the springs in motion and to make every one draw his equal share to carry the machine forward. But then 'tis an amusement in this silent country and a continual exercise of our patience and economy.

Another thing my Lord that recommends this country very much—we sit securely under our vines and our fig trees without any danger to our property. We have neither publick robbers nor private, which your Lordship will think very strange, when we have often needy Governors, and pilfering convicts sent amongst us. The first of these it is suspected have some-times an inclination to plunder, but want the power, and though they may be tyrants in their nature, yet they are tyrants without guards, which makes them as harmless as a scold would be without a tongue. . . . We can rest securely in our beds with all our doors and windows open, and yet find every thing exactly in place the next morning. We can travel all over the country by night and by day, unguarded and unarmed, and never meet with any person so rude as to bid us stand. We have no vagrant mendicants to seize and deafen us wherever we go, as in your Island of Beggers. Thus my Lord we are very happy in our Canaans if we could but forget the onions and fleshpots of Egypt. There are so many temptations in England to inflame the appetite and charm the senses, that we are content to run all risques to enjoy them. They always had I must own too strong an influence upon me, as your Lordship will believe when they could keep me so long from the more solid pleasures of innocence and retirement.

7. Good Living in Eighteenth-Century Virginia

PHILIP VICKERS FITHIAN, *a theological student from Princeton, came south to serve as a tutor in the household of one of the wealthiest men in colonial America. Robert "Councillor" Carter, "King" Carter's grandson, produced tobacco and, later, wheat. He was also the landlord for scores of tenants in the Shenandoah Valley, owner of a large ironworks in Baltimore, and the operator of a thriving spinning and weaving center at Aries, one of his many quarters. Fithian's description of Nomini Hall, the center of this large and diversified operation, illustrates the planters' other side—they were hard-working, dedicated capitalists.*

SOURCE: Hunter Dickinson Farish, ed., *The Journal and Letters of Philip Vickers Fithian. A Plantation Tutor of the Old Dominion, 1773–1774*, new ed. (Williamsburg, Va., 1965), pp. 79–81. Reprinted by permission of The University Press of Virginia.

I have all along intended, & shall now attempt to give a short discription of Nomini-Hall, & the several Buildings, & improvements adjoining it; as well for my own amusement, as also to be able with certainty to inform others of a Seat as magnificent in itself & with as many surrounding Conveniences, as any I have ever seen, & perhaps equal to any in this Colony—Mr *Carter* now possesses 60000 Acres of Land; & about 600 Negroes—But his Estate is much divided, & lies in almost every county in this Colony; He has Lands in the neighbourhood of Williamsburg, & an elegant & Spacious House in that City—He owns a great part of the well known Iron-Works near Baltimore in Maryland—And he has one or more considerable Farms not far from Anopolis. He has some large tracts of Land far to the West, at a place call'd "Bull Run," & the "Great Meadows" among the mountains. He owns Lands near Dumfries on the Potowmack; & large Tracts in this & the neighbouring Counties.—Out of these Lands, which are situated so remote from each other in various parts of these two large Provinces, Virginia, & Maryland, Mr Carter has chosen for the place of his habitation a high spot of Ground in Westmoreland County at the Head of the Navigation of the River Nomini, where he has erected a large Elegant House, at a vast expence, which commonly goes by the name of *Nomini-Hall.* This House is built with Brick, but the bricks have been covered with strong lime Mortar; so that the building is now perfectly white; It is seventy-six Feet long from East to west; & forty-four wide from North to South, two Stories high; the Pitch of the lower story seventeen Feet, & the upper Story twelve. . . .

It has five Stacks of Chimneys, tho two of these serve only for ornament. There is a beautiful Jutt, on the South side, eighteen feet long, & eight Feet deep from the wall which is supported by three tall pillars—On the South side, or front, in the upper story are four Windows each having twenty-four Lights of Glass. In the lower story are two Windows each having forty-two Lights of Glass, & two Doors each having Sixteen Lights—At the East end the upper story has three Windows each with eighteen Lights; and below two Windows both with eighteen Lights & a Door with nine. . . .

. . . There are four Rooms on a Floor, disposed of in the following manner. Below is a dining Room where we usually sit; the second is a dining-Room for the Children; the third is Mr Carter's study; & the fourth is a Ball-Room thirty Feet long—Above stairs, one Room is for Mr & Mrs Carter; the second for the young Ladies; & the other two for occasional Company—As this House is large, & stands on a high piece of Land it may be seen a considerable distance; I have seen it at the Distance of six Miles—At equal Distances from each corner of this Building stand four other considerable Houses, which I shall next a little describe. First, at the North East corner, & at 100 yards Distance stands the School-House; At the North-West Corner, & at the same Distance stands the stable; At the South-West Corner, & at the same Distance, stands the Coach-House; And lastly, at the South-East corner, & at an equal distance stands the Work-House. These four Houses are the corner of a Square of which the Great-House is the Center. . . .

Due East of the Great House are two Rows of tall, flourishing, beautiful, Poplars, beginning on a Line drawn from the School to the Wash-House. . . . These Rows of Poplars form an extreemly pleasant avenue, & at the Road, through them, the House appears most romantic, at the same time that it does truly elegant—The Area of the Triangle made by the Wash-House, Stable, & School-House is perfectly levil, & designed for a bowling-Green, laid out in rectangular Walks which are paved with Brick, & covered over with burnt Oyster-Shells—In the other Triangle, made by the Wash-House, Stable, & Coach House is the Kitchen, a well-built House, as large as the School-House, Bake-House; Dairy; Store-House & Several other small Houses; all which stand due West, & at a small distance from the great House, & form a little handsome Street.

Slave Craftsmen and Economically Diversified Plantations

EVEN THE PHYSICAL APPEARANCE AND LAYOUT *of the large tobacco plantation made abundantly clear the extent to which it was self-contained. Fithian might have noted that Nomini Hall was also surrounded by thirty-three outbuildings, including a mill, brewery, spinning center, wheat silo, and ironworks. Extensive outbuildings such as these prompted the German traveler Dr. Johann Schoepf to observe that "a plantation in Virginia has often more the appearance of a small village." One of the most complete accounts of a self-contained plantation is George Mason's portrait of the workshops at Gunston Hall. A rare and invaluable view of the black artisans who operated these shops is provided by Mason's contemporary, Bernard Moore, a well-to-do planter and land speculator who had seen better days. Facing economic ruin in the late 1760s (the tobacco market had been declining sharply since 1750), Moore published a lottery scheme which laid bare the most essential economic and social arrangements in his extended plantation family, and dramatized the remarkable degree of acculturation and occupational specialization among Virginia slaves by the third quarter of the eighteenth century.*

8. SELF-SUFFICIENCY AT GUNSTON HALL

SOURCE: Edmund S. Morgan, *Virginians at Home: Family Life in the Eighteenth Century* (Charlottesville, Va., 1952), pp. 53–54. Reprinted by permission of The University of Virginia.

. . . My father had among his slaves carpenters, coopers, sawyers, blacksmiths, tanners, curriers, shoemakers, spinners, weavers and knitters, and even a distiller. His woods furnished timber and plank for the carpenters and coopers, and charcoal for the blacksmith; his cattle killed for his own consumption and for sale supplied skins for the tanners, curriers, and shoemakers, and his sheep gave wool and his fields produced cotton and flax for the weavers and spinners, and his orchards fruit for the distiller. His carpenters and sawyers built and kept in repair all the dwelling-houses, barns, stables, ploughs, barrows, gates &c., on the plantations and the out-houses at the home house. His coopers made the hogsheads the tobacco was prized in and the tight casks to hold the cider and other liquors. The tanners and curriers with the proper vats &c., tanned and dressed the skins as well for upper as for lower leather to the full amount of the consumption of the estate, and the shoemakers made them into shoes for the negroes. . . . The blacksmiths did all the iron work required by the establishment, as making and repairing ploughs, harrow, teeth chains, bolts &c., &c. The spinners, weavers and knitters made all the coarse cloths and stockings used by the negroes, and some of finer texture worn by the white family, nearly all worn by the children of it. The distiller made every fall a good deal of apple, peach and persimmon brandy. . . . All these operations were carried on at the home house, and their results distributed as occasion required to the different plantations. Moreover all the beeves and hogs for consumption or sale were driven up and slaughtered there at the proper seasons, and whatever was to be preserved was salted and packed away for after distribution.

9. A WEALTHY PLANTER'S SLAVE ARTISANS

SOURCE: *Virginia Gazette* (Purdie and Dixon, eds.), December 1, 1768.

A SCHEME of a LOTTERY for disposing of certain LANDS, SLAVES and STOCKS, belonging to the subscriber.

PRIZES	VALUE	CONTENTS OF PRIZES
1 of	£ 5000	To consist of a forge and geared gristmill, both well fixed, and situate on a plentiful and constant stream, with 1800 acres of good land, in King and Queen county, near Todd's Bridge, which cost 6000 £.
1 of	£ 1375	To consist of 550 acres of very good land, lying in King William County, on Pamunkey river, called Gooch's, part of 1686 acres purchased of William Claiborne, deceased; the line to extend from said river to the back line across toward Mattapony.
1 of	£ 1925	To consist of 550 acres of very good land, adjoining and below the said tract, lying on Pamunkey river, whereon a good dwelling house, 70 feet long and 20 feet wide, with three rooms below and three above, also all other good and convenient outhouses, 1000 fine peach trees thereon, with many apple trees and other sorts of fruit, a fine high and

PRIZES	VALUE	CONTENTS OF PRIZES
		pleasant situation, and the plantation in exceedingly good order for cropping; the line to extend from said river to the back line toward Mattapony.
1 of	£ 1750	To consist of 586 acres, below the aforesaid two tracts, whereon is a fine peach orchard, and many fine apple trees; the plantation in exceedingly good order for cropping, and very fine for corn and tobacco, and abounds with a great quantity of white oak which will afford, it is thought, 1000 £ worth of plank and staves.
65 of £ 50	£ 3250	To consist of 6500 acres of good land, in Caroline county; to be laid off in lots of 100 acres each.
4 of £ 75	£ 300	To consist of 812 acres of good land, in Spotsylvania county, in the fork between Northanna and the north fork, with a large quantity of low grounds and meadow land; to be laid off in lots of 203 acres each.
1 of	£ 280	a Negro man named Billy, about 22 years old, an exceeding trusty good forgeman, as well at the finery as under the hammer, and understands putting up his fire; also his wife named Lucy, a young wench, who works exceeding well both in the house and field.
1 of	£ 200	a Negro man named Joe, about 27 years old, a very trusty good forgeman, as well at the finery as under the hammer, and understands putting up his fire.
1 of	£ 200	A Negro Man named Mingo, about 24 years old, a very trusty good finer and hammerman, and understands putting up his fire.

PRIZES	VALUE	CONTENTS OF PRIZES
1 of	£ 180	A Negro man named Ralph, about 22 years old, an exceeding good finer.
1 of	£ 220	A Negro man named Isaac, about 20 years old, an exceeding good hammerman and finer.
1 of	£ 250	A Negro man named Sam, about 26 years old, a fine chaffery man; also his wife Daphne, a very good hand at the hoe, or in the house.
1 of	£ 200	A Negro man named Abraham, about 26 years old, an exceeding good forge carpenter, cooper, and clapboard carpenter.
1 of	£ 150	A Negro man named Bob, about 27 years old, a very fine master collier.
1 of	£ 90	A negro man named Dublin, about 30 years old, a very good collier.
1 of	£ 90	A negro man named London, about 25 years old, a very good collier.
1 of	£ 90	A negro man named Cambridge, about 24 years old, a good collier.
1 of	£ 90	A Negro man named Harry, a very good collier.
1 of	£ 100	A Negro man named Toby, a very fine master collier.
1 of	£ 120	A Negro man named Peter, about 18 years old, an exceedingly trusty good waggoner.
1 of	£ 190	A Negro man named Dick, about 24 years old, a very fine blacksmith; also his smith's tools.
1 of	£ 80	A Negro man named Sampson, about 32 years old, the skipper of the flat.
1 of	£ 70	A Negro man named Dundee, about 38 years old, a good planter.
1 of	£ 85	A Negro man named Caroline Joe, about 35 years old, a very fine planter.
1 of	£ 110	A Negro woman named Rachel, about 32

PRIZES	VALUE	CONTENTS OF PRIZES
		years old, and her children Daniel and Thompson, both very fine.
1 of	£ 70	A Negro woman named Hannah, about 16 years old.
1 of	£ 75	A Negro man named Jack, a good planter.
1 of	£ 75	A Negro man named Ben, about 25 years old, a good house servant, and a good carter, &c.
1 of	£ 120	A Negro man named Robin, a good sawer, and Bella his wife.
1 of	£ 70	A Negro girl named Sukey, about 12 years old, and another named Betty, about 7 years old, children of Robin and Bella.
1 of	£ 75	A Negro man named York, a good sawer.
1 of	£ 80	A Negro woman named Kate, and a young child called Judy.
1 of	£ 60	A Negro girl (Aggy) and boy (Nat) children of Kate.
1 of	£ 75	A Negro named Pompey, a young fellow.
1 of	£ 110	A fine breeding woman named Pat, lame of one side, with child, and her three children, Let, Milley, and Charlotte.
1 of	£ 60	A fine boy named Phil, son of Patty, about 14 years old.
1 of	£ 50	A Negro man named Tom, an outlandish fellow.
1 of	£ 280	A Negro man named Caesar, about 30 years old, a very good blacksmith; and his wife, named Nanny, with two children, Tab and Jane.
1 of	£ 110	A Negro man named Edom, about 23 years old, a blacksmith, who has served four years to the trade.
1 of	£ 160	A Negro man named Moses, about 23 years old, a very good planter; and his wife Phebe, a fine young wench, with her child, Nell.

PRIZES	VALUE	CONTENTS OF PRIZES
1 of	£ 50	A Negro woman named Dorah, wife of carpenter Jemmy.
1 of	£ 35	A Negro named Venus, daughter of Tab.
1 of	£ 25	A Negro named Judy, wife of Sambo.
1 of	£ 20	A Negro named Lucy, outlandish.
1 of	£ 25	A Negro man named Toby, a good miller.
1 of	£ 100	A team of exceeding fine horses, consisting of four, and their geer; also a good waggon.
1 of	£ 80	A team of four horses, and their geer, with two coal waggons.
10 of £ 20	£ 200	To consist of 100 head of cattle, to be laid off in 10 lots.

124 prizes £18,400
1716 Blanks

1840 TICKETS, at £ 10 each is £ 18,400

Managers are JOHN RANDOLPH, JOHN BAYLOR, GEORGE WASHINGTON, FIELDING LEWIS, ARCHIBALD CARY, CARTER BRAXTON, BENJAMIN HARRISON, RALPH WORMELEY, RICHARD HENRY LEE, THOMAS WALKER, THOMAS TABB, EDMUND PENDLETON, PETER LYONS, PATRICK COUTTS, NEIL JAMIESON, ALEXANDER DONALD, DAVID JAMESON and JOHN MADISON, Gentlemen.

The above LOTTERY will be drawn on Thursday the 15th of this instant in Williamsburg.

N.B. Not any of the cattle mentioned in this lottery are to be under the age of two years, nor none to exceed four or five years old.

BERNARD MOORE

The Setting for Acculturation: The Upcountry Tobacco Quarter

TWO SLAVES listed near the end of Bernard Moore's lottery were worth only a tenth as much as the planter's artisans. Tom and Lucy were *"outlandish" (the term used for Africans who were new arrivals, and not yet introduced to plantation slavery); they, like the vast majority of Africans, did not learn about whites and slavery in the dynamic environment of the home plantation. Instead, as strangers to the English language and to specialized skills, recently imported slaves were immediately forced into the dull, simple, and repetitive routines of field labor on small and remote tobacco-growing plantations. Usually from 500 to 1,500 acres in size, these tracts (called "quarters") were economically specialized (producing staples, some corn, and little more), located up-river from the bustling activity and diversity of the home plantation and unique to the Chesapeake Bay region. Surrounded by woods, swamps, rivers, and reserve land, the quarter described in the following newspaper advertisement was a world of its own.*

FOR SALE

A TRACT of good tobacco land in th county of Orange, *about 8 miles above the courthouse . . . containing by estimation 1000 acres, with a plantation thereon sufficient to work 8 hands. A large swamp runs through the whole of this tract, where is a great quantity of limestone, also a great deal of fine meadow land on both sides of the swamp.*[1]

The focus narrows and the nature of the historical record changes to non-narrative sources—newspaper advertisements and plantation accounts. An inventory and two overseer contracts complete the picture of the eighteenth-century tobacco plantation and its upcountry quarters, where the African as a "new Negro" (or simply "share" or "hand") slowly began to learn about whites and their ways.

10. NEGROES, STOCK, TOOLS, FOWL

SOURCE: Charles Payne's Inventory, Fauquier County, Va., March 18, 1784, Norton Papers, Colonial Williamsburg Research Center.

1. *Virginia Gazette* (Purdie, ed.), August 8, 1777, T. Barbour, advertiser.

PLANTATION ACCTS. WITH CH[ARLES] PAYNE, OVERSEER AT EFF[INGHAM] FORREST.

Taken March 18th 1784

Negroes	*stock*
old Charles	Horses 10 (mostly mares)
Betty	Black Cattle (including)
Greenwich	"1 Red butt with a white face," and
Peter	1 Pided Cow 8 yrs. old.
Frank	
Anthony	total: 33 No Cattle
Timmy a boy	Hogs: 34
Sam a boy	Sheep: 78
Cardis	
Milly	
Black Hannah	
Candis Child	

No. 12

Acct. of Plantation Tools: 4 old Dutch Plows, 4 pr. Iron Traces, 1 pr. Iron Wedges, 4 Narrow Axes—two barrs Iron, 1 Broad Axx, 4 hilling hoes, 3 old Do. for Weading, 4 old hoes M. Muse put here, 5 Mattocks of M. Muse 1 Grubing hoe, 2 Drawing Knives, 2 Chissels, 1 hand Saw 2 Augers, 1 adds, 1 froe, 1 Scthe, 3 Murren hides, Two of which are Calves Skins, 2 Spinning Wheels

Fowls in the Care of old Betty
10 guse, 7 Fatning for Mrs. Nortons Use
5 Turkies for breading
3 fatning for Mrs. Norton
5 Dungle hens
8 Ducks

11. No "Grumbling or Feigning Excuses"

Source: An Agreement between Charles Dabney and Ancel Clarkson, August 21, 1772, Dabney Papers, Southern Historical Collection, University of North Carolina Archives.

Articles of agreement between Charles Dabney and Ancel Clarkson doth covenant and agree to overlook the plantation whereon he now Lives belonging [to] the Est[ate] of Edward Ambler the year 1773 for his two share[s] of Tabo. one of Corn and two of the wheat he sends to Market, and to allow fourteen shares for Negroes, and the said Clarkson will further Oblige himself to be Strictly Obedient to the said Dabney's Orders or Directions in every Respect regarding the management of the said Business without either grumbling or feigning Excuses and in all things Shall endeavour to promote the Interest of his employer in all respect[s] as is the Duty of an Overseer. And in Case the said Clarkson shall fail to comply with the above Articles it shall and may be [lawful] for the said Dabney to Turn him off the plantation at any Time of the year allowing him at the Rates of Thirty [pounds] the year in Witness whereof I have hereunto it my hand this Twenty first day of Aug[us]t 1772

his

LARKSON

mark

Colonial Planters as Estate Managers and Patriarchs: Plantation Authority in South Carolina and Virginia

THE STRICK OBEDIENCE AND NO GRUMBLING insisted upon by Dabney in his contract with the overseer Ancel Clarkson calls attention to the profound disagreement between planters and overseers that was part of the setting or background in which Africans became Negroes. But management problems—which made the colonial plantation particularly vulnerable to the field slaves' quiet and persistent acts of sabotage —varied from colony to colony, and changed significantly from the colonial to the antebellum eras. Before Independence, relations among tobacco (but not rice) planters, stewards, overseers, and blacks were typically chaotic. The tobacco gentry was caught in a paradox: their distinctive reaction to colonial status and the failure to achieve real self-determination in the Empire sharpened a need to be "great Fathers," while reinforcing an obstinate, defensive belief that patriarchal authority ought to be absolute and indivisible. Unfortunately it was essential for effective estate management that they do just the opposite: delegate authority to the overseers—who were directly responsible for the field slaves' performance and the masters' profits—so they could do their job well. Tidewater planters failed to resolve their authority problems in the

Empire and on their own plantations, but they left useful accounts of slaves reporting directly to them, and letters filled with bitter and revealing descriptions of plantation management and master-slave relationships.

The last document in this section, Josiah Smith, Jr.'s letterbook (one of the few documents on eighteenth-century rice cultivation to survive), presents a different picture of plantation management. Smith, commuting between Charleston and Georgetown, pursued his own business interests while managing two plantations for George Austin (once Henry Laurens' slave-trading partner), who lived in England. The tone of Smith's letterbook and the patterns of authority and decision-making it reveals are antebellum: the slaveowner was nonresident; his steward or manager visited his plantations infrequently, and then reported on crop prices, the nature of the market, major decisions on equipment and buildings, and on little else. Most important, the overseer and black driver (an institution prevalent on large nineteenth-century plantations but, in the colonial period, unknown outside of South Carolina) were clearly in charge of the daily plantation activities. Consequently, Smith's letterbook is a harbinger of the more impersonal and objective character of documents on antebellum plantations and master-slave relations that contrast sharply with the evidence on the old-fashioned paternalism of colonial Maryland and Virginia.

TOBACCO PATRIARCHS VERSUS THEIR STEWARDS AND OVERSEERS

12. "NEGROES ARE VERY UNWILLING TO GIVE UP . . . PRIVILEGES"

SOURCE: John Blair, Jr., (steward) to Charles Dabney, April 1, 1769, Dabney Papers, Southern Historical Collection, University of North Carolina Archives.

SIR,

I am no longer in the management of your brother's estate in Louisa as you Imagine on the Contrary I am well acquainted with the cause of the difference between Smith & the Negroes under him; the Cause of this—Wingfield who was Overseer on that plantation before him was so good natured to the Negroes under him he suffered them to Impose on him very much & it is well known to every person that was acquainted with his management that the [four years] he lived in the Business, the Estate Suffered many [?] by his not keeping them to their duty. This I saw was a falt in him I often told him of it but instead of his mending he grew worse and the last year he lived in the plantation, the Negroes were almost free upon which with the demise of my Father, I fired him. . . . The Negroes are very unwilling to give up the privileges they were allowed in Wingfield's time. Indeed they seem to be determined to Maintain them & because Smith has Endeavoured to keep them to their work, they have fell on every plan they possibly could to get him turned off. And I believe that George [a black sent to the owner to represent the quarter slaves] was prevailed on by the other Negroes to come down to you thinking as he was the Oldest Negro on that plantation a complaint from him would be listened to & I am Inclined to think the Stories he has told you are false as you Inform me in your Letter that he said there were many at the land [?] Absent from the Upper plantation which was without the least foundation. There is not a Negro absent from the plantations at this time nor neither was there then Except himself, as the Negroes have taken such a dislike to Smith he is to go as in the fall, & I have Employed another Overseer to Succeed him.

These Sir are the reasons why Smith and the Negroes has disagreed & for these reasons have been obliged to correct them to keep them to their duty.

It gives me great concern to think a report of this Negro who is prejudiced to the highest degree should [lead you to] conclude the Negroes in Louisa have not been treated with that humanity that the Brutes are Intitled to and I must say when you come up this fall [if] you Still are of opinion that I have not done my duties as a Steward I shall then Continue no longer in the Business.

13. "Negroes Are . . . an Ungrateful Set of Beings"

Source: Hugh Washington to Battaile Muse (steward), May 21, 1788, Muse Papers, Duke University Archives.

I once wrote to You on the subject of the Negroes ill treatment by the common Overseers; who in general have not the least humanity in regard to the Slaves under them, & I do Know that they require much looking after, to prevent their using them ill.

I never loo[ke]d on You in the light of a common Overseer,

but as a Gent:man who had undertaken the charge of overlooking them, as well as the Negroes.

Formerly there has been several of them to complain to me of their treatment, by their Overseers, but it was always in Your absence (at least they told me You was from home) & I always advised them to make their complaints to You, who was best able to redress them, if they had realy cause for complaint.

You answer'd my Letter & beg'd me not to suffer them to come with their complaints (as they had no cause) & I have never listen'd to one of them since, but Hudson, who said they had a very cruel Overseer now, this Year who never wou'd allow them to lay by, if they were sick. I will take Oath that I told him I did not believe him, & also order'd him, to return home early in the Morning, (as it was the Evening when I saw him) or I shou'd get our Overseer to send him off, in a way he wou'd not like.

I know from experience that Negroes are in general an ungrateful set of beings, that there is no such thing as satisfying them in regard to their Overseers; but indeed Sir the common run of Overseers if left to themselves, wou'd be cruel to them.

14. An Enlightened Patriarch Discusses "Humanity" toward Slaves

Source: Thomas Fairfax to Battaile Muse, December, 1792, and April 3, 1793. Muse Papers, Duke University Archives.

December, 1792

. . . I have now answerd I believe every part of yours except one, which as it seems to Contain a tacit charge against me, I must not let it pass unnoticed. After enumerating many in[s]tances of mismanagement on the plantation you Say (in fact) that I have been in part the Cause of it, by giving ear to the tales of negroes which has lesened the overseers authority.

This is altogether a mistake veiwed in what light it may be; the principle is erronious and the deduction from it equally so even allowing the principle true. When you say that the misconduct on the place proceeded from want of authority in the overseer you imply that his will was good, but that he cou'd not make the negroes do their work, but let me ask did it require a greater exertion of authority to make them fallow ground or gather Corn, or turn hogs out of the meadow or haul wood [for] fuel instead of fence rails &c than to make them thresh rey or tread out wheat? . . .

So far from Contributing to weaken the Controul of the overseer over the negroes, I never gave them the smallest encouragement and I am Surprised you shoud Suppose a thing that has so little foundation. As to giving a hearing to Slaves in any matter of Complaint they may have against their Overseer, it is quite another point. No man who possesses the principles of Justice and humanity would ever deny those who are dependent on him (whether Slaves or freemen) the privilege of making known their grievances to him. Whether these grievances are real or imaginary, let him determine.

The Master who will deny his slaves this priviledge does in reality deny them that Common justice which every man whether White or black is entitled to.

April 3rd 1793

I am Sorry we do not appear to understand each other yet about that matter of Russel [an overseer]; and I don't know why it should be So for the Case appears very plain. I will just recapitulate the matter in as concise a manner as it will admit of and then if you will calmly consider it, I dont doubt you will find the Statement right; I say calmly, because without moderation it is impossible to view any Argument in its right light; tho I must Confess the point in hand is hardly worth so much writing about.

When in Berkeley, I wrote to you among other matter, that I could not prevail upon Russel to break up the meadow as soon as it ought to be, or something to that purpose and desired you also to take a look at the hog pen. In your letter by Gabriel is a passage in the following words—"I wish the two observations you make respecting the meadow & hogs was the only injury the Estate was to sustain from the last six months carrying on the business. I think the loss of 100 Acres land usually fallowed; Grain badly put in; Stock neglected; meadow rooted up with hogs; Creature[s] [be]ing in the orchard; Fences burnt; Corn not gather'd at Christma[s] [w]ill prove in a few years no small loss to the owner of the Estate. This Conduct has arose greatly from the authority taken from the overseer by hearing every tale that de-

ceitful negroes will advance."—In my answer to this I observed, if
I remember right, that you charged me with being the Cause in
part of all the preceeding list of evils, by having lessen'd the overseer's authority I also observed that the principle was erroneous
and also the deduction, even supposed the principle true. Now
what was the principle? it was that I had lessen'd the overseers
authority; and what was the deduction? it was that all the afore-
mentioned evils were in consequence of it. I denied having impaired Russels authority and do still. . . . You say I am the only
man you ever served, that disapproved of your Conduct; now I
shall be much obliged to you to point out when and where I have
ever found fault with your management or conduct; if you or any
man whatever brings a charge against me that is not well founded;
it wou'd be very Strange indeed if I did not take notice of it. As to
humanity toward Slaves, it appears to be an indefinite term in this
Country and there are very few masters perhaps whose sentiments
and mine wou'd agree upon this point. What I might Call a want
of humanity, others might call a necessary Coercion. . . .

RICE COUNTRY ESTATE MANAGERS

15. "This Method I Think to Be the Most Proper"

Source: Josiah Smith, Jr., to George Austin, Josiah Smith, Jr., Letterbook, Southern Historical Collection, University of North
Carolina Archives.

July 22, 1773

Sir:

. . . I had the Oppor[tuni]ty of contracting for Ten New Negroes on your account, Say 3 women at 300 & 7 Men at 350
which I had the Liberty of Picking on board the ship since the
prices have advanc'd to £380 & 10 days ago some very prime men
sold at £400. The 3 Women and 3 Men I got out of a Ship from
Whydah which are not at Ashepoo Planta[tion]. The other 4 men
I got 5 days since out of a Ship from Anamaboo & shall send them
by first boat. . . . The whole Ten appear to be clever Slaves & Seem
very willing to work. The weather has been & still continues to be
very dry in most parts of our Province and thereby most of our

Provision Crops will be totally lost and a great Call for Corn must necessarily be next Spring . . . from Shipnah [?] the Overseer writes me that he had not a drop of Rain for near two months till the 8th Instant when they had a very heavy Shower attended with Sever Lightning & Thunder a Clap of which fell on the Barn & torn Out one of the Gable Ends but did no other damage. . . .

Yours

Bills of Exch[ange] lately sold at par for
4 months sight, a Sad Circumstance this
Likely to be Worse.

Jan 31, 1774

SIR:

Your Schooner was a full Month on her first trip for Rice to Pedee, occasion'd by contrary Winds & bad Weather, she got to Town the 10th Instant with 112 Bls of your Rice, which I could not put off on landing at 60/. altho' the Rice was very good, but after storing it a day or two, I prevail'd on David & John Deas to take it at 60/. 100 payable 1st May, which was the best terms I could obtain, & had they refus'd, it must now have remain'd sweating in the Store-house; before this load comes down, I rec'd a Letter from Wm Smith, your Overseer at Ashepoo, intreating that I wou'd hurry up the Austin to [Shipnah], as he had then near Eighty Barrels Rice lying at the Landing for her, which he was oblig'd to place there, to make room in the Barn for beating out more of the Crop, the Schooner return'd from thence & landed 105 Bls your Rice this day, the which appears but indifferent in quality. I have put it into a dry Cellar, hir'd by the Month, in order to save some Expence in the Storage, which wou'd be high on the Wharfs; and unless you should soon direct me to sell at the going market, it must remain in the Cellar, till your limitation for 60/. expires; I really am fearful that your resolutions of not having your Rice sold here under 60/. this side of May, will in the end prove a disadvantage for by keeping it on hand so long it must suffer in its quality & lose in its weight by the Mite and Weavle, and perhaps sell at last for a less price than it wou'd now go off at, the risque of lying at the Plantation is not small, from Fire, pilferage & other damage; I therefore think twou'd be no bad Scheme to have the Risque divided, by placing at least one half your Crops in Charles Town under my own Eye & then twou'd be ready for Sale, in case the price should suddenly start up to 60/. or perhaps I may ease you from the Risque of Fire and Expence of Storage in town by lending 2 or 300 Barrels thereof to some of our substantial Traders, to be again paid in Rice of equal quality & weight in the Month of May. . . .

. . . It gives me no little Concern, to find you complaining of the small Profits you receive on your planting Interest here; cou'd I be the means of making them more, twoud give me much Pleasure, but when we consider that, there is an Almighty Power, who over-rules all things according to his sovereign Will & Pleasure, who smiles upon some while he frowns upon others, we cannot expect to get what that Power chuses to withhold from us; these short-comings do not arise, either thro' means of your Lands or Ne-groes, for of these I believe, you possess as valuable as most planters here, & as to management, I wont pretend to say, that matters are so strictly conducted, as they may be by some planters, nor can it be expected that Plantations own'd by Persons [who] are non-residents, should produce so much Profit as those con-stantly under the Inspection of the Proprietors who reside on the Spot & at same time are able Planters, who are ever employ'd in contriving every thing that can make for their Advantage, save every Expence that can possibly be avoided, & often by hard-driv-ing, save a Crop from Destruction. These are the Persons that have enrich'd themselves very much, especially of late years by the hard Labour & Sweat of wretched Slaves, under Proper Seasons & the Smiles of a kind Providence, while many others of the like profession have come far short of them, by great losses in Ne-groes, adverse Seasons & other Expence. As to my Endeavours, I have ever done what I apprehended was my duty to do, with matters you have entrusted me with, not willfully running you to a greater Expence in Plantation Affairs, than I thought was neces-sary & useful on them; your expressions of tenderness for your Slaves added to my own inclinations that way that always induc'd one to make their Lives a little comfortable, directing your Over-seers not to overdrive or otherwise oppress them, charging them always to be well fed, & properly attended to when sick: & of this I believe they can boast, beyond most other Plantation Gangs; this method of treating them, I think to be the most proper for contin-using them in usefullness, & under them more willing to do their duty, than unmerciful driving thereto:

July 22, 1774

SIR:

. . . I now think ther is little probability of obtaining more than 50/–the price at home continuing very poor, and a very small supply of Vessels to take off the large Quantity now on hand here; am therefore, about sending the Austin to Pedee for another Load to which Place I made a Visit about 4 weeks since, when I found the Rice to wear a pleasing Aspect, about 100 Acres being very good, and 70 more that had been troubled early by the worm, appeared to be in a very thriving way; the Provisions also, consid-ering the badness of the Ground in which they are planted, looked well. The four runaways had been taken about a month before I got there, a Negro of Mr Pawley's had discovered their Camp to Brown, who getting a Couple of his Neighbour Overseers & taking two of your able Fellows, came upon the Rogues quite unexpect-edly; they had provided a pretty secure retreat at the head of a small Creek that runs from the thoroughfare into the thick woods near the Northern extremity of your Land, and with a small Canoe found in their Possession, they had well stored their Camp with Fish and Grain of several sorts; although the Grass was very bad in all your fields none of your People had run from it, they being kept to their work by mere dint of encouragement of a Beef & some Rum, added to lenient treatment by the Overseer. . . . This Letter I send by a young man of your Town . . . to him I must refer you for any particular Public transactions among us, which are in general of a spirited nature, America being resolved never to submit to British Taxation or other Claims without the Consent of her owne representatives and all the Colonies from Georgia to Nova Scotia are now firmly united. Britain must expect a most vigrous opposition, until matters are brought again to their former agreeable Standard.

C. Africans Become "New Negroes": "Outlandish" Slaves as Learners of English and as Organized Runaways

THE AVAILABLE SOURCES on slave behavior in the colonial era describe rebellious slaves and few others. The slaves described were lazy and thieving; they feigned illnesses, destroyed crops, stores, and tools, and sometimes attacked or killed overseers. Others were runaways of various types: truants (who usually returned voluntarily), "outlaws" (a legal term for "outlying," "lurking" slaves who refused to give themselves up), and runaways who were actually fugitives. These men completely rejected the plantation world and went to town to pass as free men or to board a ship. The "outlandish" Africans represented another —and unique—type of runaway. They banded together in cooperative efforts to establish villages or hideouts on the frontier; in South Carolina, particularly, they sometimes fled south across Georgia to Spanish territory in Florida. The reactions of some slaves were total; they became killers, arsonists, and insurrectionists.

Styles of rebellion, as an indication of ways blacks reacted to slavery, varied according to their origin (birthplace), level of acculturation, and position in the work hierarchy, and may be distinguished, for clarity and convenience, as inward or outward. Slaves who rejected slavery entirely, by running to the frontier as many Africans did, or by getting jobs in the anonymity of the colonial cities, as did many assimilated artisans, reacted outwardly; but "plantation negroes" who directed their rebelliousness at the plantation, or were merely truants, were resisting inwardly.

One of the very best sources for studying the socialization of Africans and its influence on their reactions to bondage are the newspaper advertisements for fugitive slaves. Slaveholders who used the newspapers to recapture valuable property were neither explaining nor defending slavery. In sparse, graphic language, they simply listed the runaway's most noticeable physical and psychological characteristics, while commenting on his birthplace, type of work, and proficiency in speaking English.

Students interested in the history of women, native Americans, blacks or the other usually nameless, faceless people who were an integral part of our past might consider the value of "unconscious" (nonnarrative) evidence, which in this case lends itself so well to a quantitative analysis of such intimate and revealing details about slaves as their heights, postures, complexions, habits of grooming and dress, and emotional peculiarities. These characteristics are indispensable for understanding *the change of physical norms, demographic makeup, and acculturation levels in colonial slave populations.*

The acculturative process whereby Africans became "new Negroes," and a much smaller number became assimilated slaves, was marked by three stages. First, the "outlandish" Africans reacted to slavery on the basis of the communal lives they had been living when enslaved. They are the only slaves in colonial America who were described in newspaper notices for runaways in groups larger than two or three. Nearly all Africans became field workers, "new Negroes," who represented the second level of acculturation. Since there seemed to be a "fit," or degree of congruence, between their cultural background and the plantation's communal norms, few Africans ever became more than "new Negroes." Their styles of rebellion are more complicated than those of the "outlandish" slaves, who seemed to want to get away from whites and slavery as quickly and completely as possible. Plantation slaves most often directed their limited, sometimes self-defeating, acts against the plantation itself. This inward-directed rebelliousness of the "new Negro" (because it was often aimed as much at themselves as at the plantation, their only convenient "target") reflected his job and his level of acculturation. The very few Africans who were educated and trained in a skill, and so eventually were more completely assimilated, were representative of the third level of acculturation. These men were usually artisans, whose imaginative exploits as fugitives dramatized the reciprocal relationships between the acquisition of skills and more advanced assimilation.

16. LEARNING ENGLISH

SINCE *the "outlandish" slaves and their new owners had evidently talked informally about Africa, the notices are also filled with information about what Africans chose to tell whites about their lives before enslavement. Another type of advertisement, written by jailers describing fugitives "taken up" (recaptured but not reclaimed by their lawful owners), also provides invaluable insights into how Africans continued to think in their own language categories, while struggling as slaves to make themselves understood in their captors' language. The jailers' descriptions of them—often naked or clothed only in loincloths, perhaps carrying a hoe or knife—reveal another facet of an upbringing that remained intact in slavery: an ability to survive cooperatively in the wilds of North America.*

SOURCES: *Virginia Gazette* (Purdie and Dixon, eds.), December 24, 1772; ibid., October 7, 1773; *South Carolina Gazette* (Timothy, ed.), January 3, 1771; *Virginia Gazette* (Rind, ed.), September 22, 1768; ibid. (Hunter, ed.), July 19, 1754.

Chesterfield, December 15, 1772

RUN away from the Subscriber on *Sunday* the 22nd of November, a new Negro fellow of small Stature, and pitted with the Smallpox; he calls himself BONNA, and says he came from a place of that Name in the *Ibo* country, in *Africa*, where he served in the Capacity of a Canoe Man. . . .

RICHARD BOOKER

RUN away from the Subscriber about the 1st of *September*, in the upper End of *King William* [County], two new Negro Men, of the *Ibo* country, named CHARLES and FRANK, who have been in the Province about twelve Months, and it is supposed cannot tell their Master's Name. *Charles* is a large Fellow, with his Country Marks in his Face, and has lost or broke off one or two of his fore Teeth, which he says was done by a Cow in his Country. Frank is a smaller Fellow, well set, and has sharp Teeth. They carried with them a *Dutch* Blanket, had each a coarse hat, and other usual Summer clothes. . . .

JOSEPH HILLYARD

TAKEN up, about one Mile from my Plantation, in St. Matthew's Parish, Berkley County, two NEGRO-FELLOWS, of the Guiney Country, who call themselves POMPEY and SAMBO: they are about five Feet ten Inches high, speak but very little English. They say that their Master's Name is JAMES BUTLER, and lives by the side of a River, and that their old Master lives on the other Side. By what I can learn by a Guiney fellow of mine, they have been run away ever since the Spring before last. They are entirely naked, and their Feet and Legs are swelled very much by lying in the Cold, on which Account I thought it would not be prudent to send them to the Work-House. If the Owner of the above Fellows, should find any Difficulty in conveying a Letter to me, they may write to Mr. JAMES COURTONE, jeweller, in CHARLES-TOWN.

WILLIAM HEATLY

COMMITTED to the gaol of this county, on the 9th instant, a Negro man who calls himself SANDY, says he belongs to *Thomas Wilsom*, or *Wilson*, in the neighborhood of *Perrin Turner* and

Thomas Waters, but in what part of the country can give no account; that he has made two crops for his master, and has been absent from his service for two moons; seems to be about 25 years old, has lost two of his under fore teeth, and those above are sharp, and a considerable distance from each other. He is cloathed in rolls breeches, a *Virginia* cotton shirt, and a *Negro* cotton jacket. The owner may have him, on proper application to

JOHN DANIEL, Gaoler

Surry County

COMMITTED to the Gaol of this County on the 24th of *April* last, Two, likely Negroe Fellows, which have been posted according to Law; they speak but little *English*, and give an indifferent Account from whence they came. There are sufficient Reasons to believe they came from *North* or *South Carolina*, or *Georgia*; they say their father's Name is *Davis*, and that he is dead. . . . They say they have been Ten Moons from home. . . .

WILLIAM CLINCH, Sheriff

Group Resistance by Runaways and Insurrectionists

IN THE TRIBAL SOCIETIES *in which most slaves before 1750 were raised, Africans received ritual scars and filed teeth (usually called "country marks") in coming-of-age rites. On the personal level the rite of passage was an unforgettable ordeal in which the emotional ties of a group of young adults were reoriented from their families to the village society. The ceremonies, calculated to burn the lesson of companionship and community into the very souls of the young participants, also left indelible scars that were visible. These "country marks," deep striations on face and chest, announced: "I am because we are, and since we are, I am." The West African scholar John Mbiti further explains that the rites united the celebrant with the rest of the community both living and dead, and "humanely speaking nothing can separate him from this corporate society."*

On the community level, the rites were a matter of survival. Most colonial slaves came from small-scale, technologically simple societies living in a precarious relationship with their environment. The facts of individual differences, of varied and uneven rates of growth among their young men of the same age, constituted a grave threat to the basic ordering of the society, particularly during the grim and perilous days of the international slave trade. By means of this ceremony "the individual or age group is cut off, isolated and then restored," reports one anthro-

pologist, "but never again to be the same; in this restoration individual distinctions and differences are translated into social ones." Consequently, Africans initially viewed slavery as a collective problem, and were inclined to resist it in organized groups of fugitives. (In fact, in more than 1,100 advertisements in eighteenth-century Virginia newspapers the only runaways in groups of three or more were "outlandish" Africans; virtually all of the remaining fugitives, acculturated Africans as well as American-born, ran off alone.) Fugitive Africans occasionally carried their tools and clothing, either to "find their way to their own country," or to replicate, in the remote areas of the colonies, village life as they knew it in West Africa. Although this tendency was more pronounced in South Carolina than in the Chesapeake Bay region, the only historical evidence of a settlement of runaways (similar to the macambos or villages of fugitives in the Jamaica mountains and northeastern Brazil) was reported in Virginia. In 1729 the royal governor described a most unusual attempt by runaways "to fix themselves in the fastnesses of the neighbouring Mountains" (near present-day Lexington in the Shenandoah Valley). And ten years later, a group of Angolans in South Carolina led an uprising on the Stono River in order to form a village of runaways or to break out of the colony and march south to freedom among the Spanish in Florida.

17. "To Find the Way Back"

Source: *Virginia Gazette* (Purdie and Dixon, eds.), September 12, 1771.

TWENTY POUNDS REWARD

RUN away from the Subscriber, near *Petersburg* on the 18th of last *May*, two new Negroes, namely, a FELLOW named *Step* about six feet high, has his Country Marks on his Temples and has lost some of his fore Teeth. He appears to have a very honest Countenance, and is supposed to be about twenty Years of Age; he had with him, when he went away, a white Plains Waistcoat and Breeches, Osnabrug shirt and a tolerable good bound Hat. The other a GIRL named *Lucy* supposed to be about twelve Years of Age, and had on a white Plains Petticoat and striped *Virginia* Cloth Waistcoat. Neither of them can speak good *English*, as they have not been long in the country. They went off with several others, being persuaded that they could find the Way back to their own Country. They were discovered, about six weeks after their going off, near *Blanton's* Ferry, in *Mecklenburg* county, where the Gang was dispersed, and three of them taken, one of whom belonged to me. The said Negroes are outlawed. FIVE POUNDS for each will be given if taken within this Colony, and TEN POUNDS for each if in any other.

GEORGE ROBERTSON

18. "THEIR NEW SETTLEMENT"

SOURCE: Lieutenant Governor Sir William Gooch to the Board of Trade, Williamsburg, June 29, 1729, Colonial Office Papers, 5/1322, 19 ff, Virginia Colonial Records Project, Colonial Williamsburg Research Center microfilm. Reprinted by permission of the Controller of Her Britannic Majesty's Stationery Office.

MY LORDS:

. . . Sometime after my Last a number of Negroes, about fifteen, belonging to a new Plantation on the head of James River formed a Design to withdraw from their Master and to fix themselves in the fastnesses of the neighbouring Mountains. They had found means to get into their possession some Arms & Ammunition, and they took along with them some Provisions, their Cloaths, bedding and working Tools; but the Gentleman to whom they belonged with a Party of Men made such diligent pursuit after them, that he soon found them out in their new Settlement, a very obscure place among the Mountains, where they had already begun to clear the ground, and obliged them after exchanging a shot or two by which one of the Slaves was wounded, to surrender and return back, and so prevented for this time a design which might have proved as dangerous to this Country, as is that of the Negroes in the Mountains of Jamaica to the Inhabitants of that Island. Tho' this attempt has happily been defeated, it ought nevertheless to awaken us into some effectual measures for preventing the like hereafter, it being certain that a very small number of Negroes once settled in those Parts, would very soon be encreas'd by the Accession of other Runaways and prove dangerous Neighbours to our frontier Inhabitants. To prevent this and many other Mischiefs I am training and exercising the Militia in the several counties as the best means to deter our Slaves from endeavouring to make their Escape, and to suppress them if they should.

THE STONO REBELLION

TEN YEARS *after the defeat of the African villagers in Virginia, one of the most destructive insurrections in the history of American Negro slavery, the Stono Rebellion, broke out in the lush, malarial, rice-growing region south of Charleston (St. Paul's Parish, Colleton County). A group of Africans led by several Angolans rebelled while working on a road crew. Perhaps aware of the Spanish King's Proclamation promising freedom to all slaves who would flee to the presidio at St. Augustine, Florida, they organized on Sunday, September 9, 1739, and surprised two men at a warehouse. Arming themselves, they marched south along the Pon Pon River road, killing men, women, and children, and burning plantations.*

19. A CONTEMPORARY OVERVIEW

SOURCE: "Extract of A Letter from South Carolina Dated October 2," *Gentleman's Magazine* (London), n.s. 10 (1740): 127–129.

Sometime since a Proclamation was published at *Augustine* in which the King of *Spain* (tho' at Peace with *Great Britain*) promised Protection and Freedom to all Negroe Slaves, who would report thither. Certain Negroes belonging to Capt. *Davis* eloped to *Augustine*, and were receiv'd there. . . . Amongst the Negroe Slaves, there are a People brought from the Kingdom of *Angola* in *Africa*, many of these speak *Portugueze* (which Language is as near *Spanish* as *Scotch* is to *English*) by reason that the *Portugueze* have considerable Settlements, and the Jesuits have a Mission and School in that Kingdom, and many Thousands of the Negroes there profess the *Roman Catholick Religion*. Several *Spaniards*, upon diverse Pretences, have some time past been strolling about *Carolina*, two of them, who will give no Account of themselves, have been taken up and committed to Gaol in *Georgia*. Since the good Reception of the Negroes at *Augustine* was spread about, several attempted to escape to the *Spaniards*, and were taken, one of them was hang'd at *Charles-Town*. In the latter End of July last Don Pedro, the Colonel of the Spanish Horse, went in a Launch to *Charles-Town*, under Pretence of a Message to General Oglethorpe and the Lieutenant-Governor.

On the *9th* Day of *September* last, being *Sunday*, which is the

Day the Planters allow them to work for themselves, some *Angola* Negroes assembled, to the Number of Twenty, and one, who was called *Jimmy*, was their Captain, they surpriz'd a Warehouse belonging to Mr. *Hutchenson*, at a Place called *Stone how*; they there killed Mr. *Robert Bathurst* and Mr *Gibbs*, plunder'd the House, and took a pretty many small Arms and Powder, which were there for Sale. Next they plunder'd and burnt Mr *Godfrey's* House, and killed him, his Daughter and Son. They then turned back, and marched Southward along *Pons Pons*, which is the Road thro' *Georgia* to *Augustine*; they passed Mr *Wallace's* Tavern about Day break, and said they would not hurt him for he was a good Man and kind to his Slaves; but they broke open and plunder'd Mr *Lemy's* House and kill'd him, his Wife, and Child. They marched on towards Mr *Rose's*, resolving to kill him; but he was saved by a Negroe, who having hid him, went out and pacified the others. Several Negroes joined them, they calling out Liberty, marched on with Colours displayed, and two Drums beating, pursuing all the white People they met with, and killing Man, Woman and Child, when they could come up with them. Colonel *Bull*, Lieutenant-Colonel of *South Carolina*, who was then riding along the Road, discover'd them, was pursued, and with much Difficulty escaped, and raised the Country. They burnt Col. *Hext's* House, killed his Overseer and his Wife. They then burnt Mr *Sprey's* House, then Mr *Sacheverell's*, and then Mr *Nash's* House, all lying upon the Pons Pons Road, and killed all the white People they found in them. Mr. *Bullock* got off, but they burnt his House. By this time many of them were drunk with the Rum they had taken in the Houses. They increased every Minute by new Negroes coming to them; so that they were above Sixty, some say a Hundred; on which they halted in a field, and set to Dancing, Singing, and beating Drums, to draw more Negroes to them, thinking they were now victorious over the whole Province, having marched ten Miles, and burnt all before them without Opposition: But the Militia being raised, the Planters with great Briskness pursued them, and when they came up, dismounting, charged them on Foot. The Negroes were soon routed, though they behaved boldly; several being killed on the Spot, many ran back to their Plantations, thinking they had not been missed; but they were then taken and shot; such as were taken in the Field also were, after being examined, shot on the Spot; and this is to be said to the Honour of the *Carolina* Planters that, notwithstanding the Provocation they had received from so many Murders, they did not torture one Negroe, but only put them to an easy Death. All who proved to be forced, and were not concerned in the Murders and Burnings, were pardon'd; and this sudden Courage in the Field, and the Humanity afterwards, have had so good an Effect, that there hath been no farther Attempt, and the very Spirit of the Revolt seems over. About 30 escaped from the Fight, of which ten marched about 30 Miles Southward, and being overtaken by the Planters on Horseback fought stoutly for some time, and were all killed on the Spot, the rest are yet untaken; and in the whole Action about 40 Negroes and 20 whites were kill'd. . . .

20. The Royal Governor Reports

Source: Lieutenant Governor Sir William Bull to the Board of Trade, Charleston, October 5, 1739, Records in the British Public Record Office Relating to South Carolina, 1711–1782 ("Sainsbury Transcripts"), vol. 20, pp. 179–180, South Carolina State Archives (C.O. Papers, S.C. Original Correspondence, Secretary of State, 1730–1746, No. 5/388). Reprinted by permission of the Controller of Her Britannic Majesty's Stationery Office.

My Lords,

I beg leave to lay before your Lordships an account of our Affairs, first in regard to the Desertion of our Negroes. . . . On the 9th of September last at Night a great Number of Negroes Arose in Rebellion, broke open a Store where they got arms, killed twenty one White Persons, and were marching the next morning in a Daring manner out of the Province, killing all they met and burning several Houses as they passed along the Road. I was returning from Granville County with four Gentlemen and met these Rebels at eleven o'clock in the forenoon and fortunately deserned the approaching danger time enough to avoid it, and to give notice to the Militia who on the Occasion behaved with so much expedition and bravery, as by four a'Clock the same day to come up with them and killed and took so many as put a stop to any further mischief at that time, forty four of them have been killed and Executed; some few yet remain concealed in the Woods expecting the same fate, seem desperate. . . .

It was the Opinion of His Majesty's Council with several other Gentlemen that one of the most effectual means that could be used at present to prevent such desertion of our Negroes is to encourage some Indians by a suitable reward to pursue and if possible to bring back the Deserters, and while the Indians are thus employed they would be in the way ready to intercept others that might attempt to follow and I have sent for the Chiefs of the Chickasaws living at New Windsor and the Catawbaw Indians for that purpose. . . .

> My Lords,
> Your Lordships Most Obedient and Most Humble Servant
> WM BULL

Rec'd Dec. 10th
Read Dec. 12 [1739]

21. THE ASSEMBLY RESPONDS AND REWARDS INDIAN SLAVE-CATCHERS

SOURCE: A Commons House of Assembly Committee Report, in a Message to the Governor's Council, Journal of the Upper House, No. 7 (November 29, 1739), pp. 266–267, South Carolina State Archives.

1.   That upon Inquiry your Committee find that a negro man named July belonging to Mr. Thomas Elliott was very early & chiefly instrumental in saving his Master & his Family from being destroyed by the Rebellious Negroes and that the Negro man July had at several times bravely fought against the Rebels and killed one of them. Your Committee therefore recommend that the Sd Negro July (as a reward for his faithful Services and for an Encouragement to other Slaves to follow his Example in case of the like Nature) shall have his Freedom and a Present of a Suit of Cloaths, Shirt, Hat, a pair of stockings and a pair of Shoes.

2.   That the several Slaves hereafter named (that is to say)

Ralph, Prince, Joe, Larush & Pompey belonging to the Sd Mr Thos Elliott, Sampon belonging to Mr Wilkinson, two Negro Men & a Negro Woman (whose names your Committee do not know) belonging to Mr Thomas Rose, Two Negro Men (whose names are also unknown to your Committee) who belong to the Estate of Mr John Haynes decd. And one Negro Man (his name not known by your Committee) belonging to the Estate of Mr Christopher Wilkinson decd a Negro man belonging to Mrs Wilkson Widow named Mingo; a Mustee Man have behaved themselves very well & been a great source in opposing the Rebellions Negroes; For which your Committee recommend that they be rewarded as follows (that is to say) the Men to have each a Suit of Cloths, hat, shirt, a pair of Shoes, and a pair of Stockings, And the Women to have each a Jacket & Petticoat, a Shift, a pair of Stockings, & a pair of Shoes and also the sum of £20 in Cash to each of the Slaves above named. . . .

5.   That a Negro Man belonging to Mr John Smith named Quash did endeavour to take one of the Rebellious Negroes for which your Committee are of opinion that he should be rewarded with the sum of £10 in Cash.

6.   That the Cloaths (herein before recommended by your Committee) to be given to the Slaves (as a Reward for their Fidelity) be made with blue Strouds faced up with Red & trimmed with brass Buttons.

7.   That several of the Neighbouring Indians did assist in hunting for, taking and destroying the sd Rebellious Negroes, For which your Committee propose that the sd Indians be severally rewarded with a Coat, a Flap, a Hat, a pair of Indian Stockings, a Gun, 2 Pounds of Powder & 8 Pounds of Bullets, Which Indians Names are as follows (that is to say) Tobb, Old Jack, Peter, Tom and Philip and five other Indians (whose names your Committee do not know) that came down to Stono with Captain Coachman. . . .

10.   Your committee also recommend that 2 Pounds of Paint be given to be divided among the Sd. Indians.

D. "Plantation Negroes," House and Field

KNOWING LITTLE *of the society beyond their world, too limited in such acculturative resources as conversational English "to pass as free" in town, field slaves usually directed their rebellious reactions inward in two ways: in a psychological sense of internalized violence that was often self-defeating or even self-destructive, and in a thrust against their only "home," the plantation setting itself—crops, tools, animals, and overseers. Generally, the field hands' laziness, boondoggling, and pilferage represented a limited, perhaps self-indulgent, type of rebelliousness. These were reactions to unexpected abuses or to sudden changes in plantation routine, and as such only token acts against slavery itself.*

Styles of rebellion may be distinguished as inward and outward in a more subjective sense, one that focuses on the psychological implications of a pattern of resistance for the slave as an individual. The house and field slaves' actions were typically short-range, direct attempts to deal immediately with their material environment: to ease hunger and fatigue or to get revenge on an overseer or owner. These punitive, sporadic, and sometimes desperate inward reactions usually worsened the situation of the "plantation Negro" (a term used for both house and field slaves). A slave committed a transgression and could then do little more than wait to be discovered and "corrected." But the view that the field slave's resistance was typically aimless and self-defeating should not be pushed too far. Loosely supervised on the upcountry quarters by overseers who were not given the means adequately to manage slaves, field hands sometimes carried on campaigns of sabotage. As Landon Carter's diary indicates, these organized and systematic activities were especially effective if the job was not routine, the master was insecure, and the overseers lacked real authority.

Field Slaves' Reactions to Slavery

THE BEST SOURCE *on the behavior of "new Negroes" in the colonial period is Landon Carter's diary, which tells a dreary story of the slaves' quiet and persistent—and noncooperative—actions. Jack P. Greene, the editor of the diary, argues that Carter was essentially an insecure, deeply embittered man: "for some reason he had failed—and he knew he had failed—to make any lasting impression upon his generation, to achieve that recognition among his contemporaries that would assure him a place in history." One should add to this characterization that Carter's failure as a statesman (he was the most prolific political*

*writer of the Virginia Revolutionary generation) underscored his need
to succeed as the patriarch of a large plantation household.*

But Carter's execution of the patriarchal role was awkward and at
times disastrous. Patriarchs who were more personally secure, for example, were able to overlook their slaves' minor transgressions. But
benevolence and indulgence did not come easily to Carter. And in his
extensive surveys of Sabine Hall (a common practice among the Tidewater's hardworking gentry), he was incredibly diligent in sniffing out
and correcting his slaves' most trivial shortcomings. Convinced that his
slaves were taking advantage of him whenever and wherever they could
—which, of course, they were—he made endless item counts of their
productivity.

Thus the diary provides an invaluable opportunity to evaluate from
the master's point of view the advantages and shortcomings of the
patriarchal role and of a familial, domestic concept of slavery.

22. Passive Resistance

Source: *The Diary of Colonel Landon Carter of Sabine Hall,
1752–1778,* ed. Jack P. Greene, 2 vols. (Charlottesville, Va.,
1966), 1:290–291, 369–370, 371–373, 379; 2:648, 840–841. Reprinted by permission of The University Press of Virginia.

25 [*March 1766*]. *Friday.*   My man Bart came in this day, he
has been gone ever since New Year's day. His reason is only that I
had ordered him a whipping for saying he then brought in two
load of wood when he was coming with his first load only. This he
still insists on was truth although the whole plantation asserts the
contrary, and the boy with him. He is the most incorrigeable villain
I believe alive, and has deserved hanging; which I will get done if
his mate in roguery can be tempted to turn evidence against him.

Bart broke open the house in which he was tyed and locked up;
he got out before 2 o'clock but not discovered till night. Talbot is
a rogue. He was put in charge of him. I do imagine the gardiner's
boy Sam, a rogue I have suspected to have maintained Bart and
Simon all the while they have been out [as runaways] And I sent
this boy with a letter to the Island ferry at breakfast, but he never
returned although he was seen going back about 12 and was seen
at night . . . pretending to be looking for his Cattle. I kept this
fellow up two nights about these fellows before And have given
Rit the Miller a light whipping as having fed them by the hands of
Gardiner Sam . . .

27 [March 1766]. Sunday. Yesterday my son brought a story from Lansdown old Tom, that Johnny my gardiner had harboured Bart and Simon all the while they were out, Sometimes in his inner room and sometimes in my Kitchen Vault. Tom had this from Adam his wife's grandson That they were placed in the Vault in particular the day my Militia were hunting for them . . .

16 [March 1770]. Friday. I do believe my old Carpenters intend to be my greatest rascals. Guy does not do about any jobb be it ever so trifling that he does not make three weeks or a month of it at least. The silling my Mudhouse, a jobb of not more than 3 days, he has already been above a fortnight about, and this morning when my people went to help to put the sills in, though he said he was ready for them, he had the rotten sills to cut out and because I told him he should certainly be called to account for it as I came back truly he was gone and no body knew where and had been gone for sometime but not about my house.

Mr. Tony, another rascal, pretends he is full of pain though he looks much better than any Negro I have.

17 [March 1770]. Saturday. Tony came abroad and was well entertained for his impudence. Perhaps now he may think of working a little.

Guy actually ran away. Outlawries are sent out against him for tomorrow's publication.

22 [March 1770]. Thursday. Guy came home yesterday and had his correction for run[ning] away in sight of the people. The 2 sarahs came up yesterday pretending to be violent ill with pains in their sides. They look very well, had no fever, and I ordered them down to their work upon pain of a whipping. They went, worked very well with no grunting about pain but one of them, to wit Manuel's sarah, taking the advantage of Lawson's ride to the fork, swore she would not work any longer and run away and is still out. There is a curiosity in this Creature. She worked none last year pretending to be with Child and this she was full 11 months before she was brought to bed. She has now the same pretence and thinks to pursue this same course but as I have full warning of her deceit, if I live, I will break her of that trick. I had two before of this turn. Wilmot of the fork whenever she was with Child always pretended to be too heavy to work and it cost me 12 months before I broke her. Criss of Mangorike fell into the same scheme and really carried it to a great length for at last she could not be dragged out. However by carrying a horse with traces the Lady took to her feet run away and when catched by a severe whipping has been a good slave ever since only a cursed thief in making her Children milk my Cows in the night . . .

26 [*April 1770*]. *Thursday.* Gardner Johnny was so pleased in being turned to the hoe that he came this morning at day break to tell me he was going and the rascal took his row next to hindmost man in my field. But to show him I did not intend the hoe to be his field of diversion I gave him the place of my fourth man and have ordered my overseers to keep him to that. I observed it made him quicken the motion of his arm which up here used to be one, two, in the time of a soldier's parade. I am necessarily obliged to put postilion Tom into the garden but I have him to learn. However I cannot be worse off than with Johnny for with him I had not for some years got anything in my garden and hardly ever a piece of work done like a workman who has been at least 20 years a gardner. His perpetual pleasure is to be always stupidly drunk and right hand man to young Robin Smith who has sold him every thing even to my plows for the sake of his throat and in this stupid state has he for many years neglected to do me the least pennyworth of service. I have therefore thought it time to remove him to where he may be made to work or else I will sell him also for a greater villain cannot live. . . . It is the same at all my out plantations. Although I have many to work and fine land to be tended, I hardly make more than what cloaths them, finds them tools, and pays their Levies [taxes]. Perhaps a few scrawney hogs may be got in the year to be fattened up here, If these things do not require the greatest caution and frugality in living I am certain nothing can do . . .

3 [*February 1772*]. *Monday.* . . . Carpenter Guy was this evening found dead in the snow at the head of the meadow. All that we can learn as yet by enquiry is that he went to Currie's to see his wife as usual on Monday night last. . . . There is a circumstance that seems to want clearing up, to wit, some blood found on the

snow . . . there is a probability that he had been drunk and perhaps he may have been fighting.

He was a good workman but not an honest one and the last Job of his work shews this, for his single covering to my adjoining building though not more than a week done is as leaky as a riddle; and so all his late work is. He is of a drunken race, always stupid; but all this only makes me wish he had not had a wife abroad; for without being drunk it is quite Idle to think that he who had come so far in a snow however deep should have gone down the hill which lead to my house after he had been upon it, as he must have know[n] every foot of the way as well.

27 [*June 1774*]. *Monday.* I must not leave a very Particular case that has happened within this week to be only recorded in my Memory. A very old Slave of mine by name Jack Lubbar, whose age, though one can[not] be certain about, though in the year 1734 I found him too old a man to keep as a foreman to my Mangorike Gang and therefore privately bid him by degrees to fall astern of the rest, which is now 40 years agoe. Ever since then he has been only as a Slave gratefully endeavouring to serve a very kind Master; At last about 20 years ago I removed him only to his care as an overlooker at my Fork quarter with 4 hands and myself; in which service he so gratefully discharged his duty as to make me by his care alone larger crops of Corn, tobacco, and Pease twice over than ever I have had made by anyone, even as high as 12,000 weight tobacco and 187 barrels corn with the 5 hands and himself besides 90 and 100 bushels of Pease a year; and besides shoats and piggs used by my house 40 and more hogs for bacon. At this Plantation he continued till his age almost deprived him of eyesight which made him desire to be removed because those under him mostly his great grandchildren, by the baseness of their Parents abused him much. I then about 12 years ago brought him and his wife, our old midwife, to my henhouse at home, where I received untill about 3 years ago the good effects of his care. At last I removed him and his old woman to the Fork again there to live quite retired only under my constant kindness. But ever active as his life has been, he then became a vast progger in Catching fish, Beavers, otters, Muskrats, and Minxes with his traps, a Constant church man in all good days and as erect and fast a Walker as

almost any man in the Parish. In this manner has the good old man continued with as well a stored garden and patches of pease and belly timber, as it is called, and has spent the latter part of his time till about a fortnight ago he hurt his shin which had for a great while been very tender. This raised a swelling attended with a fever; however a sound constitution, though ancient, did not require so much application but of the mildest kind to restore him again to his health and his industry; and about a week ago this day hearing that a minx had committed great destruction on my fouls there, he went into the run where the animal was suspected to reside, and set his traps for him. The standing in the water so long to do that work, though he was accustomed to it, gave him a cold which sat on his bladder much about his Pubis, and occasioned a Stoppage in his urine besides a costiveness. I never heard of it till the wednesday following. The poor old creature then took to his bed, and although every endeavour was used to get him a Passage except the use of the Cathetor, which I had not, he could not be brought to make a drop of water, not even by constant warm baths, and on friday he was pronounced to be dying. . . . my Poor honest Slave Jack Lubber; whichsoever way, let God's will be done. I hope I do my duty, more I know I cannot do.

VIOLENT RESISTANCE

OCCASIONALLY *an individual or small group of plantation Negroes picked up whatever weapons were available (staves, hoes, muskets) and attacked the whites around them. This kind of inward resistance was usually self-destructive, although it must have made a profound impression on those blacks who survived and probably passed into the slaves' oral traditions. The first document is a newspaper story about an uprising of field hands on a small plantation in Hanover County, Virginia. The second newspaper account tells about a man who methodically stalked and killed his master before he simply "went home" to certain capture and death.*

23. A HANOVER COUNTY, VIRGINIA, UPRISING, CHRISTMAS, 1769

SOURCE: *Virginia Gazette* (Rind, ed.), January 25, 1770.

Sometime about Christmas last, a tragical affair happened at a plantation in North Wales, Hanover county, belonging to Bowler

Cocke, Esq; the particulars of which, according to the accounts we have received, are as follow, viz. The Negroes belonging to the plantation having long been treated with too much lenity and indulgence, were grown extremely insolent and unruly; Mr. Cocke therefore had employed a new Steward. The Steward's deputy (a young man) had ordered one of the slaves to make a fire every morning very early; the fellow did not appear till sunrise; on being examined why he came not sooner, he gave most insolent and provoking answers, upon which, the young man going to chastise him, the fellow made a stroke at him with an axe (or some such weapon) that was in his hand, but happily missed him. The young man then closed with him, and having the advantage, a number of other slaves came to the Negro's assistance, and beat the young man severely. At last the ringleader (a very sensible fellow) interceded for him, on which they desisted. The young man then made off as fast as he could, to procure assistance to quell them. Whilst he was gone, they tied up the Steward, and also a poor innocent, harmless old man, who overlooked a neighbouring quarter, and on hearing the uproar . . . [illegible] across the creek to know the . . . [illegible] they whipped [them] till they were raw from the neck to the waistband. In some time the young man returned, with about twelve white men, and two little boys carrying each a gun. They released the two unhappy sufferers, and then proceeded to a barn, where they found a large body of the Negroes assembled (some say forty, some fifty) on whom they tried to prevail by persuasion, but the slaves, deaf to all they said, rushed upon them with a desperate fury, armed with clubs and staves; one of them knocked down a white man, and was going to repeat the blow to finish him, which one of the boys seeing, levelled his piece, discharged its contents into the fellow's breast, and brought him to the dust. Another fellow having also knocked down another of the Whites, was in the same manner, shot by the other boy. In short, the battle continued sometime desperate, but another of the Negroes having his head almost cut off with a broad sword, and five of them being wounded, the rest fled. The accounts vary; some say three were killed upon the spot, and five wounded, others that two were killed, and five wounded, one of whom died soon after. It is said they had threatened to kill the Steward as soon as he came to the plantation. The ringleader was one of the slain.

24. A Rebel Who Went "Home"

Source: *Virginia Argus*, September 5, 1800.

A HORRID MURDER.

Capt. John Patteson, Inspector at Horsley's Warehouse in the town of Diuguids-ville and county of Buckingham, was lately murdered in a cruel manner by Abram, a negro man slave, the property of the said Patteson.—The circumstances of this attrocious deed is in substance thus related by the wretch who perpetrated it—being his confession at the time he was apprehended—repeated immediately after his trial and condemnation, and on the morning of his execution. Says he—"In consequence of some punishment inflicted on me by my master for some misdemeanor of which I was guilty, a considerable time prior to the fatal catastrophe, I ever after medidated [*sic*] his destruction: —On the evening in which it was effected, my master directed me to set off [for] home (about 7 miles distant from the warehouse, where I generally attended) and carry a hoe which we used at the place—I set off, and was determined to dispatch him that night—after proceeding some distance I concluded to way-lay him—having the hoe in possession accordingly, I lay on, or behind a log, convenient to the road on which my master was to pass, and fell into a slumber—after waiting there a considerable time, I heard the trampling of horses' feet; I concluded therefore my master was near—I got up and walked forwards—my master soon overtook me, and asked me (it being then dark) who I was; I answered Abram; he said he thought I had been gone from town long enough to have been further advanced on the road; I said, I thought not; I spoke short to him, and did not care to irritate him—I walked on however; sometimes by the side of his horse, and sometimes before him. In the course of our travelling an altercation ensued; I raised my hoe two different times to strike him, as the circumstance of the places suited my purpose, but was intimidated—when I came to the bridge (across a small stream) I thought that place favorable to my views, but seeing a light, and some people at a house a little distant from thence, I resisted the impulse. When I came to the fatal spot, being most obscured by the loftiness of the trees, I turned to the side of the road; my master observed it, and stopped; I then turn'd suddenly round, lifted my hoe, and struck him across the breast; the stroke broke the handle of the hoe—he fell—I repeated my blows; the handle of the hoe broke a second time—I heard dogs bark, at a house which we passed, at a small distance; I was alarmed, and ran a little way, and stood behind a tree, 'till the barking ceased; in running, I stumbled and fell—I returned to finish the scene I began, and on my way picked up a stone, which I hurl'd at his head, face, &c. again and again and again, until I thought he was certainly dead—and then I went home." . . .

Household Slaves' Reactions to Slavery

FOR BLACKS, *household status was often a harrowing experience. Their work, which was usually monotonous and unrewarding, increased the number of degrading encounters with whites that intensified the impact of slavery for all concerned. Unlike the field hand, who could find a degree of protection in number and anonymity, the servant (as colonists preferred to call house slaves) was usually profoundly unsure about whites and the permanence of his "privileged" status, and often found himself in situations that threatened to expose a nature sharply divided between an enervating fear and aggressive hostility. For whites, the intimate presence of so many blacks insidiously influenced domestic affairs, particularly the master's behavior toward his wife and children. Household slavery—that dimension of American Negro slavery that changed least over time—was the epitome of Professor Frank Tannenbaum's dynamic view of the all-important human element in slave societies, where, he reminded us, slavery was not merely for blacks, but for whites as well.*

25. THOMAS JEFFERSON ON HOUSEHOLD SLAVERY

THE RECIPROCAL—*and often harmful—nature of human relations in the great mansions of his society was an issue Jefferson described briefly in Notes on Virginia. In this, his only book, Jefferson placed slavery in colonial Virginia in the context of family relations and so uncovered its essential nature: an intensely private—a family—affair for both servant and master.*

SOURCE: Thomas Jefferson, *Notes on Virginia,* Query XVIII, in Adrienne Koch and William Peden, eds., *The Life and Selected Writings of Thomas Jefferson* (New York, 1944), pp. 277–278. Reprinted by permission of Random House, Inc.

QUERY XVIII.

The particular customs and manners that may happen to be received in that State?

It is difficult to determine on the standard by which the manners of a nation may be tried, whether *catholic* or *particular*. It is more difficult for a native to bring to that standard the manners of his own nation, familiarized to him by habit. There must doubtless be an unhappy influence on the manners of our people produced by the existence of slavery among us. The whole commerce between master and slave is a perpetual exercise of the most boisterous passions, the most unremitting despotism on the one part, and degrading submissions on the other. Our children see this, and learn to imitate it; for man is an imitative animal. This quality is the germ of all education in him. From his cradle to his grave he is learning to do what he sees others do. If a parent could find no motive either in his philanthropy or his self-love, for restraining the intemperance of passion towards his slave, it should always be a sufficient one that his child is present. But generally it is not sufficient. The parent storms, the child looks on, catches the lineaments of wrath, puts on the same airs in the circle of smaller slaves, gives a loose to the worst of passions, and thus nursed, educated, and daily exercised in tyranny, cannot but be stamped by it with odious peculiarities. The man must be a prodigy who can retain his manners and morals undepraved by such circumstances.

26. FUN AND CRUEL GAMES AT WILLIAM BYRD'S WESTOVER

JEFFERSON'S VIEW *of household slavery should not be accepted uncritically. Servants did not typically engage in "degrading submissions," nor were masters usually blustering despots. Their respective roles were more intricate than that. What is most apparent, as the focus narrows to the households of a few wealthy slaveowners, are the individuals themselves and the contexts—setting, duration, and frequency—of black and white role behaviors. Caught in a cruel and irrational system that none of them really understood, sometimes they were able to cope, but more often they merely struggled.*

William Byrd II, a quick-witted, talented man, occasionally entertained himself by harassing his servants in cruel and gamelike encounters involving the blacks' family lives and the execution of their duties. Byrd, who had spent his early years living freely in London among

*various prominent and notorious literary figures and rakehells, returned
to Virginia after his father's death. He seems to have made the transition from one life and scene to another without difficulty, or so historians have told us—but perhaps not. His keen humor, haughty demeanor,
and machismo style made life miserable for the house slaves and his
young and petulant wife, Lucy Parke Custis. Planters' wives usually
supervised the servants, but not at Westover. To relieve the unaccustomed and unenlightened boredom of plantation life, while keeping
Lucy Parke in her place, Byrd undermined his wife's authority by
playing games of uproar with Anaka, Little Jenny, and Eugene.*

SOURCE: Louis B. Wright and Marion Tinling, eds., *The Secret
Diary of William Byrd of Westover, 1709–1712* (Richmond,
1941), pp. 1–2, 7, 22, 46, 78–79, 113, 192, 307. Reprinted by permission of the editors.

8 [*February 1709*]. I rose at 5 o'clock this morning and read
a chapter in Hebrew and 200 verses in Homer's *Odyssey*. I ate milk
for breakfast. I said my prayers. Jenny and Eugene were whipped.
I danced my dance. I read law in the morning and Italian in the
afternoon. . . .

22 [*February 1709*]. I rose at 7 o'clock and read a chapter in
Hebrew and 200 verses in Homer's *Odyssey*. I said my prayers, and
ate milk for breakfast. I threatened Anaka with a whipping if she
did not confess the intrigue between Daniel and Nurse, but she prevented by a confession. I chided Nurse severely about it, but she
denied, with an impudent face, protesting that Daniel only lay on
the bed for the sake of the child. I ate nothing but beef for
dinner. . . .

17 [*April 1709*]. . . . Anaka was whipped yesterday for stealing the rum and filling the bottle up with water. . . .

10 [*June 1709*]. I rose at 5 o'clock this morning but could not
read anything because of Captain Keeling, but I played at billiards
with him and won half a crown of him and the Doctor. George
B–th brought home my boy Eugene. . . . In the evening I took a
walk about the plantation. Eugene was whipped for running away
and had the [bit] put on him. I said my prayers and had good
health, good thoughts, and good humor, thanks be to God Almighty.

3 [*September 1709*]. . . . I read some geometry. We had no court this day. My wife was indisposed again but not to much purpose. I ate roast chicken for dinner. In the afternoon I beat Jenny for throwing water on the couch. . . .

1 [*December 1709*].   I rose at 4 o'clock and read two chapters in Hebrew and some Greek in Cassius. I said my prayers and ate milk for breakfast. I danced my dance. Eugene was whipped again for pissing in bed and Jenny for concealing it. . . .

3 [*December 1709*].   I rose at 5 o'clock and read two chapters in Hebrew and some Greek in Cassius. I said my prayers and ate milk for breakfast. I danced my dance. Eugene pissed abed again for which I made him drink a pint of piss. I settled some accounts and read some news. . . .

17 [*June 1710*]. . . . I set my closet right. I ate tongue and chicken for dinner. In the afternoon I caused L–s–n to be whipped for beating his wife and Jenny was whipped for being his whore. In the evening the sloop came from Appomattox with tobacco. I took a walk about the plantation. I said my prayers and drank some new milk from the cow. . . .

27 [*February 1711*].   I rose at 6 o'clock and read two chapters in Hebrew and some Greek in Lucian. I said my prayers and ate boiled milk for breakfast. I danced my dance and then went to the brick house to see my people pile the planks and found them all idle for which I threatened them soundly but did not whip them. . . . In the afternoon Mr. Dunn and I played at billiards. Then we took a long walk about the plantation and looked over all my business. In the evening my wife and little Jenny had a great quarrel in which my wife got the worst but at last by the help of the family Jenny was overcome and soundly whipped. At night I ate some bread and cheese. I said my prayers and had good health, good thoughts, and good humor, thank God Almighty.

27. Sex and Slavery at Nomini Hall

THE DELIGHTFUL JOURNAL *of the tutor Philip Fithian illuminates a critical but unfamiliar dimension of American Negro slavery: sexual relations between whites and blacks. In this instance, one senses that Fithian's remarks about Robert "Councillor" Carter's young son Ben and his mother's "plump, sleek, likely" sixteen-year-old maid Sukey describe a common occurence—the master's son learning the facts of life from a black girl or woman he had grown up with in the household. Sexual encounters between free and slave were common. To cite only one source covering a long span of time, fugitive slave notices in eighteenth-century Virginia newspapers, miscegnation was extensive and increasing late in the century. There are scores of advertisements for mulattoes; a much larger number for light-skinned blacks (called "yellow," "bright," or "mustee-complexioned"); and, by the late 1700s when the demographic make-up of the slave population was generally more American than African, a lighter-complexioned runaway was the norm. White men forcing themselves on black women (or being willingly accepted as their lovers) was the usual pattern, but not always. There are a number of examples of slave men making love to, or living with, free white women (in sources sufficiently obscure to suggest that they reveal only the tip of an iceberg); there are a few records of fugitive slaves in Virginia running off with white women; there are some divorce petitions filed in the Maury County, Tennessee, Equity Court by white men whose white brides had given birth to mulattoes; and a witness in a slave trial (trial of Larkin, March 11, 1850) in the Spartanburg, South Carolina, Judicial District mentioned casually that Jason, killed in a fight with another slave, had lived with a white woman who bore him a child—evidently with the knowledge of the community. This topic is an important one and warrants further research; and documents, such as Fithian's journal, which convey a sense of how intimate blacks and whites actually were in slave society households are a good place to begin.*

SOURCE: Hunter Dickinson Farish, ed., *The Journal and Letters of Philip Vickers Fithian*, new ed. (Williamsburg, Va., 1965), pp. 39, 85–86, 184–185, 187. Reprinted by permission of The University Press of Virginia.

Fryday 24 [December 1773]. In the Evening I read the two first Books of *popes* Homer. Dr Jones supped with us, & is to stay the Night. The conversation at supper was on Nursing Children; I find it is common here for people of Fortune to have their young Children suckled by the Negroes! Dr Jones told us his first and only Child is now with such a Nurse; & Mrs Carter said that Wenches have suckled several of hers—Mrs Carter has had thirteen Children She told us to night and she has nine now living; of which seven are with me. Guns are fired this Evening in the Neighbourhood [a Christmas season custom], and the Negroes seem to be inspired with new Life. The Day has been serene and mild, but the Evening is hazy.

Supp'd on Oysters.

Sunday 27 [March 1774]. An odd Jumble of affairs happened this morning—*Bob* drest himself & came into our Room & in his usual way began to be pretty free in telling us *News*. Amongst a vast quantity of other stuff he informed *Ben* & I that he heard Mr *Randolph* has the P . . . we both join'd severely reprimanding for attempting to propagate so unlikely a tale—Why, Brother Ben, said the mischievous Wretch, I heard in this Neighbourhood, yesterday a Report concerning you not much to your—but I will conceal it. This enraged Ben; he at first however persuaded him but soon began to threaten loudly unless he told the whole—why then, Brother, said Bob, it is reported that two Sundays ago you took Sukey (a young likely Negro Girl maid to Mrs Carters youngest Son) into your stable, & there for a considerable time lock'd yourselves together!—Before Bob had done, the Bell rung for Breakfast & we parted.

Monday 5 [September 1774]. There is wonderful *To do*, this morning among the Housekeeper & children, at the great house. They assert that a Man or a Spirit came into the Nursery about one o-Clock this morning—That if it was indeed a Spirit the Cause of his appearance is wholly unknown; but if it was Flesh & blood they are pretty confident that the design was either to rob the House, or commit fornication with *Sukey* (a plump, sleek, likely Negro Girl about sixteen)—That the doors & windows were well secured, but that by some secret manner, unknown to all, the *Thing* opened the Cellar door, went through the Cellar, & up the narrow dark Stairs (Which are used only on necessary occasions, as when the great Stair way is washing or on some such account)—That it left the said Cellar door. . . . That it had previously put a small wedge in the Lock of the Nursery Door, where several of the young Ladies, & the said *Sukey* sleep, so that when they were going to bed they could not Lock nor bolt the door, but this they all believed was done in mischief by the children, & went thereupon to bed, without suspicion of harm, with the door open—that Sukey some time in the Night discovered Something lying on her Side which she knew to be a Man by his having Breeches—That She was greatly surprised, & cry'd out suddenly to the others that a Man was among them, & that the Man *tickled* her, & said *whish, whish*—That on this She left the Bed & run & squeased herself in by the side of Miss Sally the Housekeeper, but that by this time the Whole Room was awake & alarmed—That when the thing knew there was a discovery it stamped several times on the floor, shook the Bedstead by the side of which it lay, rattled the Door several Times & went down stairs walking very heavy for one barefoot. That on its leaving the Room the Hous[e] Keeper went to Ben Carter's Chamber, & that he rose & they all went down & found the Doors & windows as I have mentioned. . . . All this with many other material accidents is circulating through the family to Day; some conclude it was a Ghost because it would not speak—But, more probably it was one of the warm-blooded, well fed young Negroes, trying for the company of buxom *Sukey*—The Colonel however, at Breakfast gave out that if any one be caught in the House, after the family are at Rest, on any Pretence what ever, that Person he will cause to be hanged!

Fryday 9 [*September 1774*]. *Ben* with great Humour either out of a *Bravado* or for Revenge gave out in the Family to day that it is the opinion of a certain *Female*, of considerable Note in the family, that all the male Children which shall be born in this unlucky year, tho' they may be fair to the Sight, will be yet unable, from a Debility of Constitution, to do their Duty, with respect to Women, either married or single—That She has two reasons for this opinion,
1. Because the Air appears to her extremely *barren, weak, & ungenerative*—2. Because the Peaches, & other Fruit, are observed this year to have in them very few Kernels, at the same time that the Peaches are sweet & fair—I think that *Ben*, by this strategem, whether it be real or otherwise, is evil with the invidious Vixen which suspected him of entering the Nursery to visit black-faced Sukey—

A *Special Kind of Household Slavery:*
Colonial Patriarchs and Their Waitingmen

ALL VIEWS *of household slaves as "Toms" should be kept in abeyance until the waitingmen, the wealthy slaveholders' personal body servants, are considered. Among "plantation Negroes," they were the most distinctive: their jobs were sometimes challenging (as well as demeaning), and they often traveled beyond the confines of the plantation world. This mobility broadened the waitingman's outlook, sheltered his individuality, and helped maintain his sanity (in the midst of households such as William Byrd's Westover, or when confronting demanding patriarchs, such as Landon Carter or George Washington).*

The waitingman's position was a difficult one, and pressures on him began early. In the last few years of his presidency, Washington in the course of three letters instructed his steward at Mount Vernon in the art of selecting a valet:

> *. . . [a] likely and well disposed young fellow of [a] man's growth, or near it. . . . Honesty with some degree of acuteness are desirable; but in whom among my people there are to be found, I know not. Sam has sense enough, and has had a little experience, but he wants honesty, and every other requisite; particularly industry. —Cyrus, besides being a dower slave, is strongly suspected of roguery and drinking; —otherwise he would do very well, as he is likely, young, and smart enough.*

> *If Cyrus continues to give evidence of such qualities as would fit him for a waitingman, encourage him to persevere in them; and if they should appear to be sincere and permanent, I will receive him in that character when I retire from public life if not sooner. —To be sober, attentive to his duty, honest, obliging and cleanly, are the qualifications necessary, to fit him for my purposes. —If he possess these, or can acquire them—he might become useful to me, at the same time that he should exalt, and benefit himself.*

> *I will direct him to be taken into the house, and clothes to be made for him. —In the meanwhile, get him a strong horn comb and direct him to keep his head will combed, that the hair, or wool may grow long.*[2]

Men like Cyrus were continually and critically assessed, and their attitudes carefully scrutinized. So many waitingmen were actually "Super-Negro"—barber, doctor, bootblack, hostler, traveling companion, and, in some cases, "right-hand man" about the plantation, with important responsibilities as an intermediary between the master and the field slaves. All this had to be accomplished while maintaining the "proper attitude": the servant had to be "brisk" and "active" in

2. Cited in W. D. Conway, ed., *George Washington and Mount Vernon*, 4 vols. (Brooklyn, N.Y.: Long Island Historical Society Memoirs, 1889), 4:21, 216, 244.

anticipating a master's every whim, but in doing so he could never appear "bold." Many waitingmen kept continual vigilance over feelings of self-denial, frustration, and bitterness, and some manifested them through such neurotic symptoms of acute anxiety as stuttering, facial tics or uncontrollable hand movements. Even a man who was relatively free would encounter serious difficulties in fulfilling the valet's diverse roles to the satisfaction of a colonial patriarch such as George Washington. For a slave to execute these roles adequately, while keeping a lid on feelings and convictions whose expression might endanger his job, was often an exercise in futility. Some realized this and ran off (only fugitive watermen were advertised in eighteenth-century Virginia more frequently than waitingmen), and were later described in newspaper notices.

It has been fashionable to see house servants as men and women who, for the illusory material advantages of better food, clothing, and shelter, exhibited "accommodationist" behavior, defined by John Dollard as

> the renunciation of protest or aggression against undesirable conditions of life and the organization of the character so that protest does not appear, but acceptance does. It may come to pass in the end that the unwelcomed force is idealized, that one identifies with it and takes it into the personality; it sometimes even happens that what is at first resented and feared is finally loved.[3]

The following descriptions of runaway waitingmen indicate that household behaviors and strategies were extremely complex, and that many servants were not accommodating "Toms." Colonel John Tayloe's ex-waitingman Will, for example, ran off from the Neabsco Furnace. He was a "very likely" twenty-one-year-old mulatto, stout and strongly made, with a "remarkable Swing in his Walk." Will was "ingenuous": he had a "surprising Knack of gaining the good Graces of almost every Body who will listen to his bewitching and deceitful Tongue, which seldom or ever speaks the Truth." After leaving Tayloe's service as a valet and traveling companion, the slave had been "chiefly employed as a Founder, a Stone Mason, and a Miller, as Occasion required."[4] Christmas was another well-made mulatto, thirty years old, very pleasant and "well featured." "He can read" and "is very fluent of Speech," his master reported; "speaks with great Propriety, and is so artful that he can invent a plausible Tale at a Moment's Warning." When the valet's master was ill, Christmas became "very idle" and "wanton in

---

3. John Dollard, *Caste and Class in a Southern Town*, 3d ed. (New York, 1949), p. 255.
4. *Virginia Gazette* (Purdie and Dixon, eds.), April 1, 1774, Thomas Lawson, advertiser.

Licentiousness." Finally, after "several gross Acts of ill Behavior," he ran away.[5] And Romeo, a well-proportioned mulatto, turned up his upper lip when he spoke "or was alarmed." This waitingman generally appeared thoughtful, was "seldom seen to laugh," and was fond of prescribing and administering to sick Negroes, who nicknamed him "Doctor." Romeo could read, write, and knew something of figures, and he often used "his talents in giving passes and certificates of freedom to runaway slaves."[6]

The most complete documentation on a colonial waitingman describes Landon Carter's Nassau, who was almost constantly at war with himself, his master, and his difficult and conflicting roles on the plantation. While serving for years as a barber, doctor, valet, and "right-hand man" to the notoriously meticulous and cranky patriarch of Sabine Hall, Nassau seemed to spend few of his waking hours sober.

Carter's insecurity made Nassau's life difficult. Once he was forced to strip the clothing from a slave; on another occasion, he had to whip a runaway. But Nassau also protected slaves who had incurred Carter's wrath; and as a doctor, he was more highly regarded than Carter, whose purges and vomits were legendary. During one siege of illness both men worked side by side. Carter constantly nagged his waitingman, who moved about the quarters, bleeding slaves and drinking steadily. After more than a week of this, Nassau ran off, which he had done on several occasions before, always returning voluntarily. But during the Revolutionary War, he ran off and did not return; and Carter published an interesting notice from his church's pulpit.

28. "MY MAN" NASSAU

SOURCE: The Diary of Colonel Landon Carter of Sabine Hall, ed. Jack P. Greene, 2 vols. (Charlottesville, Va., 1966), 1:363, 373, 491–492; 2:665, 778. Reprinted by permission of The University Press of Virginia.

26 [February 1770]. Monday. At night found Nassau most excessively drunk so that I suffered as much as an old man could suffer, it being very cold without fire and without the least assistance for Tom coming round with my horse got not here till yesterday . . .

5. Ibid., March 19, 1772, James Mercer, advertiser.
6. Virginia Independent Chronicle, March 4, 1789, Austin Brockenbrough, advertiser.

23 [March 1770]. Friday.   I came home but without Nassau and Nat, a drunken father and Son. The latter first mired my horse up to his saddle in crossing a marsh that none but a blind drunkard could ever venture upon and Mr. Nat so engaged with boon companions as never to get my chariot by which means I was to plung home 5 or 6 miles upon this mired horse without one person to assist me. I got home near sunset and about 8 o'clock came the Chariot with the drunken father and Son. This morning I ordered the son his deserts in part. The father I shall leave till another opportunity for though my old Servant I am too old a Master to be thus inhumanely treated . . .

18 [September 1770]. Tuesday.   On Fryday last I went with Corotoman Carter etc., to Mt. Airy, and left Nassau at home to attend Mr. Carter just taken with a lax. But I was surprized he would not let the boy Ben that waited upon me ride the bald face horse, Pretending the horse ran away with him. Lee thought this a good thing in Nassau; but I suspected what has happened. He kept his horse to ride out for a drunk; And so he did all day just till I got home when no Piper was ever drunker, and so confounded improvident there was no bearing him. At my going to bed he could not wait upon me And went off, and has stayed away till this morning. He will not tell where he has been; but I believe it must have been Robin Smith's, because I went there to enquire and though they denied him I do suppose they concealed him.

I clapped a pair of handcuffs upon him and locked him up for a serious day of Correction. I have been learning to do without him, and though it has been but very badly yet I can bear it and will . . .

1 [April 1772]. Wednesday.   My people were last night 11 sick, and Nassau one of them. . . . This man is of great use to me among these sick people, and might be more so, but he grows tired with any patient long ill, and always says they are better untill they die . . .

23 [September 1773]. Thursday.   I have been obliged to give Nassau a severe whipping this day. He has been every day drunk ever since Mulatto Betty was taken ill. . . . I have threatened him, begged him, Prayed him, and told him the consequences if he neglected the care to one of the sick people; that their deaths through such want of care must be an evidence against him at the great and terrible day, talked a great deal to him in most religious and affectionate way; and this day by day; and yet all will not do; he seems resolved to drink in spight of me, and I believe in order to spight me. He knows he never gets a stroke but for his drinkings, and then he is very sharply whipped; but as soon as the cuts heal he gets drunk directly. I am now resolved not to pass one instance over and think myself justified both to God and Man. I confess I have faults myself to be forgiven, but to be every day and hour committing them, and to seek the modes of committing them admits of no Plea of frailty; I hope then I may still save his soul. . . .

29. An Attempt to Sell Nassau South

Source: *Virginia Gazette* (Rind, ed.), March 10, 1768.

My man *Nassau*, who I have with much care bred up to be of great service amongst my sick people, having fallen into a most abandoned state of drunkenness, and indeed injured his constitution by it, is become now rather a prejudice to me, as he cannot be trusted in the business he has been long practiced in. As I intend to indulge his appetite, which he cannot be cured of by any persuasion, I will, as soon as I can, send him to some of the islands, where no doubt he may get his liquor with less pains than he now seems to take: Therefore I advertise, that I am in want of a young man with a good disposition, that can shave and bleed well, and I am satisfied such a person will find it so much his interest, by pursuing my directions, amongst the sick, that, with the wages which I shall give him, he will think the place nothing disagreeable to him.

LANDON CARTER

30. Nassau Takes Matters into His Own Hands

Source: Fragment from the Carter Papers, Earl Gregg Swem Library, The College of William and Mary in Virginia.

Clerk of Lunenburgh Parish Upper Church is request[ed] to publish this outlawry at his Church this day—19 Oct 1777—and next Sunday, and Certify the same reddy to be sent for—L. Carter.
[illegible] . . . the only time he ever absented himself for above

a day or so, for now some years, it is very remarkable, he was taken up in Lancaster County. And more he has Carried off every kind of wearing apparel except a Straw hat and a dirty shirt (which might have escap'd his packing up) and has taken with him even a set of raisors which he had purchased: So that this trip must have been some time projecting, with a design to go to the Bay side, in order to get on board of Some of the ships of the Enemies of this and the rest of the United States. These are therefore in this name of this Common Wealth, to order the said Nessa [illegible] for[th]with to return to his said Master. And if he does not, we do hereby require you the Sheriff and good people aforesaid, to make due serch and inquiry after the said Nassau, in order that he may be taken. And if upon finding where he shall be, as it must be empossible for him to Subsist without purloining the property of some one of this Common Wealth to support himself during his outlying; If the Said Nassau Shall refuse to be taken, We hereby declare the law after due publication of this Outlawry, for two Several Sundays in the Several Church[es].

E. Assimilated Slaves: The Artisans

SLAVE ARTISANS *resisted bondage in significantly different ways than did field or house slaves. Their jobs were varied and challenging, mastered only by expertise and self-discipline. They usually escaped the full impact of the plantation's norms and their masters' values because they worked in commercial areas—workshops, courthouses, wharves, warehouses, industries, and towns—where they became increasingly at ease and familiar with whites and their customs. Artisans also worked at their own pace without direct supervision, and they spent considerable time by themselves, or with other blacks, while acquiring their distinctive characteristics: work and leisure-time skills (several were musicians), fluent English, and what their masters referred to as a "sensible" or "artful" demeanor. Slave artisans were often relatively advantaged, competent, and resourceful men, and not typically "accommodated" or passive. They organized the first large-scale insurrection in the nineteenth century (Gabriel Prosser's), and frequently appeared in fugitive slave advertisements.*

As runaways these men were fugitives and not truants (as were Landon Carter's slaves who remained "outlying" or "lurking" for a day or so and then returned voluntarily). That is, they actually left the immediate environs of the plantation and ran off, usually downriver to a port town in order to obtain a job, and "pass as free," or to board a ship and escape slavery completely.

The documents begin with descriptions of the few African artisans who in their own lives went through the major stages of acculturation. Whether this was accountable to skills they brought with them from Africa—a distinct possibility that is nearly impossible to document—or to the fact that they were sufficiently intelligent, opportunistic, and fortunate to learn English and the other skills that made them formidable runaways cannot be determined. But their brief stories are a useful reminder of the critical importance of acculturation as a major variable in slave behavior in the colonial period.

In the second group of documents, the runaway artisans include a carpenter, a shoemaker, a jockey, a sailor, and Peter Deadfoot, the complete man.

31. Slave Artisans Who Were Once "New Negroes"

Sources: *Virginia Gazette* (Dixon and Hunter, eds.), January 23, 1778; *Virginia Herald & Fredericksburg Advertiser*, April 11, 1793.

RUN away some time in *September* last, from *James Armstrong* of *Fauquier* County, a Negro man named AYRE, belonging to the estate of the late Mr. *Allen Macrae*, deceased, about 35 years of age, 5 feet 7 inches high, rather slim made, and of a yellowish complexion, has a remarkable twist with his mouth when he speaks, and although an *Affrican*, affects to pronounce the *English* language very fine, or rather to clip it. As he can both read and write, it is more than presumable he may have forged a pass, and by that means may have travelled where he pleased as a free man. His common wearing apparel was of striped country cloth, and had on half worn hat, and country made shoes, all of which he may doubtless have had the address to alter or change, long e'er now. Whoever apprehends and so secures the said runaway Negro, so as to be had again, shall receive ten dollars if taken within 20 miles of his home, and if at a greater distance, or out of the State of *Virginia* 20 dollars, if delivered to the aforesaid *James Armstrong*, his overseer, or brought to the *Neabsco Furnace*, all reasonable charges will be thankfully paid, by

Thomas Lawson.

RUN AWAY from the Subscriber on the 31st ult., an African Negro named JASPER, by trade a carpenter, speaks very plain English as he came young into the country. He is about 50 years of age, and I think about 5 feet 5 or 6 inches in height, short limb'd and well made for strength; he can read tolerably well, and is both sensible and very artful; he has a surly countenance, especially if offended, and is of a morose temper, fond of liquor, and when drunk is very turbulent; has had the small pox, for which he was innoculated, and is a little marked with it in his face; he has also a remarkable scar above half-round his neck, given by a knife in a scoffle he had with another Negro some time past.—The dress he went off in is uncertain; he took with him two coats, one with short skirts, a drab coloured duffle; the other a white Virginia cloth, long skirted; whatever other articles is unknown. I make no doubt but he will endeavour to pass for a free man, and is most probable will endeavour to get into some of the northern states, in order to facilitate his escape; I believe he has procured some forged pass or writing—Any person who will apprehend the said runaway within the state . . . shall receive a reward of TEN POUNDS—and if without the state TWENTY.

FRANCIS JERDONE
Louisa county, April 3, 1793.

32. AMERICAN-BORN ARTISANS

SOURCES: *Virginia Gazette* (Purdie and Dixon, eds.), April 16, 1767; ibid., September 1769; *Virginia Gazette and General Advertiser*, July 15, 1795; *Virginia Gazette* (Purdie and Dixon, eds.), March 7, 1771; ibid. (Rind, ed.), September 22, 1768.

RUN AWAY from the subscriber near *Williamsburg*, last Saturday night, a Negro fellow named BOB, about 5 feet 7 inches high, about 26 years of age, was burnt when young, by which he has a scar on the wrist of his right hand, the thumb of his left hand burnt off, and the hand turns in; had on a double breasted dark coloured frieze jacket, yellow cotton breeches. He was lately brought home from *Hartford* County in *North Carolina*, where he has been harboured for three years past by one *Van Pelt*, who lives on *Chinkopin* creek; he passed for a freeman, by the name of *Edward* or *Edmund Tamar*, and has got a wife there. He is an extraordinary sawer, a tolerable good carpenter and currier, pretends to make shoes, and is a very good sailor. He has been gone for eight years, a part of which time he lived in *Charlestown, South Carolina*. He can read and write; and, as he is a very artful fellow, will probably forge a pass. All masters of vessels are hereby cautioned from carrying him out of the colony, and any person from employing him. . . .

WILLIAM TREBELL

RUN AWAY from the subscriber in *Albemarle*, a Mulatto slave called *Sandy*, about 35 years of age, his stature is rather low, inclining to corpulence, and his complexion light; he is a shoemaker by trade, in which he uses his left hand principally, can do coarse carpenters work, and is something of a horse jockey; he is greatly addicted to drink, and when drunk is insolent and disorderly, in his conversation he swears much, and in his behavior is artful and knavish. He took with him a white horse, much scarred with traces, of which it is expected he will endeavour to dispose; he also carried his shoemakers tools, and will probably endeavour to get employment that way. . . .

THOMAS JEFFERSON

TEN GUINEAS REWARD *and all reasonable expenses paid, if taken out of the state, for apprehending* CHARLES GREEN, FORTY years old, a yellow man of middle stature. He is a most excellent Hostler, in the general way, and Gardner—a remarkable good Race-Keeper and Rider, and is handy about every kind of business a house or field servant can be employed in—He will endeavour to pass for a free person, by forging letters of emancipation, and thereby strive to get out of the state. This fellow was very well known on the turf formerly, having rode at all the race grounds of consequence in Littleberry Hardyman's life, and I do suppose he will make his living in the line of his old profession, if he can with safety, in this state, *North* or *South-Carolina*, or by his other qualities, if he should go to the North.

JOHN TYLER

Green-Way, June 11, 1795

RUN away from the Sloop *Tryal*, in *Rappahannock* River, on the second of *December* last, a bright Mulatto Man Slave named SAM, property of Mr. *Charles Yates* of *Fredericksburg*, who bought him last *May* of Colonel *Warner Lewis* of *Gloucester* County, since which Time he has been constantly with me, until he ran off. He is about twenty-five Years old, six feet two inches high, strong limbed, well made, very likely Fellow; he has a Scar on his Forehead over one of his Eyes, I think it is the left, some Colour in his Cheeks when warm, and has a long Shock of Wool on his Head, which he often shears about the Crown. He was bred partly to the Plantation and Farming Business, and sometimes, as he informed me, was employed as an Axe Man and Sawer, about Ship building. His Dress was such as Sailors wear, and was imported ready made, an under Jacket of spotted Swanskin, or Cotton, and is too short for him in the Arms: he had also a milled double Yarn Cap, of two Colours, and took with him his Bedding, a new spotted Rug which he had stolen, and several Yards of mixed coloured Broadcloth, cut from a whole Piece that he had stolen, the Remainder of which he distributed amongst the Sloop's Crew to bribe them to Secrecy. His Thefts were certainly the Cause of his Flight, to avoid the Gallows, for he was never punished whilst with me, nor ever complained, neither had he any Cause to be dissatisfied at his Treatment; and it is probable his Apprehensions will make him endeavour to escape out of the Colony, under the Character of a Seaman. I have heard he was at *Norfolk* on *Christmas* Day, and there pretended to have belonged to a Vessel lately wrecked on the Sea Coast. With such a Story some Person in Want of Hands might be induced to engage him. Should it have been so, any One knowing it shall be well rewarded for the Information. . . .

STAFFORD LIGHTBURN JUNIOR

STAFFORD COUNTY, August 20, 1768.

RAN away last *April*, from one of the subscriber's quarters in *Loudoun* (where he had been a short time sawing) a Mulatto slave belonging to *Samuel Selden*, jun. named *Peter Deadfoot*, though it is supposed he has changed his name, as he the day before attempted to pass for a freeman, and got as far as *Noland's* ferry, on his way to *Philadelphia*, by a forged pass, in which he was called *William Swann*. He is a tall, slim, clean limbed, active, genteel, handsome fellow, with broad shoulders; about 22 years of age, a dark Mulatto, with a nose rather flat than otherwise, very sensible, and smooth tongued; but he is apt to speak quick, swear, and with dreadful curses upon himself, in defence of his innocence, if taxed with a fault, even when guilty; which may be easily discovered, by any person taxing him with being run away. He is an indifferent shoemaker, a good butcher, ploughman, and carter; an excellent sawyer, and waterman, understands breaking oxen well, and is one of the best scythemen, either with or without a cradle, in *America*: in short, he is so ingenious a fellow, that he can turn his hand to any thing; he has a great share of pride, though he is very obliging, is extremely fond of dress; and though his holiday clothes were taken from him, when he first attempted to get off, yet, as he has probably passed for a freeman, I make no doubt he has supplied himself with others, as such a fellow would readily get employment; it has been reported that he was seen on board a vessel in *York* river, near *York* town; but for my own part, I suspect that he is either in *Prince William* county, *Charles* county in *Maryland* (in both which places he has relations) or in the neighbourhood of *Winchester*. Whoever apprehends the said slave, and conveys him to me in *Stafford* county, shall receive if taken within ten miles of my house, Five Pounds; if above fifty miles, Ten Pounds; and if above one hundred miles, Twenty Pounds reward, besides what the law allows.

THOMSON MASON

II

The Era of the American Revolution

IN VIRGINIA *from 1775 to 1800 the violent crosscurrents of the Revolutionary Era—set in motion by sharp economic changes (an upswing of urbanization and the substitution of wheat and general farming for tobacco), the impact of the natural rights philosophy on whites and blacks alike, and a rapidly acculturating black population brought slaves to the flash point of rebellion on two occasions.*

In the fall of 1775 Virginians fought a small-scale war against their ex-Royal Governor, John Murray, Earl of Dunmore, who in the course of events offered to free slaves who would join him and fight against their masters. About 1,000 did so, and they were attached as fighters and engineers (trench diggers and porters) to a force of British seamen, marines, and Scotch Highlanders, who conducted amphibious raids from British warships on the virtually defenseless Tidewater plantations. But Dunmore's emancipation proclamation and the critical situation it momentarily created did not incite a general slave uprising. The reactions of rebellious slaves during the military campaigns in Virginia (particularly during the British invasions of 1777 and 1781) indicated that blacks still reacted to slavery individually. They ran off alone and joined whichever army—British, American, or French—was most convenient, and seemed to promise more control over their lives, if not outright freedom.

Large-scale, armed insurrection, however, waited on certain conditions that were at best only latent in 1775 but more fully developed in 1800. In the summer of that year Gabriel Prosser and his brothers, Solomon, a blacksmith, and Martin, a preacher, planned an elaborate night attack on the new capital at Richmond. It failed abysmally, but generated a remarkable number of explanations by whites. The most probing and insightful one was written by St. George Tucker, an aristocrat and lawyer, who provided an overview for the entire tumultuous period in a letter to the state legislature. Tucker also concluded with a prophetic statement about the religious inspiration for insurrection—which (while pointing to the sources of Gabriel's failure) did not become a reality until Nat Turner's rebellion thirty years later.

33. A Moral Philosopher Examines Two Virginia
Slave Rebellions, 1775 and 1800

FOR WHITES *a puzzling and ominous development among their most trusted slaves was the assimilated blacks' transformation between 1775 and 1800 from solitary fugitives to organized insurrectionists. Writing in 1801 about this change in outlook, and attempting brilliantly to connect the artisans' personal motivation to their historical setting, St. George Tucker analyzed the events of 1775 and 1800 for the state legislature. Comparing the blacks' reactions to Dunmore and Gabriel, he discussed their exceptionally rapid material and spiritual development in the "few short years" following the Revolutionary War, which he attributed to the growth of towns and skilled trades, and a complementary increase in the extent of slave literacy.*

SOURCE: [St. George Tucker], *To a Member of the General Assembly of Virginia, on the Subject of the Late Conspiracy of the Slaves,* Baltimore, Maryland, 1801, Virginia State Archives microfilm.

There is often a progress in human affairs which may indeed be retarded, but which nothing can arrest . . . it is marked only by comparing distant periods. The causes which produce it are either so minute as to be invisible, or, if perceived, are too numerous and complicated to be subject to human control. Of such sort is the advancement of knowledge among the negroes of this country. It is so striking, as to be obvious to a man of the most ordinary observation. Every year adds to the number of those who can read and write; and he who has made any proficiency in letters, becomes a little centre of instruction to others. This increase of knowledge is the principal agent in evolving that spirit we have to fear. The love of freedom, sir, is an inborn sentiment . . . long may it be kept under by the arbitrary institutions of society, but, at the first favorable moment, it springs forth, and flourishes with a vigour that defies all check. This celestial spark . . . is not extinguished in the bosom of the slave. It may be buried in the embers; but it still lives; and the breath of knowledge kindles it into flame. Thus we find, sir, there never have been slaves in any country, who have not seized the first favorable opportunity to revolt.

In our infant country, where population and wealth increase

with unexampled rapidity, the progress of liberal knowledge is proportionally great. . . . The fact is, they [the blacks] are likely to advance much faster in this vast march of the mind. The growth and multiplication of our towns tend a thousand ways to enlighten and inform them. The very nature of our government, which leads us to recur perpetually to the discussion of natural rights, favors speculation and enquiry. By way of marking the prodigious change which a few years has made among this class of men, compare the late conspiracy with the revolt under lord Dunmore. In the one case, a few solitary individuals flocked to that standard, under which they are sure to find protection. In the other, they, in a body, of their own accord, combine a plan for asserting their claims, and rest their safety on success alone. The difference is, that then they fought for freedom merely as a good; now they also claim it as a right. . . .

We have hitherto placed much reliance on the difficulty of their acting in concert. Late experience has shewn us, that the difficulty is not insurmountable. Ignorant and illiterate as they are, they have maintained a correspondence, which, whether we consider its extent, or duration, is truly astonishing. If their gradual improvement did not continually facilitate communication, the want may be at any time supplied by a few desperate intriguers, or bigoted enthusiasts.

Fanaticism is spreading fast among the Negroes of this country, and may form in time the connecting link between the black religionists and the white. Do you not, already, sir, discover something like a sympathy between them? It certainly would not be a novelty, in the history of the world, if Religion were made to sanctify plots and conspiracies.

Rebellion 1775: Governor Dunmore's Emancipation Proclamation

GOVERNOR DUNMORE *routed a scratch force of colonial militia outside Norfolk in mid-November 1775. At this apparently auspicious moment he decided to issue an emanicipation proclamation (an action he had contemplated for more than eight months) from on board the man-of-war* William *in Norfolk harbor. A week later he marched into the small village, raised the King's standard, and invited those able and willing to bear arms (including indentured servants and slaves) to join him. Contemporary and present-day accounts vary considerably about how many slaves eventually responded. But according to Professor Benjamin*

Quarles about 800 joined, and the number may have grown to about 1,500. Three weeks after the Proclamation, Dunmore used between 300 and 400 fugitive slaves at the Battle of Great Bridge in Norfolk County.

The planters were deeply troubled. Edmund Pendleton wrote to Richard Henry Lee, "letters mention that slaves flock to him [Dunmore] in abundance; but I hope it is magnified." And George Washington warned that "if the Virginians are wise, that arch traitor . . . Dunmore should be instantly crushed, if it takes the force of the whole army to do it; otherwise like a snowball rolling, his army will get size."[1]

But the ex-Royal Governor's "Black Regiment" was little more than a group of fugitives temporarily thrown together by white officers to perform a desperate holding action. For several weeks Dunmore burned a few plantations, ransacked outbuildings, and destroyed some crops and herds and little more. Generally his brief pursuit of the war along Virginia's relatively unprotected coasts was unimaginative and conducted (through no fault of his own) on a limited scale. The ex-colonists' objective, to "circumscribe within narrow bounds [Dunmore's] sphere of mischief," was soon accomplished. When a virulent smallpox ravaged his small force on Gwinn's Island, the ex-Governor sailed from Virginia and did not return.

Dunmore's raids may have been of minimal economic and military importance, but his "damned," "infernal," "Diabolical" proclamation inspired an unprecedented torrent of bitter anti-Negro propaganda. Newspaper editors, presumably addressing a receptive audience, became obsessed with the idea of slaves armed by "outsiders" with guns and unnatural thoughts of freedom.

34. "God Save the King"

Source: Peter Force, ed., *American Archives*, 6 vols. (Washington, D.C., 1840), 3:1386.

PROCLAMATION BY THE GOVERNOUR OF VIRGINIA.

By his Excellency the Right Honourable JOHN, *Earl of* DUNMORE. *His Majesty's Lieutenant and Governour-General of the Colony and Dominion of* VIRGINIA, *and Vice-Admiral of the same.*

1. Edmund Pendleton to Richard H. Lee, November 27, 1775, in *American Archives*, ed. Peter Force, 6 vols. (Washington, D.C., 1840), 4th ser., 4:202; George Washington to Joseph Reed, December 15, 1775, cited in George W. Williams, *History of the Negro Race in America from 1610–1880* (New York, 1885), p. 341.

A PROCLAMATION.

As I have ever entertained hopes that an accommodation might have taken place between *Great Britain* and this Colony, without being compelled, by my duty, to this most disagreeable, but now absolutely necessary step, rendered so by a body of armed men, unlawfully assembled, firing on His Majesty's Tenders; and the formation of an Army, and that Army now on their march to attack His Majesty's Troops, and destroy the well-disposed subjects of this Colony: To defeat such treasonable purposes, and that all such traitors, and their abettors may be brought to justice, and that the peace and good order of this Colony may be again restored, which the ordinary course of the civil law is unable to effect, I have thought fit to issue this my Proclamation, hereby declaring, that until the aforesaid good purposes can be obtained, I do, in virtue of the power and authority to me given, by His Majesty, determine to execute martial law, and cause the same to be executed throughout this Colony. And to the end that peace and good order may the sooner be restored, I do require every person capable of bearing arms to resort to His Majesty's standard, or be looked upon as traitors to His Majesty's crown and government, and thereby become liable to the penalty the law inflicts upon such offences— such as forfeiture of life, confiscation of lands, &c., &c.; and I do hereby further declare all indented servants, Negroes, or others (appertaining to Rebels) free, that are able and willing to bear arms, they joining His Majesty's Troops, as soon as may be, for the more speedily reducing this Colony to a proper sense of their duty to His Majesty's crown and dignity. I do further order, and require, all His Majesty's liege subjects to retain their quit-rents, or any other taxes due, or that may become due, in their own custody, till such time as peace may be again restored to this at present most unhappy Country, or demanded of them for their former salutary purposes, by officers properly authorized to receive the same.

Given under my hand, on board the Ship *William*, off Norfolk, the 7th day of November, in the sixteenth year of His Majesty's Reign.

DUNMORE

GOD *Save the King*

35. Ex-Colonists' Public Reactions

Sources: *Virginia Gazette* (Dixon and Hunter, eds.), November 25, 1775; ibid. (Purdie, ed.), March 22, 1776.

Williamsburg, November 25, 1775

A COPY of the above proclamation having fallen into my hands, I thought it was necessary, for the welfare of two sorts of people, that its public appearance should be attended with comments of the following nature. . . .

The second class of people, for whose sake a few remarks upon this proclamation seem necessary, is the *Negroes.* They have been flattered with their freedom. . . . To none . . . is freedom promised but to such as are able to do Lord *Dunmore* service. The aged, the infirm, the women and children, are still to remain the property of their masters, masters who will be provoked to severity, should part of their slaves desert them. Lord *Dunmore's* declaration, therefore . . . leaves by far the greater number at the mercy of an enraged and injured people. But should there be any amongst the Negroes weak enough to believe that *Dunmore* intends to do them a kindness, and wicked enough to provoke the fury of the Americans against their defenceless fathers and mothers, their wives, their women and children, let them only consider the difficulty of effecting their escape, and what they must expect to suffer if they fall into the hands of the Americans. . . . Long have the Americans, moved by compassion, and actuated by sound policy, endeavoured to stop the progress of slavery. Our Assemblies have repeatedly passed acts laying heavy duties upon imported Negroes, by which they meant altogether to prevent the horrid traffick; but their human intentions have been as often frustrated by the cruelty and covetousness of a set of English merchants, who prevailed upon the King to repeal our kind and merciful acts, little indeed to the credit of his humanity. Can it then be supposed that the Negroes will be better used by the English. . . . No, the ends of Lord *Dunmore* and his party being answered, they will either give up the offending Negroes to the rigour of the laws they have broken, or sell them in the West Indies, where every year they sell many thousands of their miserable brethren, to perish either by the inclemency of the weather, or the cruelty of barbarous masters. Be not then, ye Negroes tempted by this proclamation to ruin yourselves. I have given you a faithful view of what you are to expect; and I declare before GOD, in doing it, I have considered your welfare, as well as that of the country. Whether you will profit by my advice I cannot tell; but this I know, that whether we suffer or not, if you desert us, you most certainly will.

Williamsburg, March 22, 1776

We hear that lord Dunmore's *Royal Regiment of Black Fusileers* is largely recruited . . . who, after doing the drudgery of the day (such as acting as scullions, &c. on board the fleet) are ordered upon deck to perform the military exercise; and, to comply with their *native* warlike genius, instead of the drowsy drum and fife, will be gratified with the use of the sprightly and enlivening *barrafoo*, an instrument peculiarly adapted to the martial tune of "Hungry Niger, parch'd Corn!" and which from henceforward is to be styled, by way of eminence, the BLACKBIRD MARCH.

Rebellion 1800: Gabriel Prosser's Conspiracy

IN THEIR QUEST *for an "Independence on every one but Providence," colonial tobacco planters encouraged Africans to change their customs as quickly as possible, while learning English and the other skills that were the basis for their economically diversified plantations. Paradoxically, acculturation ultimately produced slaves—educated, mobile, and resourceful in commercial settings—who were unsuited for plantation slavery. In the closing years of the century this situation became dangerous, when conditions prompted a radical change in the way assimilateds resisted slavery.*

Between 1775 and 1800 revolutionary conflict and ideology were resolved for most free men but, as St. George Tucker explained, not for the slave artisans, an elite group that had come to realize that regardless of their relatively privileged position, and the whites' efforts to ameliorate the worst abuses of slavery, the institution would survive and grow. Assimilateds, who customarily resisted alone, for the first time viewed slavery as a collective problem, and organized one of the largest and most ambitious rebellions in the history of our country.

Gabriel Prosser's insurrection failed. Elaborate plans—to march in three columns to the new capital of Richmond, to fire its warehouse district, storm the arsenal, and make the Governor, James Monroe (the future President), a hostage—were destroyed by a fierce rainstorm, and by an even more catastrophic division between the leaders and their potential followers.

Divisive problems that plagued Gabriel's scheme throughout, and which eventually brought disaster, were laid bare in the encounters during recruitment, when leaders and rank-and-file shared views of what concerned them most—military rank, arms, and who was to be killed or spared once slaves were on top.

The story opens and closes with documents from the trial of King, a waitingman for the Governor's aide-de-camp. Additional trial depositions describe the organization and destruction of the conspiracy. The concluding section, "Aftermath: All Confidence . . . Is Destroyed," includes trial evidence, the official correspondence between the Mayor of Norfolk and Governor Monroe, and A. W.'s letter (a rare surviving example of written communication between slaves insurrectionists).

SOURCES: All but one document for this section, on Gabriel Prosser's Conspiracy, including A.W.'s letter (a manuscript fragment), are in a file marked "Negro Insurrection" among the Executive Papers, September–December, 1800, Virginia State Library. "Extract of a letter from a gentleman in this city to his friend in New-York, dated September 20, 1800" (the first part of Document No. 39) was reprinted in the *Virginia Argus* (Richmond), October 14, 1800.

36. RECRUITMENT

At the Trial of Philip Narbonne Nicholas' King. The Application by Philip N. Nicholas, esqr. to the court of Oyer and Terminer, which tried and condemned a negroe man Slave named *King*, belonging to the said Nicholas, who was charged before that court with "advising, consulting, plotting and conspiring to rebel, and make an insurrection among the slaves against the laws and Government of this Commonwealth &c." To recommend the said King to the clemency of the Executive, being refused by the said Court, the undersigned members of the said court, willing to do whatever with propriety they can do to gratify the Wish of the said Nicholas, have thought it fit to make the following statement of the Evidence adduced on the said trial as well on the part of the Commonwealth, as on the part of the said "King" to be submitted to the Executive. This statement is made with the aid of some notes, but principally from recollection; and while they will not pretend that *every mi-*

nute circumstance is detailed in it, they feel assured that no *material circumstance is ommitted.*

Evidence on the part of the Commonwealth. Ben alias Ben Woolfolk, a slave, First Witness [deposed]:

That about 5 or 6 weeks before on a Sunday morning, he the witness came to Richmond and brought with him some articles for market. That after the market was over, and after the bell had rung for Sermon at the Capitol, about 9, or 10 or 12 of the clock, he left the market house to return homewards, having procured a bottle of Spirits. That when he got near to the house of one Vanne he met with the prisoner—an indifferent conversation is commenced between them—as, from the prisoner: "Do you not know me, my name is King, commonly called Governor's King." Answer: "I did not, but I have often heard my brother speak of you." Prisoner: "I know your brother very well." Witness: "Will you drink a draw with me." Prisoner: "I can't drink it without water, I will drink some with water." That water was procured, and the prisoner drank some mixed with spirit from the witness' bottle. There were other Negroes around, or near them, the conversation continued, but had not grown more interesting when a young Gentleman came up on horse back, and after addressing to the Prisoner a short but pretty tart reprimand for his not having gone to wait on dinner at Mr. Randolph's as he had been directed, ordered the prisoner to go immediately into the lett[?], the prisoner in reply, muttered some excuse, as "that his cloaths were bad"; or "he had not had his new cloaths"; or he had not fit cloaths to wait at Mr. Randolph's, and went away before the Gentleman, who followed. That the witness continued in the same place, where he was again, in a short time joined by the prisoner. The prisoner spoke contumeliously of his master, and of the white people; his language and deportment encouraged the witness, and he asked him "are you a true man?" Prisoner: "I am, a true-hearted man; your brother knows me if you do not" Witness: "Can you keep a *proper*, or *important* secret?" Prisoner: "Yes." Witness: "The negroes are about to rise, and fight the White people for our freedom." Prisoner: "I never was so glad to hear anything in my life, they ought to have taken that consideration a long time ago; I am, and will be ready to join them at any moment; I could slay the white people like sheep." The witness enjoined him to keep it a profound secret, which he promised to do, not to mention it to or in the presence of any woman. If he knew or should meet with any sound or true hearted men, he might endeavour to enlist such, but he must know them well first. And witness did not see or converse with him afterwards—he took the prisoner to be sober, or he should not have told him the secret.

At the Trial of Sam Byrd, Jr.

Ben Woolfolk deposed: The prisoner was the second person from whom I received information of the intended insurrection. I went to the prisoner's house sometime last spring in the company with George Smith, was informed by the prisoner that he had fallen upon a plan (which ought long since to have been adopted) of freeing the Negro from slavery. That he intended hiring his own time for the greater part of the ensuing summer which would enable him to go about and engage a number of men in the adjacent counties and in Petersburg. That at this time he pulled a list out of his pocket containing the names of a number of Negroes enlisted by him. That in conversations with the prisoner afterwards at different times the subject of the insurrection was mentioned. That the prisoner mentioned that the Katawba Indians and French would join them against the white people. That the prisoner (as he said) was to be engaged as a recruiting officer and was to go in person to engage the Indians. That at the meeting at Mr. Young's spring in July last, the prisoner being asked what number of men he had enlisted answered that he had not his list about him, but supposed he had about five hundred, who were to be assembled by him and given up to Gabriel on the night to be appointed for the attack. The prisoner told the witness he had been to Louisa [County] and had enlisted a good many Men there.

At the trial of James, Ben Woolfolk deposed: That he was asked by George Smith to go to Elisha Price's to a feast. He was in company with this man and a number of others. He asked the prisoner if he was one of George Smith's men; he said yes, by God I am. He asked him if he thought he could kill white people stoutly; yes, says he, by God I can, and I will fight for my freedom as long as I have breath, and that is as much as any man can do. One of his children was with us minding or attending a white child of his masters. His child gave him offence for which he whipt him. The white child cried at his whipping his son, I suppose (says the prisoner to the white child) if you were big enough you would have my shirt off, but I hope you never will be big enough.

[At] the Trial of Gilbert, the property of William Young, Prosser's Ben deposed: That Gabriel went to Mr. Young's with the witness and after sending for the prisoner he came. Gabriel asked him if he had studied on the business, he answered he had. Gabriel asked him if he had a sword, he replied that his master had one hanging up in the house, which he would get and make himself a belt for it; he (the prisoner) wanted to be a captain but Gabriel refused him this command, saying he stuttered too much to give the word of command.

Mr. Price's John deposed: That on a Sunday after a sermon at Mr. Young's, Prosser's Gabriel gave an invitation to some of the Negroes to drink grog down at the spring; after being there sometime Gabriel asked the prisoner amongst others to join him to fight for his country; the prisoner consented to join Gabriel, and to endeavour to get him men, and he also promised to meet Gabriel at Prosser's Tavern, at a time to be appointed and observed that they would slay as they went.

Paul Graham's Ben alias Ben Woolfolk deposed: That the prisoner agreed to join George Smith in the first place, but in consequence of the business not being carried into execution so soon as he expected he enlisted with Gabriel. That the prisoner had a pistol and on the day proceeding the very rainy Saturday night, he came to town and purchased powder for the purpose of the insurrection. He expressed much regret that his master, who was up in the County, had rode away the horse he intended for himself, but said as it was [so] he would take the [pie]bald. That he was determined his master and mistress should be put to death by the men under him (as he could not do it himself) they having raised him.

37. ORGANIZATION AND STRATEGY: THE YOUNG'S SPRING MEETING

Confession of Ben Alias Ben Woolfolk, Sept. 17th 1800. On this day of the sermon George called on Sam Byrd to inform him how many men he had; he said he had not his list with him, but he supposed about 500. George wished the business to be deferred some time longer. Mr. Prosser's Gabriel wished to bring on the business as soon as possible. Gilbert said the summer was about over, and he wished them to enter upon the business before the winter got too cold. Gabriel proposed that the subject should be refered to Martin his brother to decide upon—Martin said there was this expression in the Bible: delays breed danger. At this time he said the country was at peace, the soldiers were discharged, and the arms all put away; there was no patroling the country, and that before he would any longer bear what he had borne, he would turn out and fight with his stick. Gilbert said he was ready with his pistol, but it was in need of repair. He gave it to Gabriel, who was to put it in order for him.

Others spoke to the company and informed them I wished to have something to say. I told them that I had heard in the days of old, when the Israelites were in servitude to King Pharoah they were taken from him by the power of God—and were carried away by Moses. God had blessed him with an angel to go with him; but that I could see nothing of that kind in these days. Martin said in reply I read in my Bible where God says if we will worship him we should have peace in all our land, five of you shall conquer an hundred and a hundred a thousand of our enemies. After this they went into consultation upon the time they should execute the plan. Martin spoke and appointed for them to meet in three weeks which was to be of a Saturday night. Gabriel said he had 500 bullets made. Smith's George said he was done with the corn and would then go on to make as many crossbows as he could. Bowler's Jack said he had got 50 spears as bayonets fixed at the end of stocks. The plan was to be as follows, we were all to meet at the brewry shop on the brook, 100 men were to stand at the brook bridge, Gabriel was to take 100 men and go to Gregory's tavern and take the arms, which were there, 50 men were to be sent to Rocketts to set that on fire in order to alarm the upper part of the town and induce the people to go down there, while they were employed in extinguishing the fire Gabriel and the other officers and soldiers were to take the Capitol and all the arms they could find and be ready to slaughter the people on their return from Rockets. . . .

"The above communications were put down precisely as delivered to us by Ben alias Ben Woodford [Woolfolk]. Given under our hands this 17th day of September 1800.

GERVAS STORRS
JOSEPH SELDEN

Confessions of Ben Alias Ben Woolfolk, Sept. 17th 1800 nos. 4. As far as I understood all the whites were to be massacred, except the Quakers, the Methodists and the Frenchmen; and they were to be spared on account as they conceived of their being friendly to liberty and also they had understood that the French were at war with this country for the money which was due them and that an army was landed at South Key which they hoped would assist them. They intended also to spare all the poor white women who had no slaves.

At the trial of Gabriel, Prosser's Ben deposed: That they were to kill Mr. Prosser, Mr. Mosby and all the neighbours, and then proceed to Richmond where they would kill every body, take the treasury, and divide the money amongst his soldiers—after which he would fortify Richmond and proceed to discipline his men, as he apprehended force would be raised elsewhere to repel him. That if the white people agreed to their freedom they would then hoist a white flag, and he would dine and drink with the merchants of the city on the day when it should be so agreed.

38. THE STORM BREAKS

Major William Mosby to Governor James Monroe,
September 1, 1800

On Saturday the 30th of August last about 10 or 11 o'clock I received information from Mr. Mosby Sheppard in Richmond, that the negroes that night intended to rise, kill and destroy the white people and that their place of rendezvous was on the brook near M. Thomas H. Prosser's and that Mr. Prosser, Mr. Johnston and myself were the first that were to fall a sacrifice, and that they were then to move on to Richmond. I asked him how he came by this information. He answered that he had received it from a Negro immediately from the country, who had come down that morning for the express purpose and that he was agitated in such a manner when telling him that he was induced to believe it was true. I confess that I was very much alarmed, and communicated the news to Captain William Austin who promised to go on to the brook that night with his troop of horse in order to meet Mr. Dabney William-son and myself with what men we could raise, but there came on the most powerful rain perhaps that ever fell in the same space of time which prevented our junction. However Captain Gregory and myself together with some others who had met at Priddie's Tavern for the purpose patroled as far as Mr. Prosser's and from there down to the brook but made no discovery. We then returned to the tavern again where I staid perhaps 'till 8 or 9 o'clock next morning. I then went home and being very much fatigued I laid myself down. I had been on the bed but a very little while before a negro woman of my own came to me—the first words she spoke were "You must not tell." She then asked me if I had heard that the negroes were going to rise. I told her, I had. I then asked her where they were to meet, she said "somewhere below Mr. Prosser's and as they did not meet last night they would meet tonight." I asked her how many she understood were to meet there, she said "three or four hundred, some from town and some from the country," and that there were to be a number of them mounted on horseback who were to go at a distance and kill and destroy all as they went, and as I understood, to kill them in their beds, and that the main body were to move on to Richmond. This, sir, is the information I re-ceived at the beginning of the alarm, delivered, as near as can be recollected, in the words I received it.

Thomas Newton, Mayor of Norfolk, to Governor James Monroe, September 24, 1800

Sir, the bearers here of Obadiah Gunn and Robt Wilson brings with them Negro Gabriel taken from on board the three masted Schooner *Mary*, Richard Taylor, master, belonging to Richmond. Mr. Hooper is part owner of the schooner from whom the charac-ter of Taylor may be known.

It appears that he left Richmond on Saturday night, and run on ground on the bar in Ward's Reach 4 miles below Richmond. On

Sunday morning Gabriel hailed the schooner and was brought on board by one of the Negroes belonging to her, he was armed with a bayonet fixed on a stick which he threw into the river. Captain Taylor says he was unwell and in his cabbin when Gabriel was brought on board. Negro Billy says he was asleep and when he awakened he found him on board he questioned him, conceiving him to be Gabriel that he said he was called Gabriel but his name was Daniel. Isham and Billy two Negro hands informed me, they told the Captain Taylor it was their opinion he was the person the reward was offered for. Captain Taylor says that he came on board as a freeman, that he asked him for his papers but he did not shew any, saying he had left them; Captain Taylor is an old inhabitant been an overseer and must have known that neither free blacks nor slaves could travel in this country without papers and he certainly must have had many opportunities of securing Gabriel in eleven days even if he had suspected his hands would not assist him. But they declared a willingness to me to have done it, in hopes of obtaining a reward. He passed Osborne's, Bermuda Hundred, City Point and I suppose many vessels where he could have obtained force to have secured him. His conduct after his arrival here is also blameable, he was boarded by a Captain Inchman below this place to whom he never mentioned a circumstance of Gabriel whom he could then have secured, after he came up to town, he went along-side a ship with 25 men on board, at ten o'clock he still never mentioned the matter. One of his men, Negro Billy, was sent on shore and he sent no information. He wrote to Captain Ashley but gave him none also. Billy being acquainted with a young man by name of Norris, a blacksmith, told him when he was on shore of his suspicions that Gabriel was on board. A Mr. Woodward happened to be in the shop when Norris told him of the circumstance, he immediately took such steps which was about two o'clock that m[ornin]g, Gunn and Robert Wilson, two constables, proceeded on board the schooner *Mary* and took him, he was at liberty on board and might have made his escape. Taylor says he had just begun to write a letter to Captain Tucker of this place, to know what he was to do with him, the part he wrote is inclosed and I confess I think Mr. Taylor knew much better than he acted, what to do in such a case having long had the management of negroes. . . .

His conduct appears extraordinary to me and I think deserves punishment instead of a reward. . . . I conceive that some reward should be given to Negro Billy who showed a disposition to take him by informing of him and I believe was the means of his being secured. The constables I hope will get the reward, they have been very active and constantly looking out for him. Taylor told me that he had emancipated his Negro Isham, but on exa[mining] Isham he told me that he had never given him any papers but promised him to do it, when he was a methodist, but as he was now turned again he was afraid he should not give him his freedom. Both Billy and Isham say they saw the Negroes hung before they left Richmond. Mr. Taylor must have known that circumstance and undoubtedly have heard of Gabriel before he left.

Monday 6th Oct. 1800. At the trial of Thomas Henry Prosser's Gabriel. The said Negro Man Slave Gabriel was sent to the bar in custody and being arraigned of the premises pled not guilty. Whereupon sundry witnesses were charged, sworn, and examined and the said prisoner fully heard in his defence by James Rind, gentleman counsel assigned him by the court. On consideration whereof it is the unanimous opinion of the court that the said Negro man slave Gabriel is guilty of the crime with which he stands accused and for the same that he be hanged by the neck until he be dead and that execution of this sentence be done and performed on him the said Gabriel tomorrow being the seventh instant at the usual place of execution.

39. AFTERMATH: "ALL CONFIDENCE . . . IS DESTROYED"

EXTRACT OF A LETTER FROM A GENTLEMAN
IN THIS CITY, TO HIS FRIEND IN NEW–YORK,
DATED SEPTEMBER 20TH, 1880

Having regularly attended the court which is now setting here for the trial of the negroes concerted in the late alarming insurrection, I am enabled to give you the outlines of the principal facts that have been given in evidence.

On Saturday morning the 30th ult. a negro man a few miles from Richmond, terrified with the thought of the danger to which

he was about to expose himself, informed his master that a considerable body of slaves would set off on that evening from the Brook,
six miles distant, for the purpose of massacreing all the whites of
Richmond, and to cause a general insurrection through out the
state. The master lost no time in communicating this important
project to the executive, who immediately took the necessary measures for defeating it. A corps of cavalry was dispatched to the
Brook. The night was rendered still more memorable by a tremen-
dous thunder storm which took place about the time when the
negroes assembled, and terror spread itself among them. They regarded it as a judment from Heaven.

The swelling of the waters prevented their meeting in a body,
and it was a work of no difficulty to seize the suspected and convey
them to Richmond. The number thus arrested amounted to 31. A
court of enquiry composed of two magistrates, and a criminal
tribunal of five, were instituted without delay: at the same time
suitable consel was assigned to the state and to the prisoners. . . .

The judges conduct themselves with a degree of humanity highly
honorable. The least doubt, the smallest suspicion, or contradiction
on the part of the witnesses (who are kept in separate apartments)
will often acquit Negroes who are really criminal.

Until yesterday morning no suspicion was entertained of the
negroes in town having any share in the insurrection plot: but last
night a number of them were surprized and taken into custody. . . .

Military service is performed night and day, Richmond resembles a town besiged: but I think the danger is over. All confidence
among the negroes is destroyed, they will not venture to communi-
cate one with another for fear of impeachment.

September 20, 1800

dear frind
    Tel jacob at john Williams johny is taken up and wil be hanged.
i is afraid, so all you in gloster must keep still yet. Brother X will
come and prech a sermond to you soon, and then you may no more
about the bissiness. i must be killed if the white peple catch me
and carry me to richmon

i am your tru frind
A.W.

Gloucester

This day Wm Morgain came before me & made oath that he picked up the above Letter in the road leading from Gloucester Ct. House and Ware Neck yesterday. given under my hand this 2nd day of October 1800

THOS. BOOTH

At the Trial of Philip N. Nicholas' King. . . . Mrs. Mary Martin —second witness [deposed]: That the prisoner, and another negroe who seemed to be travelling having a bundle upon his back, came into her shop one night in the next week after the time said to have been appointed for the rising of the negroes, as the Guards were going out, or about. That the prisoner addressed himself to her in a surly and abrupt style: "Give me a gill of spirits and I will pay you for it." She drew it and handed it to him, he drank it with his comrade, the apparent traveller—the latter also called for a gill of spirits, which was handed to him, and was in like manner drank between them. In the shop were other negroes, who divided with the attention of the Witness with the prisoner and his companion, who were conversing. She understood some of their conversation that the traveller was going to see his wife. The prisoner said he wished he could go to see his wife. She asked him why he could not go. He answered: "It was too far, and that the white people had turned so comical a man can't go out of his house now but he's taken up to be hanged." After some other conversation not particularly attended to by the witness, the prisoner told his comrade to tell their acquaintance where he was going. "We are all alive *as yet*, looking hard at the bacon, but he can't get at it. We are doing what we can, what we can't do with our Guns, we will do with our Bayonets. And that (touching his forehead with his finger) no body *knows* what is here *yet*." She had no bacon in her shop, nor had they any that she saw.

III

The Antebellum Era

GABRIEL'S REBELLION, *which for a brief and tragic moment highlighted many of the fiercely contradictory patterns of eighteenth-century slavery, also represented the end of an era. Signs of profound changes in the new republic were the opening of vast territories for plantations along the Gulf of Mexico; the introduction of Eli Whitney's cotton gin and the shortstaple, upland variety of cotton; and the passing of the slave trade. With the end of both the large annual importations of "outlandish" Africans and the story of their socialization as "new Negroes," the other major features of colonial slavery became history—the familial and patriarchal character of bondage, the self-contained plantations of the Chesapeake Bay region, and a slave population made up of blacks at different stages of acculturation.*

Slavery in the antebellum period also changed over time toward more absenteeism, a more rational (and, one senses, workable) division of authority, and fewer (or less-conspicuous) slave artisans and insurrectionists. Greater stress in the nineteenth century came to be placed on field labor and staple production, an economic role fixed on the South by the dynamics of the national market economy and international trade. Most important staples were profitable, and slaves, the econometricians have argued, were one of the best investments in the antebellum era.

In this setting, the rationalization of plantation management and personnel forced similar patterns throughout the staple-producing areas of the South. The superb travel accounts of Frederick Law Olmsted— landscape architect, professional traveler, and naturalist—leave an impression that beneath surface differences—accountable to the peculiarities of rice, sugar, and cotton cultivation—personnel and structures on large plantations were remarkably uniform. The letter of Isaac Step provides a view of how one slave (a supervisor) fitted into the new scheme.

A. Frederick Law Olmsted and Isaac Step Describe the South's Major Crops

40. COTTON

A HANDSOME MANSION *empty for several years and cabins for 139 slaves dominated a large, "first-rate" plantation outside Natchez, Mississippi. When Olmsted visited the estate in the early 1840s, nearly all of its adult slaves were field hands, and of the 10 of 67 who were not, 3 were artisans and the others seamstresses, cooks and cattle tenders. While occupational specialization among nonfield slaves in the colonial period was extensive, these opportunities diminished in the nineteenth century; and "petty officers" in the fields—hoe gang drivers and plow gang foremen—increased appreciably. For talented and ambitious blacks (the counterparts of Gabriel Prosser and such fugitive artisans and waitingmen as Jasper, Peter Deadfoot, Christmas, and Romeo) field supervision was the only "avenue of advancement." The other tasks outside the field, Olmsted noted, had been "studiously removed." Abandoning diversification, most large planters concentrated on the cash crop. While the colonial plantation was also a business, this Natchez estate represented a new, more rigorous and single-minded, application of economic rationality. Even though the owner had not set foot on his property for two years, operations ran smoothly because he was so "thorough and systematic in [its] management."*

SOURCE: Frederick Law Olmsted, *The Cotton Kingdom* (1861; New York, 1953), pp. 430–435. (In this and the following excerpts from Olmsted, his footnotes have been omitted.)

It was a first-rate plantation. On the highest ground stood a large and handsome mansion, but it had not been occupied for several years, and it was more than two years since the overseer had seen the owner. . . .

The whole plantation, including the swamp land around it, and owned with it, covered several square miles. It was four miles from the settlement to the nearest neighbour's house. There were between thirteen and fourteen hundred acres under cultivation with cotton, corn, and other hoed crops, and two hundred hogs running at large in the swamp. It was the intention that corn and pork enough should be raised to keep the slaves and cattle. This year, however, it has been found necessary to purchase largely, and such was probably usually the case, though the overseer intimated the owner had been displeased, and he "did not mean to be caught so bad again."

There were 135 slaves, big and little, of which 67 went to field regularly—equal, the overseer thought, to fully 60 prime hands. Besides these, there were 3 mechanics (blacksmith, carpenter, and wheelwright), 2 seamstresses, 1 cook, 1 stable servant, 1 cattle-tender, 1 hog-tender, 1 teamster, 1 house servant (overseer's cook), and one midwife and nurse. These were all first-class hands; most of them would be worth more, if they were for sale, the overseer said, than the best field-hands. There was also a driver of the hoe-gang who did not labour personally, and a foreman of the plough-gang. These two acted as petty officers in the field, and alternately in the quarters.

There was a nursery for sucklings at the quarters, and twenty women at this time who left their work four times each day, for half an hour, to nurse their young ones. These women, the overseer counted as half-hands—that is, expected to do half the day's work of a prime field-hand in ordinary condition. . . .

We found in the field thirty ploughs, moving together, turning the earth from the cotton plants, and from thirty to forty hoers, the latter mainly women, with a black driver walking about among them with a whip, which he often cracked at them, sometimes allowing the lash to fall lightly upon their shoulders. He was constantly urging them also with his voice. All worked very steadily, and though the presence of a stranger on the plantation must have been a most unusual occurrence, I saw none raise or turn their heads to look at me. Each gang was attended by a "water-toter," that of the hoe-gang being a straight, sprightly, plump little black girl, whose picture, as she stood balancing the bucket upon her head, shading her bright eyes with one hand, and holding out a calabash with the other to maintain her poise, would have been a worthy study for Murillo.

I asked at what time they began to work in the morning. "Well," said the overseer, "I do better by my niggers than most. I keep 'em right smart at their work while they do work, but I generally knock 'em off at 8 o'clock in the morning, Saturdays, and give 'em all the rest of the day to themselves, and I always gives 'em Sundays, the whole day. Pickin' time, and when the crop's bad in grass, I sometimes keep 'em to it till about sunset, Saturdays, but I never work 'em Sundays."

"How early do you start them out in the morning, usually?"

"Well, I don't never start my niggers 'fore daylight, 'less 'tis in pickin' time, then maybe I get 'em out a quarter of an hour before. But I keep 'em right smart to work through the day." He showed an evident pride in the vigilance of his driver, and called my attention to the large area of ground already hoed over that morning; well hoed, too, as he said.

. . . All worked as late as they could see to work well, and had no more food nor rest until they returned to their cabins. At half-past nine o'clock the drivers, each on an alternate night, blew a horn, and at ten visited every cabin to see that its occupants were at rest, and not lurking about and spending their strength in fooleries, and that the fires were safe—a very unusual precaution; the negroes are generally at liberty after their day's work is done till they are called in the morning. When washing and patching were done, wood hauled and cut for the fires, corn ground, etc., I did not learn: probably all chores not of daily necessity were reserved for Saturday. Custom varies in this respect. In general, with regard to fuel for the cabins, the negroes are left to look out for themselves, and they often have to go to "the swamp" for it, or at least, if it has been hauled, to cut it to a convenient size, after their day's work is done. The allowance of food was a peck of corn and four pounds of pork per week, each. When they could not get "greens" (any vegetables) he generally gave them five pounds of pork. They had gardens, and raised a good deal for themselves; they also had fowls, and usually plenty of eggs. He added, "the man who owns this plantation does more for his niggers than any other man I know. Every Christmas he sends me up a thousand or fifteen hundred dollars' [equal to eight or ten dollars each] worth of molasses and coffee, and tobacco, and calico, and Sunday tricks for 'em. Every family on this plantation gets a barrel of molasses at Christmas."

Besides which, the overseer added, they are able, if they choose, to buy certain comforts for themselves—tobacco for instance—

with money earned by Saturday and Sunday work. Some of them went into the swamps on Sunday, and made boards (which means slabs worked out with no other instrument than an axe). One man sold last year as much as fifty dollars' worth. . . .

This was the only large plantation I had an opportunity of seeing at all closely, over which I was not chiefly conducted by an educated gentleman and slave owner, by whose habitual impressions and sentiments my own were probably somewhat influenced. From what I saw in passing, and from what I heard by chance of others, I suppose it to have been a very favourable specimen of those plantations on which the owners do not reside. . . . A magistrate of the district, who had often been on the plantation, said in answer to an inquiry from me, that the negroes were very well treated upon it, though he did not think they were extraordinarily so. His comparison was with plantations in general. He also spoke well of the overseer. He had been a long time on this plantation—I think he said ever since it had begun to be cultivated. This is very rare; it was the only case I met with in which an overseer had kept the same place ten years, and it was a strong evidence of his comparative excellence, that his employer had been so long satisfied with him. Perhaps it was a stronger evidence that the owner of the negroes was a man of good temper, systematic and thorough in the management of his property. . . .

I made no special inquiries about the advantages for education or means of religious instruction provided for the slaves. As there seems to be much public desire for definite information upon that point, I regret that I did not. I did not need to put questions to the overseer to satisfy my own mind, however. It was obvious that all natural incitements to self-advancement had been studiously removed or obstructed, in subordination to the general purpose of making the plantation profitable. Regarding only the balance-sheet of the owner's ledger, it was admirable management. . . .

41. RICE: AN OWNER'S PERSPECTIVE

GEOGRAPHY AND ECONOMICS *combined to limit rice production to a small number of wealthy slaveholders concentrated along the South Carolina–Georgia seacoast (more than half of whom lived on three river systems, the Savannah, the Ashley and Cooper, and the Pee Dee–Waccamaw). The region's epicenter was Georgetown (60 miles northeast of Charleston), where the relationship between land, rivers, and ocean was ideal. Tides were indispensable for rice cultivation. They pushed fresh water up the rivers and into the fields, irrigating the rice ponds, feeding plants, and killing undesirable weeds and sprouts. Channeling the tidal flows and using effectively the low country's marshes, swamps, and swollen streams—the key to successful rice growing— required large amounts of money and labor. (In the 1860 census, 20 of the 74 planters in the entire South with 300 to 500 slaves, 8 of the 13 planters with 500 to 1,000, and the only owner in the country with more than 1,000 slaves were all rice planters.)*

Only sugar production demanded as much initial capital as rice, in which approximately $25,000 of a total investment ranging from $50,000 to $500,000 was required for a threshing and pounding mill and for the arduous, labor-consuming ditching and canal work. On the Manigault family's 260-acre Gowrie Plantation (Savannah, Georgia) more than 100 acres in embankments and 75 miles of ditches, sluice, and trunk canals controlled various flows. Until new rice areas were developed in Arkansas, Louisiana, and Texas in the mid-1880s (using powered irrigation instead of tides and soil adapted to machinery rather than slave labor), only the South Carolina–Georgia coastal region was suitable for rice planting.

Rice cultivation also created unusual demographic patterns. There was a high incidence of planter absenteeism on the rice coast, a great destroyer of the slaves' health and lives. While slaves in this country (unlike most regions in Latin America) generally reproduced themselves readily, births scarcely kept pace with deaths in the Carolina low country. Malaria, "miasma," and other related diseases cut down slaves unmercifully. From May to November, when the Anopheles *mosquito swarmed, blacks suffered and whites vacationed in pineland or seacoast resorts.*

In this setting work routines were a bundle of contradictions. The top man, who was usually an overseer but occasionally a black driver, had to be in full command of the timing of the successive floodings, cutting and harvesting, and procedures for threshing and pounding. But no one was lower than a rice field Negro, who used the crudest tools (plows did not replace hoes until the late 1850s) to do one of the dullest, most stultifying—and wettest—jobs forced upon antebellum field hands. A most distasteful and unhealthy task—in January, after the rice had been milled and barreled—sent slaves into the cold, dank salt swamps to haul buckets of organically rich muck onto the rice fields.

While visiting a Georgia rice plantation, Olmsted again encountered an operation characterized by workers' "villages," and a "practical talent for organization and administration." His guide, "Mr. X," was the son of a New England farmer, who had brought to his business in the South the "intimate and useful knowledge [of] the rugged fields, the complicated looms, and the exact and comprehensive counting houses of New England." Mr. X used an overseer because the law required him to do so. But in practice even his most trustworthy supervisors had to consult the black drivers, who were directly in charge of the field people, made the major decisions about the timing and amount of water flow into the rice fields, and sometimes even ran the plantation in X's absence. This was not an unusual practice; and those who could write probably sent reports directly to their owners, which would be fascinating reading if they had survived. At least one such letter is extant—by Isaac Step, a black driver who helped run a Sea Island rice plantation while his master was away.

SOURCE: Frederick Law Olmsted, A *Journey in the Seaboard Slave States in the Years 1853–1854*, 2 vols. (1856; New York, 1904), 2:45–46, 47–48, 58–59, 60–61, 62–63, 66–67.

Mr. X. has two plantations on the river, besides a large tract of poor pine forest land, extending some miles back upon the upland, and reaching above the malarious region. In the upper part of this pine land is a house, occupied by his overseer during the malarious season, when it is dangerous for any but negroes to remain during the night in the vicinity of the swamps or rice-fields. Even those few who have been born in the region, and have grown up subject to the malaria, are generally weakly and short-lived. The negroes do not enjoy as good health on rice plantations as elsewhere; and the greater difficulty with which their lives are preserved, through infancy especially, shows that the subtle poison of the miasma is not innocuous to them; but Mr. X. boasts a steady increase of his negro stock of five per cent. per annum, which is better than is averaged on the plantations of the interior. . . .

There is a "negro settlement" on each; but both plantations, although a mile or two apart, are worked together as one, under one overseer—the hands being drafted from one to another as their labor is required. Somewhat over seven hundred acres are at the present time under the plough in the two plantations: the whole number of negroes is two hundred, and they are reckoned to be equal to about one hundred prime hands—an unusual strength for that number of all classes. The overseer lives, in winter, near the settlement of the larger plantation, Mr. X. near that of the smaller.

It is an old family estate, inherited by Mr. X.'s wife, who, with her children, were born and brought up upon it in close intimacy with the negroes, a large proportion of whom were also included in her inheritance, or have been since born upon the estate. Mr. X. himself is a New England farmer's son, and has been a successful merchant and manufacturer. He is also a religious man, without the dementifying bigotry of self-important humility, so frequently implied by that appellation to a New Englander, but generous, composed and cheerful in disposition, as well as conscientious.

The patriarchal institution should be seen here under its most favorable aspect; not only from the ties of long family association, common traditions, common memories, and, if ever, common interests, between the slaves and their rulers, but, also, from the practical talent for organization and administration, gained among the rugged fields, the complicated looms, and the exact and comprehensive counting-houses of New England, which directs the labor. . . .

It is a custom with Mr. X., when on the estate, to look each day at all the work going on, inspect the buildings, boats, embankments and sluice-ways, and examine the sick. Yesterday I accompanied him in one of these daily rounds. . . .

After passing through tool-room, corn-rooms, mule-stables, store-rooms, and a large garden, in which vegetables to be distributed among the negroes, as well as for the family, are grown, we walked to the rice-land. It is divided by embankments into fields of about twenty acres each, but varying somewhat in size, according to the course of the river. The arrangements are such that each field may be flooded independently of the rest, and they are subdivided by open ditches into rectangular plats of a quarter acre each. We first proceeded to where twenty or thirty women and girls were engaged in raking together, in heaps and winrows, the stubble and rubbish left on the field after the last crop, and burning it. The main object of this operation is to kill all the seeds of weeds, or of rice, on the ground. Ordinarily it is done by tasks—a certain number of the small divisions of the field being given to each hand to burn in a day; but owing to a more than usual amount of rain having fallen lately, and some other causes, making the work harder in some places than others, the women were now working by the day, under the direction of a "driver," a negro man, who walked about among them, taking care that they left nothing unburned. Mr. X. inspected the ground they had gone over, to see whether the driver had done his duty. It had been sufficiently well burned, but, not more than [a] quarter as much ground had been gone over, he said, as was usually burned in task-work,—and he thought they had been very lazy, and reprimanded them for it. The driver made some little apology, but the women offered no reply, keeping steadily, and it seemed sullenly, on at their work.

In the next field, twenty men, or boys, for none of them looked as if they were full-grown, were ploughing, each with a single mule, and a light, New-York-made plough. The soil was very friable, the ploughing easy, and the mules proceeded at a smart pace; the furrows were straight, regular, and well turned. Their task was nominally an acre and a quarter a day. . . .

Leaving the rice-land, we went next to some of the upland fields, where we found several other gangs of negroes at work; one entirely of men engaged in ditching; another of women, and another of boys and girls, "listing" an old corn-field with hoes. All of them were working by tasks, and were overlooked by negro drivers. They all labored with greater rapidity and cheerfulness than any slaves I have before seen; and the women struck their hoes as if they were strong, and well able to engage in muscular labor. The expression of their faces was generally repulsive, and their *tout ensemble* anything but agreeable to the eye. The dress of most of them was uncouth and cumbrous, dirty and ragged; reefed up, as I have once before described, at the hips, so as to show their heavy legs, wrapped round with a piece of old blanket, in lieu of leggings or stockings. Most of them worked with bare arms, but wore strong shoes on their feet, and handkerchiefs on their heads; some of them were smoking, and each gang had a fire burning on the ground, near where they were at work, to light their pipes and warm their breakfast by. Mr. X. said this was always their custom, even in summer. To each gang a boy or girl was also attached, whose business it was to bring water for them to drink, and to go for anything required by the driver. The drivers would frequently call back a hand to go over again some piece of his or her task that had not been worked to his satisfaction, and were constantly calling to one or another, with a harsh and peremptory voice, to strike harder or hoe deeper, and otherwise taking care that the work was well done. . . .

The field-hands are nearly always worked in gangs, the strength of a gang varying according to the work that engages it; usually it numbers twenty or more, and is directed by a driver. As on most large plantations, whether of rice or cotton, in Eastern Georgia and South Carolina, nearly all ordinary and regular work is performed *by tasks*: that is to say, each hand has his labor for the day marked out before him, and can take his own time to do it in. For instance, in making drains in light, clean meadow land, each man or woman of the full hands is required to dig one thousand cubic feet; in swamp-land that is being prepared for rice culture, where there are not many stumps, the task for a ditcher is five hundred feet; while in a very strong cypress swamp, only two hundred feet is required; in hoeing rice, a certain number of rows, equal to one-half or two-thirds of an acre, according to the condition of the land; in sowing rice (strewing in drills), two acres; in reaping rice (if it stands well), three-quarters of an acre; or, sometimes a gang will be required to reap, tie in sheaves, and carry to the stackyard the produce of a certain area, commonly equal to one-fourth the number of acres that there are hands working together. Hoeing cotton, corn, or potatoes, one-half to one acre. Threshing, five to six hundred sheaves. In ploughing rice-land (light, clean, mellow soil) with a yoke of oxen, one acre a day, including the ground lost in and near the drains—the oxen being changed at noon. . . .

Before any field of work is entered upon by a gang, the driver who is to superintend them has to measure and stake off the tasks. To do this at all accurately, in irregular-shaped fields, must require considerable powers of calculation. A driver, with a boy to set the stakes, I was told, would accurately lay out forty acres a day, in half-acre tasks. The only instrument used is a five-foot measuring rod. When the gang comes to the field, he points out to each person his or her duty for the day, and then walks about among them, looking out that each proceeds properly. If, after a hard day's labor, he sees that the gang has been overtasked, owing to a miscalculation of the difficulty of the work, he may excuse the completion of the tasks; but he is not allowed to extend them. In the case of uncompleted tasks, the body of the gang begin new tasks the next day, and only a sufficient number are detailed from it to complete, during the day, the unfinished tasks of the day before. The relation of the driver to the working hands seems to be similar to that of the boatswain to the seamen in the navy, or of the sergeant to the privates in the army.

Having generally had long experience on the plantation, the advice of the drivers is commonly taken in nearly all the administration, and frequently they are, *de facto*, the managers. Orders on important points of the plantation economy, I have heard given by the proprietor directly to them, without the overseer's being consulted or informed of them; and it is often left with them to decide when and how long to flow the rice-grounds—the proprietor and overseer deferring to their more experienced judgment. Where the drivers are discreet, experienced, and trusty, the overseer is frequently employed merely as a matter of form, to comply with the laws requiring the superintendence or presence of a white man among every body of slaves; and his duty is rather to inspect and report, than to govern. Mr. X. considers his overseer an uncommonly efficient and faithful one, but he would not employ him, even during the summer, when he is absent for several months, if the law did not require it. He has sometimes left his plantation in care of one of the drivers for a considerable length of time, after having discharged an overseer; and he thinks it has then been quite as well conducted as ever. His overseer consults the drivers on all important points, and is governed by their advice.

42. RICE: A DRIVER'S PERSPECTIVE

SOURCE: Isaac Step to his master, Beaufort, S.C., October 22, 1849, Elliott-Gonzales Papers, Southern Historical Collection, University of North Carolina Archives.

Beaufort Oct. 22ᵈ [18]45

To Master

On the 16th of October I was at pon pon and all the rice had been don harvesting 24 fine ricks. The overseer thinks it will run 2 thousand 8 hundred the stacker says 2 thousand 9 hundred—and I think 3 thousand. A fine crop of root potatoes for I think they will last untill Christmass. I would not say the slip will turn out well for the want of the Season. A fine crop of corn they have not taken it in as yet. I think things are going on well at the place all appear to be in good order. Mistress flour & arden are in good order. I wish

Master had such an overseer Lrial [?] Hall for I think him fine. The cotton have been much injured with the drouth. I do not think they will make more than 2 or three bags, and last of all I think Mistress will raise but a few poultry. I suppose by this time they are taken in the corn. As regards [illegible] on the 19th I got in 20 bags. The crop of cotton may run 30 bags though the crop has been much injured by the drouth. I am about taken in the peas—a fine crop. The root potatoes are done. I have begun to cut the slips they are small and bad. The corn has made 30 Barrels. As far as the cotton seed whent they were fine. I may get 2 or three hundred oringes. Turkeys, one hundred, as I had lost some of them. The vessel is still hear on account of the yellow fever being so bad in Charleston. Edward has been quite sick but better at this time.

Old Mistress and Miss Mary are quite well. I was quite sorry some of my young mistress and masters were not in Beaufort to enjoy themselves at some of the fine dinner and Tea partys. Old Mistress has been grieving for her grand children in Beaufort—at every party reminds me of Master William and the Doctor.

The Miss Smith's are quite well but know not how they will get thear servant back on the main, every thing on the main are green having no frost thear.

Master will be so kind as to give my love to my wife. All her friends are well, and say howdey to her and myself just like an old Buck, hearty and prime.

> Not furgetting the old Man
> to Mistress Snow
>
> from Master
> Servant ISAAC STEP

43. SUGAR

ULRICH B. PHILLIPS *introduced his study of American Negro slavery with the proposal, "Let us begin with the weather." This insight is especially appropriate for a discussion of antebellum sugar production. Early frosts restricted cultivation to southern Louisiana plantations that extended no farther north than Baton Rouge, about a hundred miles from New Orleans. Cold weather forced planters to begin the crop late, and to delay the cutting until the last moment in October, when the cane was as mature as possible. Sugar was usually planted from stalks (ratoons, not seed) cut by the slaves during the preceding harvest, laid* in furrows about six feet apart, and covered with loose soil. Louisiana sugar suffered such disadvantages from the weather that, without a protective tariff against Cuban sugar, its market would have been sharply restricted.

Sugar plantations were the most expensive to set up, and required the most intensive labor. Sugar land cost about twice as much as cotton acreage; and the mill and steam engine required to turn cane to syrup and then to granulated sugar alone cost $40,000 or more. Another great expense was the diking and ditching required to maintain low land suitable for planting. To prevent destructive overflows from the Mississippi and its tributaries, trenches were cut running at right angles from the rivers and bayous upon which the plantation was situated. These ditches plunged for a mile or two in a straight line back into the property, increasing in depth and width as they receded into the swamp into which they were emptied.

Weather, foreign competition, capital and geography limited the number of sugar plantations by 1850 to approximately 1,535 and, as smaller plantations using less efficient horse-powered mills were absorbed by larger units with steam-powered mills, to fewer than 1,300 by 1860. Sugar was such an expensive and risky (but highly remunerative) enterprise that by 1859 nearly a third of all plantations were partnerships.

On the eve of the war, however, a technological breakthrough transformed one of the most expensive and time-consuming processes— purifying sugar by boiling it with lime in open kettles. The overwhelming problem in this method had been wood fuel. Before the boiling season in the fall (when all hands worked eighteen hours a day), slaves were constantly cutting, hauling, and stacking logs for the boiler room furnaces; and in the slack season they retrieved driftwood from the Mississippi. But in 1843 Norbert Rillieux, a brilliant Creole Negro educated in France, developed a process of boiling cane juice in vacuum pans and using the vapor of one pan to heat another. This efficient method alleviated the wood fuel problem, and was widely adopted just before the Civil War.

Sugar planters concentrated capital and labor in staple production, importing such necessities as slave food and clothing. They generally voted for the Whig party and its programs of internal improvements and protective tariffs. One of the wealthiest planters, William J. Minor of Ascension and Terrebonne parishes, who as a rule visited his plantations only during grinding season from October 15 to Christmas, even imported pork, the meat staple in a slave's diet. In 1838 he purchased from a Tennessee factor 130 barrels of pork at $8 to $21 per barrel for his "Waterloo" plantation, or almost $1,000 a year for each of his three plantations. This was Minor's largest plantation expense, among other

sums, paid to New York City and New Orleans factors, for slave clothing and medicine. Sugar planters also hired white artisans and mechanics during the grinding season. Engineers, "sugar makers," were paid
either by the barrel (a dollar or so) or from $750 to $1,500 for the
entire harvest. Minor paid his overseers between $1,200 and $1,500,
while overseers on prime cotton lands in Alabama, Mississippi, and
Georgia received between $200 and $700 yearly.

Upon a capital base of this size, slave society architecture became
grandiose. John Hampden Randolph's "Nottoway," a mansion in the
Greek Revival style, had two-story pillars and iron rails along full-sized
porches running off both floors of the house. All interior floors were
worked, dressed, and laid in the best manner, with close and even
joints; rails and stair balusters were mahogany. Randolph also ordered
four coats of paint inside and out, two rainwater cisterns of 10,000
gallons capacity, and a gas apparatus that produced a good quantity of
light. In addition, the house featured fifty-one rooms, twenty-two columns sixty feet in height, and two hundred windows with eighteen panes
of glass in each window.

Thoughtful masters insidiously incorporated their slaves' lives into
Nottoway-like settings: in Randolph's rear hall there was a twelve-bell
instrument, each tone identifying and summoning a particular servant.
In West Feliciana Parish (with only 19 sugar plantations in 1854, 83
working slaves per unit, but one of the highest yields per plantation—
500 hogsheads of 1,225 barrels each), Daniel Turnbull built a church
for his slaves, hired a Baptist minister to safeguard their souls, and even
employed a song leader to teach them gospel songs.

SOURCE: Frederick Law Olmsted, A Journey in the Seaboard Slave
    States in the Years 1853–1854, 2 vols. (1856; New York, 1904),
    2:313, 315–317, 318–319, 320–321, 323–324, 325–327.

I came to Mr. R.'s plantation by a steamboat, late at night. As
the boat approached the shore, near his house, her big bell having
been rung some ten minutes previously, a negro came out with a
lantern to meet her. The boat's bow was run boldly against the
bank; I leaped ashore, the clerk threw out a newspaper and a
package, saying to the negro, "That's for your master, and that's
for so and so, tell your master, and ask him to give it to him." The
boat bounded off by her own elasticity, the starboard wheel was
backed for a turn or two, and the next minute the great edifice was
driving up the stream again—not a rope having been lifted, nor
any other movement having been made on board, except by the
pilot and engineer. . . .

The plantation contained about nine hundred acres of tillage land, and a large tract of "swamp," or woodland, was attached to it. The tillage land was inclosed all in one field by a strong cypress post-and-rail fence, and was drained by two canals, five feet deep, running about twenty feet apart, and parallel—the earth from both being thrown together, so as to make a high, dry road between them, straight through the middle of the plantation.

Fronting upon the river, and but six or eight rods from the public road, which everywhere runs close along the shore inside the levee, was the mansion of the proprietor: an old Creole house, the lower story of brick and the second of wood, with a broad gallery, shaded by the extended roof, running all around it; the roof steep, and shedding water on four sides, with ornaments of turned wood where lines met, and broken by several small dormer windows. The gallery was supported by round brick columns, and arches. The parlors, library, and sleeping-rooms of the white family were all on the second floor. Between the house and the street was a yard, planted formally with orange trees and other evergreens. A little on one side of the house stood a large two-story, square dove-cot, which is a universal appendage of a sugar planter's house. In the rear of the house was another large yard, in which, irregularly placed, were houses for the family servants, a kitchen, stable, carriage-house, smoke-house, etc. Behind this rear yard there was a vegetable garden, of an acre or more, in the charge of a negro gardener; a line of fig trees were planted along the fence, but all the ground inclosed was intended to be cropped with vegetables for the family, and for the supply of "the people." I was pleased to notice, however, that the negro gardener had, of his own accord, planted some violets and other flowering plants. From a corner of the court a road ran to the sugar works and the negro settlement, which were five or six hundred yards from the house.

The negro houses were exactly like those I described on the Georgia rice plantation, except that they were provided with broad galleries in front. They were as neat and well-made externally as the cottage usually provided by large manufacturing companies in New England, to be rented to their workmen. The clothing furnished the negroes, and the rations of bacon and meal, were the same as on other good plantations. . . .

"Buying a plantation," were his [the owner's] words, "whether a sugar or cotton plantation, in this country, is usually essentially a gambling operation. The capital invested in a sugar plantation of the size of mine ought not to be less than $150,000. The purchaser pays down what he can, and usually gives security for the payment of the balance in six annual instalments, with interest (10 per cent. per annum) from the date of the purchase. Success in sugar as well as cotton planting is dependent on so many circumstances, that it is as much trusting to luck as betting on a throw of dice. If his first crop proves a bad one, he must borrow money of the Jews in New Orleans to pay his first note; they will sell him this on the best terms they can, and often at not less than twenty-five per cent. per annum. . . . I have myself been particularly fortunate; I have made three good crops in succession. Last year I made six hundred and fifty hogsheads of sugar, and twelve hundred barrels of molasses. The molasses alone brought me a sum sufficient to pay all my plantation expenses; and the sugar yields me a clear profit of twenty-five per cent. on my whole investment. If I make another crop this year as good as that, I shall be able to discount my outstanding notes, and shall be clear of debt at the end of four years, instead of six, which was the best I had hoped for." . . .

The soil of the greater part of the plantation was a fine, dark, sandy loam; some of it, at the greatest distance from the river, was lighter in color, and more clayey; and in one part, where there was a very slight depression of the surface over about fifty acres, there was a dark, stiffish soil. It was this to which Mr. R. alluded as having produced his best cane. It had been considered too low, wet, tenacious, and unfertile to be worthy of cultivation by the former owner, and was covered with bushes and weeds when he took it. The improvement had been effected entirely by draining and fall ploughing. . . .

The sugar-cane is a perennial-rooted plant, and the stalk does not attain its full size, under favorable circumstances, in less growing time than twelve months; and seed does not usually form upon it until the thirteenth or fourteenth month. This function (termed *arrowing*) it performs only in a very hot and steadily hot climate, somewhat rarely even in the West Indies. The plant is, at all stages, extremely susceptible to cold, a moderate frost not only suspending its growth, but disorganizing it so that the chemical qualities of its sap are changed, and it is rendered valueless for sugar-making. . . .

Planting commences immediately after the sugar-manufacturing season is concluded—usually in January. New or fallow land is prepared by ploughing the whole surface: on this plantation the plough used was made in Kentucky, and was of a very good model, ploughing seven to nine inches deep, with a single pair of mules. The ground being then harrowed, drills are opened with a double-mould-board plough, seven feet apart. Cuttings of cane for seed are to be planted in them. These are reserved from the crop in the autumn, when some of the best cane on the plantation is selected for this purpose, while still standing. This is cut off at the roots, and laid up in heaps or stacks in such a manner that the leaves and tops protect the stalks from frost. The heaps are called mattresses; they are two or three feet high, and as many yards across. At the planting season they are opened, and the cane comes out moist, and green, and sweet, with the buds or eyes, which protrude at the joints, swelling. The immature top parts of the stalk are cut off, and they are loaded into carts, and carried to the ground prepared for planting. The carts used are large, with high side boards, and are drawn by three mules—one large one being in the shafts, and two lighter ones abreast, before her. The drivers are boys, who use the whip a great deal, and drive rapidly.

In the field I found the laborers working in three divisions—the first, consisting of light hands, brought the cane by armfuls from the cart, and laid it by the side of the furrows; the second planted it, and the third covered it. Planting is done by laying the cuttings at the bottom of the furrow in such a way that there shall be three always together, with the eyes of each a little removed from those of the others—that is, all "breaking joints." They are thinly covered with earth, drawn over them with hoes. The other tools were so well selected on this plantation, that I expressed surprise at the clumsiness of the hoes, particularly as the soil was light, and entirely free from stones. "Such hoes as you use at the North would not last a negro a day," said the planter.

Cane will grow for several years from the roots of the old plants, and, when it is allowed to do so, a very considerable part of the expense is avoided; but the vigor of the plant is less when growing from this source than when starting from cuttings, and the crop, when thus obtained, is annually less and less productive, until, after a number of years, depending upon the rigor of the seasons, fresh shoots cease to spring from the stubble. This sprouting of cane from the stools of the last crop is termed "ratooning." . . .

Planting is finished, in a favorable season, early in March. Tillage is commenced immediately afterwards, by ploughing *from* the rows of young cane, and subsequently continued very much after the usual plan of tillage for potatoes, when planted in drills, with us. By or before the first of July, the crop is all well earthed up, the rows of cane growing from the crest of a rounded bed, seven feet wide, with deep water-furrows between each. The cane is at this time five or six feet high; and that growing from each bed forms arches with that of the next, so as to completely shade the ground. The furrows between the beds are carefully cleaned out; so that in the most drenching torrents of rain, the water is rapidly carried off into the drains, and thence to the swamp; and the crop then requires no further labor upon it until frost is apprehended, or the season for grinding arrives.

The nearly three months' interval, commencing at the intensest heat of summer, corresponds in the allotment of labor to the period of winter in Northern agriculture, because the winter itself, on the sugar plantations, is the planting season. The negroes are employed in cutting and carting wood for boiling the cane juice, in making necessary repairs or additions to the sugar-house, and otherwise preparing for the grinding season.

The grinding season is the harvest of the sugar planter; it commences in October, and continues for two or three months, during which time, the greatest possible activity and the utmost labor of which the hands are capable are required to secure the product of the previous labor of the year. Mr. R. assured me that during the last grinding season nearly every man, woman, and child on his plantation, including his overseer and himself, were at work fully eighteen hours a day. From the moment grinding first commences, until the end of the season, it is never discontinued; the fires under the boiler never go out, and the negroes rest only for six hours in the twenty-four, by relays—three-quarters of them being constantly at work.

Notwithstanding the severity of the labor required of them at this time, Mr. R. said that his negroes were as glad as he was himself to have the time for grinding arrive, and they worked with greater cheerfulness than at any other season. How can those persons who are always so ready to maintain that the slaves work less than free laborers in free countries, and that for that reason they are to be envied by them, account for this? That at Mr. R.'s plantation it was the case that the slaves enjoyed most that season of the year when the hardest labor was required of them, I have, in addition to Mr. R.'s own evidence, good reason to believe, which I shall presently report. And the reason of it evidently is, that they are then better paid; they have better and more varied food and stimulants than usual, but especially they have a degree of freedom, and of social pleasure, and a variety of occupation which brings a recreation of the mind, and to a certain degree gives them strength for, and pleasure in, their labor. Men of sense have discovered that when they desire to get extraordinary exertions from their slaves, it is better to offer them rewards than to whip them; to encourage them, rather than to drive them.

B. Manipulative Paternalism: The Patriarch Becomes a Personnel Manager

THE FOLLOWING DOCUMENTS *leave little doubt about the intellectual constructs—entrepreneurial and managerial, or semifeudal and paternalistic—that most adequately characterized antebellum slavery on large plantations. The most conscientious slaveholders realized that plantations were businesses that could be as standardized as the Northern, and English Midland, mills that most of them served. In the course of interminable public discussions of how this degree of economic rationality could best be achieved, overseers and owners—from the border states, through the rice coast, to the rich bottom lands of the Gulf state black belts—argued essentially the same way about plantation management: "reduce everything to a system"; and "introduce a daily accountability in every department."*

The first section, "The Antebellum Plantation System Defined: An Overview," features "Management of Negroes" articles in Southern agricultural journals that describe the manipulative techniques used to encourage compliance by "making [slaves] as comfortable at home as possible," and the plantation "a perfect society." The second section, "The Antebellum System Applied," is divided into part one, "To Introduce a Daily Accountability in Every Department," which focuses on the account books and ledgers that were a major product of new con-

*cepts in management; and part two, "Reduce Everything to a System,"
which provides a closer view of the slaves' diet, housing, health, and
quarters. Together these documents establish a mood of the plantation's
daily rhythms and activities, and from this a sense of what the large
antebellum plantation was like from the perspective of owners and
overseers. Documents illustrating sadism, small planters and poor
whites, and slave culture therefore will follow as a corrective to a view
of American Negro slavery based primarily on evidence about wealthy
planters and their slaves at work.*

The Antebellum Plantation "System" Defined: An Overview

AS PLANTERS *became more consciously manipulative toward plantation
Negroes, they realized the importance of knowing each slave as an
individual so they could more properly "elevate his pride." But on the
larger plantations (particularly in the rice and sugar regions, where the
average number of Negroes was roughly sixty or seventy per unit) it
was not often possible for the owner to know each slave well. The
answer to this dilemma was to force the field worker into a mold. "The
mass," Olmsted wrote in a perceptive note, "must be reduced to a
system."*

*The system developed by thoughtful planters who liked to write let-
ters to the editor was based on an appreciation for the subtle but
important relationship between the plantation setting, or environment,
and manipulative techniques that would make slaves acquiescent. If the
plantation was a highly standardized operation, "a piece of machinery,
then to operate it successfully all of its parts should be uniform and
exact, and the impelling force regular and steady." These visions of
1984 were seldom if ever realized—slaves were too resilient and resourceful for that. But the understanding of some whites was marvel-
ously sophisticated, insidious, and contemporary in feeling: "No more
beautiful picture of human society can be drawn than a well organized
plantation. . . . A regular and systematic plan or operation on the
plantation is greatly promotive of easy government. Have, therefore, all
matters as far as possible reduced to a system." This last is the gist of
the "Management of Negroes" genre.*

44. "HABIT IS EVERYTHING"

SOURCE: "Management of Slaves," *Southern Cultivator*, 4 (March
1846): 44 (reprinted from the *Southern Agriculturalist*).

. . . I have ever maintained the doctrine that my negroes have no
time whatever; that they are always liable to my call without ques-

tioning for a moment the propriety of it; and I adhere to this on the grounds of expediency and right. The very security of the plantation requires that a general and uniform control over the people on it should be exercised. . . . To render this part of the rule justly applicable, however, it would be necessary that such a settled arrangement should exist on the plantation as to make it unnecessary for a negro to leave it, or to have a good plea for so doing. You must, therefore, make him as comfortable at home as possible, affording him what is essentially necessary for his happiness—you must provide for him yourself, and by that means create in him a habit of perfect dependence on you. . . .

. . . Habit is everything. The negro who is accustomed to remain constantly at home, is just as satisfied with the society on the plantation, as that which he could find elsewhere. . . .

45. I "Caused Him to Maintain a Pride of Character"

Source: "On the Conduct and Management of Overseers, Drivers, and Slaves," *Farmer's Register*, 4 (June 1836): 114–115.

Santee [S.C.], April 3, 1836

Mr. Editor,

—I received your letter a month since, requesting me to give you "my system in the management of Mr.——'s plantation."

. . . Among an hundred other things, he impressed upon my mind, that I was to be his representative; to regulate his slaves in their moral and general conduct. . . .

. . . Most of my duties he had committed to writing, and I was required to keep them as a constant guide to me in the management of his plantation. . . .

. . . I always required of him [the driver], that he should dress myself [sic] better than the other negroes. This caused him to maintain a pride of character before them, which was highly beneficial. Indeed, I constantly endeavored to do nothing which would cause them to lose their respect for him. . . .

. . . Ten years ago, I bought, at auction in Charleston, a stubborn, ill looking fellow, sold as runaway. . . . I was convinced that Ben (for that was his name) had not been properly managed. I accordingly purchased him, at a reduced price, took him home, and put him to work by the side of some of my best workers. I pointed out what I would require of him; and in a flattering way, observed the other fellows, that I was now going to give them a push. "Now," said I, "Ben, I will expect you to do your best; keep close to those fellows, and if you follow them up close, you may feel proud of yourself." He seemed pleased at my remark, said he would, and commenced as if he intended to do his best. I left Ben to himself, and in a few hours after returned to where he was working: he was getting on exceedingly well, for which I complimented him. It was in this manner that I urged him on throughout his day's work. That evening he finished his task, did it well, and went home much pleased with himself. This was the first step towards the reformation of Ben. By following up my treatment, I so entirely reclaimed him in a few months, that from being a runaway and a rogue, I made him one of my primest and trustiest negroes.

46. "Attach Them to Their Homes"

Source: "On the Management of Negroes," *Farmer's Register*, 1 (February 1834): 564–565.

ON THE MANAGEMENT OF NEGROES

ADDRESSED TO THE FARMERS AND OVERSEERS OF VIRGINIA

The management of our slaves is a subject of some little difficulty, but which difficulty may be overcome by a judicious system (where there are no foreign causes operating to prevent it, which foreign causes I may hereafter speak of).

I consider our Virginia negroes as forming a most valuable class. They have some of the best traits of character of any people on the globe. For instance, they are more generally good tempered than other people—they are kind towards each other, and are almost universally good hearted: they are generally grateful for favors, have the strongest local attachments, endure fatigue and hardships with great patience, are very contented, and cheerful—and in fact, are the happiest people in the world, unless tampered with by fanatics. With all these good qualities they have as few faults as most people, and it only requires system and some little management to make them valuable as a class of laborers, and contented and happy among themselves. In the management of negroes there should always be perfect uniformity of conduct towards them. . . . Rewards should also be made a part of the system, whenever there is displayed particular good conduct; and praise now and then judiciously used, goes a great way in their management. I have known a very lazy fellow who had been frequently punished for laziness without the least effect, spurred up, and made one of the most industrious fellows on the plantation, by a little praise. One day this lazy fellow was seen to be rather brisker at his work than usual for *him*, though by no means very brisk; however, I thought I would try what effect praise would have upon him, and in riding by him said, "Well, Joe, you are improving; you are getting along quite fast." Joe, with a smile, said, "Do you think so master?" and moved on a little faster. The next day or two, when I saw him again, I said, "Why, really Joe, you are doing quite well: you are getting to be quite smart with your work." "I am glad of it master," said Joe, with cheerful face, and a much more active step than I ever saw him have before. In five or six days after that, when I went where Joe was, I found him ahead of all the other hands. "Well Joe, you have got ahead of them?" "Yes master, and I mean to keep there too;" but it was too hard a tug for Joe to smile this time. However, we have never had cause to find fault with him since about his laziness. A few kind words will often go a great way. I would recommend to my friends, the Virginia overseers, to use a little flattery sometimes instead of stripes. In the management of slaves, the temper and disposition of each negro should be particularly consulted. Some require spurring up, some coaxing, some flattering, and others nothing but good words. When an overseer first goes upon a plantation to live, he should study their dispositions well, before he exerts too much rigor. Many a noble spirit has been broken down by injudicious management, and many a lazy cunning fellow has escaped, and put his work on the shoulders of the industrious. Give me a high spirited and even a high tempered negro, full of pride, for easy and comfortable management. Your slow sulky negro, although he may have an even temper, is *the devil* to manage.

The negro women are all harder to manage than the men. The

only way to get along with them is by kind words and flattery. If you want to cure a sloven, give her something nice occasionally to wear, and praise her up to the skies whenever she has on any thing tolerably decent. In the management of negroes it is particularly necessary to elevate their notions of honesty and character as much as possible, and never to charge them with dishonesty unless you have positive proof of the fact. . . .

It is all important for the morals as well as the comfort of the slaves (to say nothing of the policy and humanity of the thing) that they should be well clothed and fed; for they will steal if they are not well fed, and the very best remedy for hog stealing is to give the rogues a plenty of pork to eat. Negroes should have some of the luxuries of life too, such as fowls, egg, etc., with which to buy coffee and sugar, a garden and fruit trees, all of which will save the master's fowls, fruit, etc., and aid in the facility of managing the slaves, and will serve to attach them to their homes.

The "System" Applied—"To Introduce a Daily Accountability in Every Department": A Technological Breakthrough in Record-Keeping

TOOLS AND MACHINES *have often been a catalyst for sweeping changes in human history. A familiar example of the relationship between technological innovation and fundamental institutional change is the acceleration of the Protestant Reformation by the printing press. In the early nineteenth century a far less dramatic but significant technological impetus to social change was set in motion by Thomas Affleck, a Scotsman from Mississippi. Affleck's printed ledgers (and their imitations) brought together in one neat package several of the miscellaneous records of crops, tools, livestock, and daily production schedules usually kept by systematic planters.*

Thomas Affleck of Washington, Mississippi, was a scientific farmer, horticulturalist, essayist, and editor of agricultural journals. He was born in Dumfries, Scotland, in 1812, and came to the United States as a young man. From humble beginnings as a clerk, merchant, nurseryman, and columnist, he became a spokesman with a national reputation for the most advanced farming practices of his day, a speaker for national agricultural groups, and a consultant with a genius for turning useful knowledge to profit (and not always ethically). In 1846 he began a highly successful yearly ledger that soon flooded an eager market, and completed a few years later an even more successful series of "Plantation Journals and Account Books for Cotton and Sugar Growers."

47. Pre Aux Cleres Plantation Record Book

THE
COTTON PLANTATION
RECORD AND ACCOUNT BOOK
No. 1
Suitable for a Force of 40 Hands, or Under
By Thomas Affleck

Third Edition

New Orleans:
Published by Weld & Co., 92 Camp Street
1851

Source: Pre Aux Cleres Plantation Record Books, Book No. 1,
1852–1854 (J. M. McKnight, Natchitoches Parish, La.). Louisiana State University Department of Archives and Manuscripts.
Italics indicate handwritten entries.

PREFATORY REMARKS

It is now two years since the first edition of the "Plantation Record and Account Book" was issued. A large edition was immediately consumed, and that, without any particular effort on the part of the publisher—marking, most approvingly, the commendation with which the work was received, and giving emphatic proof of how greatly the want of a book of the kind was felt. . . .

. . . The author has corresponded widely with Planters and Overseers of experience, with a view to receiving suggestions which might enable him to simplify and improve. The result has been some slight but important alterations.

He has been highly gratified by the repeated assurances of many of the best Overseers in the country, that his labors have afforded them the means of greatly smoothing their thorny path, and of simplifying their duties. They have assured him that, instead of finding their labors and responsibilities increased, as they at first feared, when his work was placed in their hands to be kept, both have been greatly lessened; whilst the correct keeping of the Records and Accounts has proved, from their simplicity and completeness, a pleasing task. . . .

Washington, Adams Co., Miss.,
7th Nov., 1849.

DAILY RECORD OF PASSING EVENTS on
Pre Aux Cleres Plantation, during the week commencing
on the 2̲3̲ day of May 1852.   W̲es̲ ̲B̲eaird̲ Overseer.

SUNDAY   *May 23   Was a fine warm day*

MONDAY   *May 24   was a fine warm day till noon*
four plowing corn two hands plowing cotton the rest
of the hans hoing cotton till noon after noon was
wet all hans engaged in plowing an hoing cotton when
it wasent raining

TUESDAY   *May 25   was a wet day all hans engaged hoing back*
levy before noon after noon the wemen sewing the
men engaged at difernt jobs Lue turned out to day

WEDNESDAY   *May 26   was a wet day all hans hoing cotton till late*
in the evening they were stopt till nite by a hevy rain
that fell in the evening

THURSDAY   *May 27   was a wet bad day*
all hands hoing cotton till about three o'Clock when
it set in and rained till night all hands engaged at
diferent jobs the res of the day harison haling railes

FRIDAY   *May 28   was a wet slopy day*
all hans engaged hoing cotton in the evening fell three
hevy showers harison haling rails

SATURDAY   *May 29   was a wet slopy day it rained one lite shower*
—only all hans engaged as yesterday harison jobin
about

DAILY RECORD OF COTTON PICKED on *Pre aux Cleres* Plantation, during the week commencing on the <u>16</u> day of <u>August</u> 1852.   Overseer <u>Beard</u>

Weeks Picking stray pullings: 3000 lbs.

NAME	NO.	MONDAY	TUESDAY	WEDNESDAY	THURSDAY	FRIDAY	SAT
Baille	1	170	100	85	Sick	"	160
Jeff	2	at gin	"			gin again	155
Henry	3	"	"	90	160	150	150
Ben	4	140	75	95	155	160	140
Black	5	150	45	65	165	Scas	Sick
Sophia	6	160	85	85	177	170	65
Ester	7	155	75	100	110	170	110
Casolin	8	125	75	100	145	160	130
Sarah	9	125	70	75	130	150	"
Leueasar	10	125	65	75	155	150	75
Nora	11	130	70	65	90	Sick	105
Elick	12	110	65	75	115	115	150
Hassett	13	115	70	60	140	115	135
Mary & Child	14	170	85	65	180	160	105
Nancy & child	15	140	75	90	170	150	60
Elizarst	16	120	55	80	195	130	60
Margarett	17	65	55	75	85	70	50
Emila	18	100	50	45	sick	Sick	
Tonos	19	85	40	sick	"	65	
George	20	90	"	"	"	"	
Elizarga	21	160	75	45	50	50	
Wilson	22	at Tols	45	65			
Amt. of Each days work is		2000	a/1 1500	1500	2000	2000	1500	11300

DAILY RECORD OF PASSING EVENTS ON

Pre aux Cleres Plantation, during the week commencing
on the <u>25</u> day of <u>Dec</u> 185<u>3</u>   Overseer

SUNDAY   *December 25, 1853*
                Was a damp cold day the hands taking Holiday

MONDAY   *Dec 26*
                *Was a fine day all hands went to Red Plains to a
                frolick.*

TUESDAY   *Dec 27th*
                Was a fine day all hands still taking holiday

WEDNESDAY   *Dec 28th*
                Was a fine day all hands taking holliday

THURSDAY   *Dec 29th*
                Was a fair day but Cold
                all hands at worke on levy through lake
                I have 18 of Red Plains hands helping

FRIDAY   *Dec 30th*
                *Was a fine day all hands engaged on levy but the
                grainers*
                I still have 18 of the Red Plains hands on the levy

SATURDAY   *Dec 31st*
                Was a fine day but cold
                all hands engaged as yesterday

HORSES		
Work Horses	2	2
Brood Mares,		
Colts,		
Jack,		

MULES.		
Work Mules,	8	10
Colts		

CATTLE		
Bulls,	1	
Cows,	4	6
Calves	4	6
Yearlings,		
2 and 3 year-olds,	2	
Work Oxen,	6	5
Aged Oxen		

SHEEP

Rams,
Ewes,
Wethers,
Lambs,

GOATS

HOGS

Boars,		1
Brood Sows,	3	8
Pigs,	10	20
Shoats,	5	12
Stock Hogs,		6 or
	Barows	12

POULTRY.	
Turkeys,	
Geese,	10
Ducks,	20
Fowls,	20

WAGGON SHED.				REMARKS
Waggons,	1	1		
Carts,	1	1	2	
Ox-chains,	4	4	4	
Ox-yokes	4	4	3	

PLOW SHED.			
Plows,	12	18	12
Cultivators,			
Sweeps,	3	3	6
Scrapers,			
Shovel-plows,	2	2	2
Planters,	3	3	2
Harrows,	4	4	2
Wheel-barrows,			
Hand-barrows,	2	3	2
Single-trees,	8	8	6
Double-trees,	8	8	6
Scoops,			

STABLE.			
Collars,	10	10	
Bridles,	6 or 8		all old ones
Pairs Trace-chains,	14	14	12
Sets Waggon-gears,			
Curry-combs,	4 or 5		3 or 4 old ones
Dung-forks,			

TOOL HOUSE.			
Axes,	8	8	6
Wedges,	4	4	4
Hoes,	12	12	all old ones
Grubbing-hoes	10	10	10
Spades,	7	7	
Shovels,			
Cross-cut saws,			
Hand-saws,	3	3	2
Pit-saws,			
Adzes,	1	1	1
Broad-axe,			1
Scythes,			
Briar-hooks,			

The old mule cow is 12 years old 1854 Red mula is 8 years old 1854 Black mula is 6 years old 1854 The red Cow is 9 years old 1854 Chuy is 9 years old 1854 Red Cow is 7 years old 1854 The Brown Bull and Black Stere will be 3 years old Feb 1854 The mula Bull is 2 years old April 1854 The red one is one year old Feby 1854

The ages of my mules at this date Jany 1st 1854 Buster 00 years Jim Boots is 10 years old Sal is 9 years old Nel is 9 years old Jack is 9 years old Tom is 7 years old Jim is 6 years old Beck is 6 years old The two Black Mare Mules are 3 years old Each in May 1854

THE DUTIES OF AN OVERSEER

It is here supposed that the Overseer is not immediately under his employer's eye, but is left for days or weeks, perhaps months, to the exercise of his own judgment in the management of the plantation. To him we would say . . .

"On entering upon your duties, inform yourself thoroughly of the condition of the plantation, negroes, stock, implements, etc. Learn the views of your employer as to the general course of management he wishes pursued, and make up your mind to carry out his views fully, as far as in your power. . . ."

48. E. J. CAPELL'S PLANTATION DIARY

SOURCE: Cabell (Eli J.) Plantation Diaries and Record Books, Plantation Diary, 1850, Louisiana State University, Department of Archives and Manuscripts. Italics indicate handwritten entries.

DAILY RECORDS of passing events on
Pleasant Hill Plantation during the week commencing
on *22* day of *Sept*.   185*0*   *Jones* Overseer.

SUNDAY

MONDAY   *A very dry time and verry warm. Waggon went to Clinton with 6 Bales Cotton & 5 Mules & back*

TUESDAY   *A verry warm and dry day wanting rain verry much. Finished cutting Hay in Orchard to day verry healthy in Country*

WEDNESDAY

THURSDAY   *A verry warm dry dusty day, Cotton wanting rain verry much, opening two fast, I had my Cogs put away in oat house, Put one Man to David Jacksons Jack I hear of but little Sickness*

FRIDAY   *A shower of rain after noon with a good deal of Thunder. I went to saw Mill with one waggon after* plank for fences, 3 Boys pressed 6 Bales & broke the ferrale. The Cotton pickers lossed about two hours by the rain

SATURDAY

DAILY RECORDS of Cotton picked on
Pleasant Hill Plantation during the week commencing
on 21st day of Octr. 1850   Jones Overseer.

NAME	NO.	MONDAY	TUESDAY	WEDNESDAY	THURSDAY	FRIDAY	SATURDAY	Week's Picking
Sandy	1	Ginning	Pressing	Ginning	Ginning	Ginning	Ginning	Brought
Scott	2	Clearing	Pressing	Clearing	Clearing	Hauling Corn		Forward 64
Solomon	3	Clearing	Hauling rails	Clearing	Gone to Clinton	Hauling		54
Bill	4	Clearing	Do	Clearing	Clearing	Hauling		30
Jerry	5	Clearing	Clearing	Clearing	Clearing	Do Do		90
Isaac	6	Clearing	Clearing	Clearing	Clearing	Do Do		70
Jim	7	Sick	Sick	Sick	Sick	Sick		Sick
Dotson	8	Gone after Shoes	Clearing	Clearing		Clearing	Ho Corn	60

RECORD OF THE PHYSICIAN'S VISITS to the Sick, &c.,
upon ——————— Plantation during the year 1850

PHYSICIAN	DATE OF VISIT	NAME OF PATIENT	DATE WHEN THE PATIENT ENTERED AND LEFT THE HOSPITAL		DISEASE, &C.
Myself	April 8	Jim	April 8	April 10	A cold, pain in head
Girl Mary	May 3	Fanny	May 3	May 31	In Child bed
Myself	May 28	Sarah	May 28	" 31	Loose Bowels
Myself	May 29	Sandy	May 29	" 31	Pains in Breast &c
Mrs Capell	June 6	Rachel	June 6	June 10	Monthly Disease
Myself	June 7	Anthony	June 7	June 12	Remittent Fever
Myself	June 10	Peter	June 10	June 11	Derangement from Hoeing
Myself	June 23	William	June 22	June 28	Light fever & over work
Myself	June 28	Edmund	June 28	June 29	Damag'd by getting wet
Myself	July 27	Jerry	July 27	July 29	Got wet & feels out of order
Mrs Capell	Oct. 4	Martha	Octr 4	Octr 7	Pains in her legs &c.

THE PLANTER'S ANNUAL RECORD of his Negroes
upon _Pleasant Hill_ Plantation, during the year 18<u>50</u>
<u>E. J. Capell</u> Overseer.

		MALES					FEMALES	
NAME	AGE	VALUE AT COMMENCEMENT OF THE YEAR	VALUE AT END OF THE YEAR	NAME	AGE	VALUE AT COMMENCEMENT OF THE YEAR	VALUE AT END OF THE YEAR
John	70	$50.00	75.00	Hannah	60	$100.00	125.
Tom	49	1000.00	1200.00	Mary	34	800.00	900.
Sandy	38	600.00	800.00	Fanny	23	800.00	900.
Edmund	35	1000.00	1300.00	Rachel Sen.	32	675.00	750.
Jerry	40	700.00	950.00	Lucy	28	600.00	750.
Solomon	38	700.00	950.00	Azaline	13	600.00	700.
William	24	1000.00	1100.00	Sarah	9	350.00	450.
Charles	10	500.00	650.00	Harriet	8	300.00	400.
Tom	5	250.00	275.	Melissa	3	100.00	125.
Monroe	4	200.00	225.	Carolina	3	150.00	150.
Aaron	3	175.00	200	Laura	1	100.00	125.
Jerry	1	75.00	100				

THE PLANTER'S STATEMENT OF the EXPENSES of
Pleasant Hill Plantation, during the year 18<u>50</u>   ———— Overseer.

	TO WHOM, HOW, WHEN AND WHERE PAID, &C.	SUM
Overseer's Wages,	_To Tom, Cash, Febry 1st Paid at home_	10.00
Taxes,	_To R. M. Jenkins at Thickwood Precinct on 27th of January 1851 for 1850_	53.00
Pork, Bacon, &c.,	_None purchased_	

Corn, Flour, &c.,	To 3 Barrels of Molasses @21¢ To Clauss & McCombs	25.20
	B Sara on the 7th Feby	
Implements & Tools,	To 10 New Plows part in Centi & part at home Jan 1st	51.00
	1 Two horse Waggon 1 Cart & Sundries Septr 30th	140.00
	1 Sett Harness 1 Sett Cart Do 1 Bellows for Shop Oct. 30th	60.00
Bale Rope & Bagging,	To Cash paid for 477½ yds Rope	33.14
	" for 445 yds. Bagging	56.60
Blacksmith, Carpenter, &c.,	To Cash paid Carpenter	190.00
	Cash paid Blacksmith	7.25
Physician and Apothecary,	To Cash paid J. R. Caulfield & Drug Store	21.00

THE PLANTER'S ANNUAL

Showing the result of the season's operations—the LOSS

				$	¢
To 1485 Acres of Land, with the improvements, forming Plantation, at $5.00 per acre,				7425	00
Interest on same, at six per cent.				445	50
" Negroes, as per Inventory at	page	I		20000	00
Interest on same at six per cent.				1236	00
" Stock, as per Inventory at	page	J		1940	50
Interest on same, at six per cent.				116	43
" Stock purchased during the year, as per	page	J		227	00
" Implements and utensils, as per	page	K		663	30
Interest on same at six per cent.				39	79
" Do. purchased during the year, as per	page	K		197	20
" Produce on hand at commencement of the year, as per	page	L		3366	90
" Plantation expenses, as per statement at	page	N		893	63
				$37151	25

BALANCE SHEET,
or PROFIT upon the crop of *Pleasant Hill* Plantation
at close of 1850

					$ ¢
By	Acres of Land, forming	Plantation,			
	with improvements, at $ per acre,				7425 00
"	Negroes, as per Inventory, at close of the year, as per		page	I	30025 00
"	Stock sold and used during the year, as per		page	J	54 00
"	Do. on hand at the close of the year, as per		page	J	2811 75
"	Implements and utensils do. do. as per		page	K	671 25
"	Produce of Plantation sold, as per		page	L	2187 31
"	Do. of do. on hand at close of the year, as per		page	L	4554 00
					$47728 31
					37151 25
Balance in favor of farm					$10577 06

"Reduce Everything to a System"

CONSCIENTIOUS PLANTERS *made every effort to apply to their daily operations the techniques discussed in the agricultural journals. Charles Crommelin, an Alabama black-belt cotton planter, in 1846 wrote a "Memorandum of Directions" for "my Business." He insisted that his "manager" be sober and industrious; that he personally attend to all major aspects of the plantation operation—from food preparation and the disposition of corn cribs and smokehouses to the cut and tailoring of slave clothing and fencing of springs and woodland; and, for the slaves' benefit, that he "observe with them a regular Discipline."*

Most careful planters understood that the entire operation revolved around the slaves and slave quarters. In rules for his South Carolina rice estate, P. C. Weston wrote: The proprietor "wishes the Overseer most distinctly to understand that his first object is to be, under all circumstances, the care and well being of the negroes," and then proceeded to lay down stringent rules about "tickets" for slaves who traveled, food allowances, and slaves as watchmen, trunk-minders, and nurses.[1] When planters considered hygiene, they were even more insistent about the benefits of regimentation: "Cleanliness is a matter which cannot be too closely attended to. . . . My mode of making such reviews, is the following: I appoint a certain hour for attending to this matter on each Sabbath. . . . Every Negro distinctly understands, that at this hour he will be reviewed. . . . My business here is to call their

1. P. C. Weston, Esq., "Management of a Southern Plantation," *De Bow's Review*, 22 (January 1857): 38. (See Document 53, below.)

respective names, and to see that everyone has had his head well combed and cleaned, and their faces, hands, and feet well washed."[2] Olmsted clearly recognized that statements such as these were not patriarchal. Their tone and voice was that of Big Brother of Agribusiness.

As a general rule, the larger the body of negroes on a plantation or estate, the more completely are they treated as mere property, and in accordance with a policy calculated to insure the largest pecuniary returns. . . . It may be true, that among the wealthier slaveowners, there is oftener a humane disposition, a better judgement, and a greater ability to deal with their dependents indulgently and bountifully, but the effects of this disposition are chiefly felt, even on those plantations where the proprietor resides permanently, among the slaves employed about the house or stables, and perhaps a few old favorites in the quarters. It is more than balanced by the difficulty of acquiring a personal interest in the units of a large body of slaves, and an acquaintance with the individual characteristics of each.

Olmsted was also not distracted by the material conditions of a rich man's slaves; he understood the real character of their oppression:

The treatment of the mass must be reduced to a system, the ruling idea of which will be, to enable one man to force into the same channel of labor the muscles of a large number of men, of various, and often conflicting wills.

The chief difficulty is to overcome their great aversion to labor. They have no objection to eating, drinking and resting, when necessary, and no general disinclination to receive instruction. If a man owns many slaves, therefore, the faculty which he values highest, and pays most for, in an overseer, is that of making them work. Any fool could see that they were properly supplied with food, clothing, rest and religious instruction.[3]

49. "LEADING PRINCIPLES"

SOURCE: *Southern Agriculturalist*, 6 (November 1833): 571–572, 574.

2. A Planter, "Notions on the Management of Negroes, &c," *Farmer's Register*, 4 (December 1836): 494.
3. Frederick Law Olmsted, *A Journey in the Back Country* (New York, 1860, 1863), pp. 64–65.

ART. LXXX.—ACCOUNT OF
AN AGRICULTURAL EXCURSION MADE INTO THE
SOUTH OF GEORGIA IN THE WINTER OF 1832;
BY THE EDITOR.

Having gone through with the crops cultivated at "*Hopeton*," it only remains for us to notice the general system of management pursued at this place, and to which we invite the particular attention of our readers. We will here extract also (as we have hitherto done) pretty freely from Mr. Couper's notes.

GENERAL SYSTEM OF MANAGEMENT

"Two leading principles are endeavoured to be acted on, 1st, to reduce every thing to system. 2d, to introduce a daily accountability in every department.

"In order to accomplish these objects, the negroes are classed into rateable and unrateable hands. The rateable or working hands are divided into field-hands and permanent jobbers. The field hands are divided into 7 gangs;—3 of males, and 4 of females. Each hand is rated agreeably to his or her efficiency. There are 4 rates of each sex, viz. full hands, ¾, ½ and ¼ hands, and the daily task is proportioned to the rates,—4 quarter hands being required to do the same work with one full hand.

"The male gangs consist, 1st, of the prime young and strong men, constituting the *ditching* gang, they are all full hands. 2d, of the second class of men, and 3d, of third class.

"The women gangs are divided into 4.—1st, of the prime, young and strong women, 2d and 3d, of the less efficient, and 4th, of the old and very young.

"Each gang is under a separate driver, whose authority is limited to his own gang. Over the whole is a head driver."

The object of this division is to apportion the gang to the character of the work to be performed. For instance: in ditching none but the primest men (No. 1) are employed. For moting and assorting cotton where numbers are required and not strength, No. 3 of women is employed. This is, perhaps, better illustrated in the harvesting of the cane crop. No. 1 of women cut the canes, No. 2, strip the blades, and No. 3 bind and carry. The old bind and the young carry.

Besides the field hands there are a number of jobbers.

"The permanent jobbers are thrown into classes, and one individual of each class has charge of it, and reports the work done by it. The principal classes are carpenters, coopers, blacksmiths, masons, carters, stock-minders, hospital, nursery, garden, etc. A yard-driver attends to the feeding of the stock; grinding, small issues, and keeping the buildings in order.

"Every evening the drivers and heads of classes make a report to the overseer in my presence of the employment of their respective hands. The drivers report the number of hands and their rates employed in the field, the quantity and kind of work they have done, and the field in which it is done—the number and rates of the sick—the number and rates of such hands as may have been employed in jobbing, and how they have been employed. The heads of classes report the quantity of work done by that class. These reports are taken on a slate, and are copied into the "Journal of Plantation Work," which forms a minute and daily record of the occupation and quantity of work done by the different gangs. After the reports are received, the work for the following day is arranged, and the head driver is directed what is to be done, and the manner in which it is to be executed. He distributes the orders to sub-drivers and others:—the sub-drivers to the hands composing their gangs.

"As the quantity of land in each field is accurately known, a constant check is had on the fidelity of the reports as to the quantity of work done. It only remains, by a daily inspection, to see that all operations have been well performed. . . ."

We have already noticed the systematic manner in which all the operations on this place are conducted, and have referred several times to the books kept; these were all submitted to our inspection. They consist of "journal of plantation work," "hospital book," "corn book," "stock book," "crop books and sugar-house books."

In these "accurate accounts are kept 1st, of the *articles received and issued*; 2d, of *stock*, viz. horses, mules, cattle, sheep and hogs, showing the increase and decrease; 3d, of *corn* received and issued; 4th, of *rice winnowed and shipped*; 5th, of *cotton picked*, showing the daily, monthly and annual amount from each field; 6th, of *cotton sorted, ginned, moted, packed and shipped*; 7th, of the sugar crop, showing daily, the number of acres cut, the field, the number of gallons of juice expressed, the quantity of sugar (sugar proof) boiled off, the quantity of lime, etc. used, the effect of the temper, and a column of miscellaneous remarks. In addition to these, a regular set of mercantile books is kept." ...

50. "THE MANAGER MUST . . . ATTEND *Personally* TO EVERY BRANCH OF MY BUSINESS"

SOURCE: Memorandum of Directions to the Manager of My Business for the Year 1846, Charles Crommelin Papers, Alabama Department of Archives and History.

MEMORANDUM OF DIRECTIONS TO THE MANAGER OF MY BUSINESS FOR THE YEAR 1846

The manager must soberly and industriously attend *personally* to every branch of my business. What he does not personally perform, he must see done.

He must rise early and see that the negroes do the same, and that they get early to work, and not loiter about the yard or their houses in the morning, and that they retire early at night.

He must observe with them a regular Discipline and humane treatment and see that they are properly cared for in sickness.

He must personally see that they keep their clothing mended and clean, and that they wash their clothes as often as once a week for which purpose time must be regularly set apart the latter end of each week. He must see that they are clean on Sunday and not straggling about the country dusty and ragged. And he must see that they appear clean every Monday morning in the year without any failure whatever.

He must see that they keep their houses clean, and their yards free from weeds and filth.

He must see that the Cook prepares the food for the work people in a proper manner and at the proper times.

He must see that a garden is planted and well cultivated to raise vegetables for my family, and for the use of the plantation.

He must *personally* salt the horses, mules, sheep and cattle, and give salt, ashes and copperas to the hogs. He must do this himself and must himself see that they are fed under his own inspection and that the horses and mules are curried regularly and watered at proper periods.

He must *himself* keep the keys of the cribs, smoke house and all other buildings in which any property belonging to me is stored, and must *himself* see to the giving out of food of every description.

He must have poultry raised and well taken care of that I may be furnished with it as required.

He must have special care and attention given to the dairy seeing that the milk cows are regularly fed, salted and milked, and that the butter is properly and neatly prepared and sent to me regularly and buttermilk when desired.

He must see that the negro clothing is properly cut, and well and strongly made. The Dairy, the Poultry yard and the clothing will come more especially under the attention of the manager's wife.

He must keep the ploughs and Harrows well stocked and the hoes, mattocks, &c. axes well halved and in good order.

He must keep the waggons and carts well sheltered, and their gear and the plough gear in the best order, and well greased with neatsfoot oil and always under shelter when not in use, and never on any pretence permit tools or gear to remain where last used.

He must personally see every pannel of the fence around the plantation frequently and see that the gates and gate frosts and fastenings are always in good order, and must keep the fences in good repair and the fence corners of the cultivated fields clean.

He must keep the roads and crossings in the plantation clean and in good order.

He must see that the springs are kept clean and well fenced in.

He must see that the buildings about the plantation are not destroyed for want of care, and for want of repairs at the proper time.

He must see that my woodland is not intruded upon by pilferers and that my fields are not overrun by persons who have no business in them under the pretence, frequently, of hunting, but at times killing my stock and poultry with their dogs and guns and doing other damage.

I must be the sole owner of stock of every kind and description, and of all poultry on my plantation.

The manager must see that the cat[tle], the sheep, hogs, etc., are regularly penned every night at the proper season, to enrich the land where they are penned, or to accumulate manure for other fields.

He must *himself* mark and alter all calves, sheep and hogs which require it, when young and must spay all such sows as are not specially kept for breeding at the earliest period at which it should be done.

He must keep in this book an accurate account of all money received for me and forward the same to me when received and an account of such disbursements as I may authorise to be made, and must when I am not in the immediate neighborhood of my farm as often as once in each week write to me and give me an account of the progress of my affairs, state of the crops etc. . . .

He must keep in writing an account of my stock of every kind, and count them often to see that none are missing. . . .

CH CROMMELIN
Montgomery Co
28th Dec. 1847

51. HOUSING AND FAMILY LIFE

SOURCE: A Mississippi Planter, "Management of Negroes upon Southern Estates," *De Bow's Review*, 10 (June 1851): 623–624, 625.

. . . My first care has been to select a proper place for my "Quarter," well protected by the shade of forest trees, sufficiently thinned out to admit a free circulation of air, so situated as to be free from the impurities of stagnant water, and to erect comfortable houses for my negroes. Planters do not always reflect that there is more sickness, and consequently greater loss of life, from the decaying logs of negro houses, open floors, leaky roofs, and crowded rooms, than all other causes combined; and if humanity will not point out the proper remedy, let self-interest for once act as a virtue, and prompt him to save the health and lives of his negroes, by at once providing comfortable quarters for them. There being upwards of 150 negroes on the plantation, I provide for them 24 houses made of hewn post oak, covered with cypress, 16 by 18, with close plank floors and good chimneys, and elevated two feet from the ground. The ground *under* and around the houses is swept every month, and the houses, both inside and out, white-washed twice a year. The houses are situated in a double row from north to south, about 200 feet apart, the doors facing inwards, and the houses being in a line, about 50 feet apart. At one end of the street stands the overseer's house, workshops, tool house, and wagon sheds; at the other, the grist and saw-mill, with good cisterns at each end, providing an ample supply of pure water. . . . As to their habits of amalgamation and intercourse, I know of no means whereby to regulate them, or to restrain them; I attempted it for many years by preaching virtue and decency, encouraging marriages, and by punishing, with some severity, departures from marital obligations; but it was all in vain. I allow for each hand that works out, four pounds of clear meat and one peck of meal per week. Their dinners are cooked for them, and carried to the field, always with vegetables, according to the season. There are two houses set apart at mid-day for resting, eating, and sleeping, if they desire it, and they retire to one of the weather-sheds or the grove to pass this time, not being permitted to remain in the hot sun while at rest. They cook their own suppers and breakfasts, each family being provided with an oven, skillet, and sifter, and each one having a coffee-pot (and generally some coffee to put in it), with knives and forks, plates, spoons, cups, &c., of their own providing. The wood is regularly furnished them; for, I hold it to be absolutely mean, for a man to require a negro to work until daylight closes in, and then force him to get wood, sometimes half a mile off, before he can get a fire, either to warm himself or cook his supper. Every negro has his hen-house, where he raises poultry, which he is not permitted to sell, and he cooks and eats his chickens and eggs for his evening and morning meals to suit himself; besides, every family has a garden, paled in, where they raise such vegetables and fruits as they take a fancy to. A large house is provided as a nursery for the children, where all are taken at daylight, and placed under the charge of a careful and experienced woman, whose sole occupation is to attend to them, and see that they are properly fed and attended to, and above all things to keep them as dry and as cleanly as possible, under the circumstances. The suckling women come in to nurse their children four times during the day; and it is the duty of the nurse to see that they do not perform this duty until they have become properly cool, after walking from the field. In consequence of these regulations, I have never lost a child from being burnt to death, or, indeed, by accidents of any description; and although I have had more than thirty born within the last five years, yet I have not lost a single one from teething, or the ordinary summer complaints so prevalent amongst the children in this climate.

I must not omit to mention that I have a good fiddler, and keep him well supplied with catgut, and I make it his duty to play for the negroes every Saturday night until 12 o'clock. They are exceedingly punctual in their attendance at the ball, while Charley's fiddle is always accompanied with Ihurod on the triangle, and Sam to "pat."

I also employ a good preacher, who regularly preaches to them on the Sabbath day, and it is made the duty of every one to come up clean and decent to the place of worship. As Father Garritt regularly calls on Brother Abram (the foreman of the prayer meetings), to close the exercises, he gives out and sings his hymn with much unction, and always cocks his eye at Charley, the fiddler, as much as to say, "Old fellow, you had your time last night; now it is mine."

I would gladly learn every negro on the place to read the bible, but for a fanaticism which, while it professes friendship to the negro, is keeping a cloud over his mental vision, and almost crushing out his hopes of salvation.

52. Slave Children

SOURCE: A Planter, "Notions on the Management of Negroes, &c.," *Farmer's Register*, 4 (December 1836): 495.

LITTLE NEGROES.

I have a nurse appointed to superintend all my little negroes, and a nursery built for them. If they are left to be protected by their parents, they will most assuredly be neglected. I have known parents take out an allowance for their children and actually steal it from them, to purchase articles at some shop. Besides, when they would be honest to their offspring, from their other occupations, they have not the time to attend to them properly. The children get their food irregularly, and when they do get it, it is only half done. They are suffered, by not having one to attend to them, to expose themselves; and hence many of the deaths which occur on our plantations.

I have just stated that I have a nursery for my little negroes, with an old woman or nurse to superintend and cook for them, and to see that their clothes and bedding are well attended to. She makes the little ones, generally speaking, both girls and boys, mend and wash their own clothes, and do many other little matters, such as collecting litter for manure, &c. In this they take great pleasure, and it has the tendency to bring them up to industrious habits. The nurse also cooks for them three times a day; and she always has some little meat to dress for them, or the clabber or sour milk from the dairy to mix their food. In *sickness* she sees that they are well attended to; and from having many of them together, one is taught to wait upon the other. My little negroes are consequently very healthy; and from pursuing the plan I have laid down, I am confident that I raise more of them, than where a different system is followed.

53. Food

Source: *De Bow's Review*, 22 (January 1857): 38–45.

MANAGEMENT OF A SOUTHERN PLANTATION

RULES ENFORCED ON THE RICE ESTATE OF P.C. WESTON, ESQ., OF SOUTH CAROLINA

Allowance— Food.— Great care should be taken that the negroes should never have less than their regular allowance: in all cases of doubt, it should be given in favor of the largest quantity. The measures should not be *struck*, but rather heaped up over. None but provisions of the best quality should be used. If any is discovered to be damaged, the Proprietor, if at hand, is to be immediately informed; if absent, the damaged article is to be destroyed. The corn should be carefully winnowed before grinding. The small rice is apt to become sour: as soon as this is perceived it should be given out every meal until finished, or until it becomes too sour to use, when it should be destroyed.

Allowances are to be given out according to the following schedule. None of the allowances given out in the big pot are to be taken from the cook until after they are cooked, nor to be taken home by the people:

SCHEDULE OF ALLOWANCE
Daily, (Sundays Excepted.)

During Potato-Time

To each person doing any work .... 4 quarts
To each child at the negro-houses .... 2 quarts

During Grits-Time

To the cook for public-pot, for every person doing any work 1 quart
To the child's cook, for each child at negro-houses .... 1 pint
Salt to cook for public pot .... pint
Salt to child's cook .... pint

On every Tuesday and Friday throughout the year

To cook for public-pot, for whole gang of workers, ⎤Meat,
  tradesmen, drivers, etc. .... ⎦ pounds.
To child's cook for all the children .... pounds

On every Tuesday and Friday, from April 1st to October 1st

To the plantation cook, for each person doing any ⎤Small Rice,
  work, instead of the pint of grits .... ⎦1 Pint.
To the child's cook, for each child, instead of the ½ pint
  of grits .... ½ pint
To the plantation cook, for the whole gang of   ⎤ Peas,
  workers, tradesmen, drivers, &c. .... ⎦ quarts.

Every Thursday throughout the year

To the child's cook, for all the children .... Molasses, quarts.

Weekly allowance throughout the year
—to be given out every Saturday afternoon

To each person doing any work .... Flour, 3 quarts.
To each child at negro-houses .... ″ 3 pints.
To each person who has behaved well, and has ⎤ 2 Fish, or
  not been sick during the week .... ⎦ 1 pt. Molasses.

To each nurse . . . . 4 Fish, or 1½ pt. Molasses.

To head-carpenter, head-miller, head-cooper, head-ploughman, watchman, trunk-minders, drivers, mule-minder, hog-minder, cattle-minder, and to every superannuated person . . . . } 3 Fish, or 1½ pt. Molasses each.

Monthly Allowance—on the 1st of every month

To each person doing any work, and each superannuated person . . . . Salt, 1 quart.

Ditto . . . . Tobacco, 1 hand.

Christmas Allowance

To each person doing any work, and each superannuated person . . . . } Fresh Meat, 3 lbs.
Salt   ″   3 lbs.
Molasses,   1 qt.
Small Rice, 4 qts.
Salt,   ½ bushel

To each child at negro-houses . . . . } Fresh Meat, 1½ lbs.
Salt   ″   1½ lbs.
Molasses,   1 pt.
Small Rice, 2 qts.

Additional Allowance

Every day when rice is sown or harvested, to the cook, for the whole gang of workers in the field } Meat,   lbs.
Peas,   qts.

No allowances or presents, besides the above, are on any consideration to be made, except for sick people, as specified further on.

54. HEALTH PRECAUTIONS

SOURCE: James A. Tait Memorandum Book, 1831–1840, State of Alabama, Department of Archives and History.

HEALTH AND CARE DURING THE SICKLY SEASON

Regulations for the sickly season. More care must always be taken about health during the sickly season than at other times, foggs, and hot sun to[o] much guarded against as possible, there is more danger to the negroes in picking cotton time than any other, the hot sun shining on their backs whilst stooping after the bowels [bolls], and August and Sept. being the most sickly months too; must never leave their houses till sunrise during green time or as long as the cotton is green and during August and Sept.

Must come in at twelve o'clock; to straiten up and walk in to the houses and back again is a great relief to them; besides the cotton during said months must be suned on a scaffold that is, what is picked out in the forenoon. When cotton is rank and they are picking on the further side of the field, open a path so that the dew on the cotton will not wet them till they get to their work. A free use of molasses tends to keep off fever, too, I think; it acts by sweatening the bile etc.

Negroes Houses, ought to be moved regularly once in 2 or 3 years. This is essential to health; the filth accumulates under the floors, so much in 2 years as to cause disease. This is cheaper and easyer than to pay doctors and nurse sicknesses.

The putrid Soar throat which prevailed so fataly in the winter of 1837, 38 was caused by the filth under the houses, I have no doubt.

55. Health: Vital Records from a Plantation Journal

SOURCE: Arnold-Screven Papers, Plantation Journal No. 4, Southern Historical Collection, University of North Carolina Archives.

PROCTOR'S FERRY AND BRUTON HALL
Record of Deaths

NAME	AGE	CAUSE OF DEATH	TIME OF DECEASE
Old York	60	Typhoid Pneumonia	Jan. 1851
Binah	2	dropsy	May 3 "
Jimmy (carpenter)	45	Rupture of the heart (Jimmy was carrying a heavy block complained of pain in his heart, laid down and died in a few minutes. An autopsy	May 10, 1852

			TIME OF
NAME	AGE	CAUSE OF DEATH	DECEASE
		found his heart enlarged softened & almost diaphanous and ruptured near the base of the large pulmonary artery. His lungs were filled with serum, and the pericardium also.)	
Frank	infant	Afflection Bowels	Dec. 1852
Old Hannah		old age	" 1853
Fortune	30	Child bed, Fortune was reported in labor at 5 A.M. Labor reported difficult at 10 A.M. Sent for Dr. Harris who saw her at 5½ P.M. Craristomy performed & child delivered. The mother died next day at 11 A.M.	Feb. 10th 1854
Eldy's child	infant	Died suddenly at night supposed to be smothered	Feb. 5th/54
Claudia's child, Terry	3	Inherited Veneral	Feb. 11th '54
Samson	40	Dropsy	Jan 3/54
Noble	33	Drowned Sav[annah] river	April/54
Profit	50 or more	Disease unknown	
O[ld] Jenny	60 or more	Paralysis &c.	
Alick	35	Gun shot wound with mustard seed—required after refusing to stop while running away. The shot penetrated the aorta from a distance of 40 or 50 yds	May 27th/54
July	45	Diarrhea	Sept. 11th 1854

NAME	AGE	CAUSE OF DEATH	TIME OF DECEASE	
Jupiter	60	Fever	" 10th	"
Hannibal	40	unknown	" 9th	"
Caesar	45	Killed by a blow on board Steamboat Fashion while Stealing	July	"
Child	4	Drowned in a ditch	Sept	"
Virginia	32	Typhoid Fever (during Pregnancy) Introduced by exposure in Hurricane of 7,8,9th Sepr.	Sept 29th	"
Comfort's child	9 days	Died in fits	Oct 7th	"
William	25	Died of Cholera	Dec 15th	"
*Sylvia's child	8 mos.	Inflam[mation] from Cold	Dec 26th	"
Comfort	30	Cholera	Jan 18th	1855
Abrah	50	Cholera	Jan 26	1855
Nancy's child girl	3	Bowel compl[ication]s	Jan 30	55
Prince	40	Cholera	Jan 29	55
Frank	21	Diarrhea	July	55
Doctor	40	Gangrene of foot	July 24	"
O[ld] Chloe	60	Disease of Heart	Aug 1	55
Lenny's child	2	Abcess of Head (Lunpa)	Aug 8	55
Robin	50	Tuberculosis	Sept	55
Daniel	40	Pneumonia	December	55
Sarah	50	Dropsy	December	

Record of Births

NAME	CHILD OF	WHEN BORN	
Harry	Daniel & Fortune	about 1st Feb.	1851
Frank	——Jenny. Boy	8th March	"

* Died 1854—9 full hands, 8 old & children—17 total

NAME	CHILD OF	WHEN BORN	
Lucy	William & Harrit	9th "	"
Jacob	——Binah	about 15th June	"
Harry	Lightfoot & Sylvia	" August	"
Rosa Anna	George & Peggy	12th July	1852
Claudia	Sharper & Pleasant—girl	Nov.	"
	Lightfoot & Sylvia	Aug	1854
	Sharper & Pleasant	Sept 28	"
	Comfort (Ferry)	"	"
Ritta	Sally "	Aug	"
Jack	Claudia "	Dec.	"
	Matilda "	Jan.	1855
Dead	Clara "		
Sandy	Sue	Jan. 7th	1855
Sibby	Amy Proctor['s]	July	"
	Grace Ferry	July 20	"

The "System's" Mindlessness: Three Views
of Sadism and Violence against Slaves

THOSE WHO ARGUE that slavery was essentially paternalistic must contend with the ugly accounts of uncivilized cruelty toward slaves that are endemic in plantation records of all kinds. While some scholars see beatings of slaves as an aberration, an exception to the master's generally benign, patriarchal benevolence, Kenneth Stampp seems much closer to the truth of the matter when he writes, "Barbarism was an integral part of slavery, and the master-slave relationship generated every bit as much of it as did paternalism."[4]

Patriarchal customs at one time may have sheltered some slaves from their supervisors' cruelty, but antebellum evidence suggests that brutality may have been a widespread problem. Most extant accounts and overseer agreements (as well as virtually all of the "Management of Negroes" articles) contain detailed instructions on punishment. For example:

> Punishments. ——It is desirable to allow 24 hours to elapse between the discovery of the offence, and the punishment. No punishment is to exceed 15 lashings. In cases where the Overseer supposes a severer punishment necessary, he must apply to the Proprietor, or ——, Esq., in case of the Proprietor's absence

4. Kenneth Stampp, "Interpreting the Slaveholders' World: A Review," *Agricultural History*, 44 (October 1970): 410.

from the neighborhood. Confinement (not in the stocks) is to be preferred to whipping: but the stoppage of Saturday's allowance, and doing whole task on Saturday, will suffice to prevent ordinary offences. Special care must be taken to prevent any indecency in punishing women.[5]

On a huge and thoroughly organized Mississippi plantation, Olmsted asked: "It must be very disagreeable to have to punish them as much as you do?" "Yes," the overseer replied, "it would be to those who are not used to it—but it's my business, and I think nothing of it. Why sir, I wouldn't mind killing a nigger more than I would a dog." Mindless bureaucratic cruelty of this kind was a major force in eroding whatever vestiges of paternalism remained on the large antebellum plantation; and the following accounts are a reminder that even the most "reasonable" systems are often subverted by the inane, irrational actions of petty officials.

56. "GET DOWN ON YOUR KNEES"

SOURCE: Frederick Law Olmsted, A Journey in the Back Country (New York, 1860, 1863), pp. 82–87.

The whip was evidently in constant use, however. There were no rules on the subject, that I learned; the overseers and drivers punished the negroes whenever they deemed it necessary, and in such manner, and with such severity, as they thought fit. . . . I said to one of the overseers, "It must be very disagreeable to have to punish them as much as you do?" "Yes, it would be to those who are not used to it—but it's my business, and I think nothing of it. Why, sir, I wouldn't mind killing a nigger more than I would a dog." I asked if he had ever killed a negro? "Not quite," he said, but overseers were often obliged to. Some negroes are determined never to let a white man whip them, and will resist you, when you attempt it; of course you must kill them in that case. Once a negro, whom he was about to whip in the field, struck at his head with a hoe. He parried the blow with his whip, and drawing a pistol tried to shoot him, but the pistol missing fire he rushed in and knocked him down with the butt of it. At another time a negro whom he was punishing, insulted and threatened him. He went to the house for

5. "Management of a Southern Plantation," De Bow's Review, 22 (January 1857): 40.

his gun, and as he was returning, the negro, thinking he would be afraid of spoiling so valuable a piece of property by firing, broke for the woods. He fired at once, and put six buck-shot into his hips. He always carried a bowie-knife, but not a pistol, unless he anticipated some unusual act of insubordination. He always kept a pair of pistols ready loaded over the mantel-piece, however, in case they should be needed. It was only when he first came upon a plantation that he ever had much trouble. A great many overseers were unfit for their business, and too easy and slack with the negroes. When he succeeded such a man, he had hard work for a time to break the negroes in, but it did not take long to teach them their place. His conversation on this subject was exactly like what I have heard said, again and again, by northern shipmasters and officers, with regard to seamen.

The severest corporeal punishment of a negro that I witnessed at the South, occurred while I was visiting this estate. . . . The manner of the overseer who inflicted the punishment, and his subsequent conversation with me about it, indicated that it was by no means an unusual occurrence with him. I had accidentally encountered him, and he was showing me his plantation. In going from one side of it to the other, we had twice crossed a deep gully, at the bottom of which was a thick covert of brushwood. We were crossing it a third time, and had nearly passed through the brush, when the overseer suddenly stopped his horse exclaiming, "What's that? Hallo! who are you there?"

It was a girl lying at full length on the ground at the bottom of the gully, evidently intending to hide herself from us in the bushes.

"Who are you there?"

"Sam's Sall, sir."

"What are you skulking there for?"

The girl half rose, but gave no answer.

"Have you been here all day?"

"No sir."

"How did you get here?"

The girl made no reply.

"Where have you been all day?"

The answer was unintelligible.

After some further questioning, she said her father accidentally locked her in, when he went out in the morning.

"How did you manage to get out?"

"Pushed a plank off, sir, and crawled out."

The overseer was silent for a moment, looking at the girl, and then said, "That won't do—come out here." The girl arose at once, and walked towards him; she was about eighteen years of age. A bunch of keys hung at her waist, which the overseer espied, and he said, "Ah, your father locked you in; but you have got the keys." After a little hesitation, the girl replied that these were the keys of some other locks; her father had the door-key.

Whether her story were true or false, could have been ascertained in two minutes by riding on to the gang with which her father was at work, but the overseer had made up his mind as to the facts of the case.

"That won't do," said he, "get down on your knees." The girl knelt on the ground; he got off his horse, and holding him with his left hand, strick her thirty or forty blows across the shoulders with his tough, flexible, "raw-hide" whip. They were well laid on, as a boatswain would thrash a skulking sailor, or as some people flog a baulking horse, but with no appearance of angry excitement on the part of the overseer. At every stroke the girl winced, and exclaimed, "Yes, sir!" or "Ah, sir!" or "Please, sir!" not groaning or screaming. At length he stopped and said, "Now tell me the truth." The girl repeated the same story. "You have not got enough yet," said he. "Pull up your clothes—lie down." The girl without any hesitation, without a word or look of remonstrance or entreaty, drew closely all her garments under her shoulders, lay down upon the ground, with her face toward the overseer, who continued to flog her with the rawhide, across her naked loins and thigh, with as much strength as before. She now shrunk away from, not rising, but writhing, groveling, and screaming, "Oh, don't, sir! oh, please stop, master! please, sir! please, sir! oh, that's enough, master! oh, Lord, oh, master, master! oh, God, master, do stop! oh, God, master! oh, God, master!"

A young gentleman of fifteen was with us; he had ridden in front, and now, turning on his horse looked back with an expression only of impatience at the delay. It was the first time I had ever seen a woman flogged. I had seen a man cudgeled and beaten, in the heat of passion, before, but never flogged with a hundredth part of the severity used in this case. I glanced again at the perfectly passionless but rather grim business-like face of the overseer, and again at the young gentleman, who had turned away; if not indifferent he had evidently not the faintest sympathy with my emotion. Only my horse chafed with excitement. I gave him rein and spur and we plunged into the bushes and scrambled fiercely up the steep acclivity. The screaming yells and the whip strokes had ceased when I reached the top of the bank. Choking, sobbing, spasmodic groans only were heard. I rode on to where the road coming diagonally up the ravine ran out upon the cotton-field. My young companion met me there, and immediately afterward the overseer. He laughed as he joined us, and said,

"She meant to cheat me out of a day's work—and she has done it, too."

"Did you succeed in getting another story from her?"

"No; she stuck to it."

"Was it not perhaps true?"

"Oh no, sir, she slipped out of the gang when they were going to work, and she's been dodging about all day, going from one place to another as she saw me coming. She saw us crossing there a little while ago, and thought we had gone to the quarters, but we turned back so quick, we came into the gully before she knew it, and she could do nothing but lie down in the bushes."

"I suppose they often slip off so."

"No, sir; I never had one do so before—not like this; they often run away to the woods and are gone some time, but I never had a dodge-off like this before."

"Was it necessary to punish her so severely?"

"Oh yes, sir," (laughing again.) "If I hadn't punished her so hard she would have done the same thing again to-morrow, and half the people on the plantation would have followed her example. Oh, you've no idea how lazy these niggers are; you northern people don't know any thing about it. They'd never do any work at all if they were not afraid of being whipped."

57. "The First Time . . . He Had Ever Corrected Her"

Source: *Southern Statesman* (Jackson, Tenn.), September 10, 1831.

Unnatural and horrid Murder.—on Wednesday night last, a negro woman, the property of Col. Thomas Loftin, near this place, destroyed three of her children by drowning; one a boy aged about seven years, and two girls, one an infant at the breast. On the evening of that day, she had been chastized by her master, the first time it is said, that he had ever corrected her. At a late hour of the night, she, according to her own acknowledgements, deliberately took them to a pool of water, one at a time, and held them in it, until life became extinct. In the act of taking her fourth child for the same purpose, she was discovered by her husband, when an alarm was made. The drowned children were found about two hours after the act was committed, but, every exertion to resuscitate them proved ineffectual. The woman stands committed for trial.

58. "They Are Both Doing Pretty Well"

SOURCE: Everard Green Baker Diaries, 1848–1876, Southern Historical Collection, University of North Carolina Library. Reprinted by permission.

2 June 1854.   Day before yesterday a boy belonging to Thad Sorsby stabbed Mr Hugh Hardin twice in the side because he was agoing to whip him—Hardin then shot at him but missed, then drew his knife & stabbed the boy 25 times, holding the boy in the meantime by the wrist of the hand in which he held the knife. He stabbed him 4 times on the head breaking his skull in two places, the boy first drew a deadly weapon. They are both doing pretty well and may recover.

There is strong reason to believe that 5 of the men on the place were engaged in plotting against the life of Mr. Hardin who was overseeing there. Several Gents assembled & we whipped one.

The Smaller Slaveholders and Their Black Family Members: Two Views of Antebellum Paternalism

SCHOLARS, *recently coming to grips with the fact that antebellum whites North and South were determined to keep America "a white man's country," are re-examining the harsher implications of Ulrich B. Phillips' view that slavery was a system of racial adjustment as well as a labor system.*

Only small slaveholders and non-slaveowning whites had to confront directly the realities of a biracial society, or the more remote but threatening possibilities of gradual emancipation. Their situation was somewhat comparable to that of working-class people today who on a face-to-face basis must adjust to biracial neighborhoods, schools, and other public services, which they feel are forced upon them by wealthy liberals who live in segregated suburbs and send their children to private schools. The great planter, secure in his mansion or holiday resort in Holly Springs, Mississippi, or Hendersonville, North Carolina, was above the din and abrasiveness of race relations among poor whites and slaves; he could afford to take a certain liberal and benevolent view of freedmen and race adjustment in general. But whites who lived in towns serving plantations or on small farms or, particularly, poor whites, the "buckra," who were sometimes economically indistinguishable from some of the free blacks in their neighborhoods, saw freedmen as an immediate threat. If blacks were free, this class reasoned, they would have to be colonized outside the United States: "I reckon the majority would be right glad [to abolish slavery]," an Alabama farmer told Olmsted, "if we could get rid of the niggers. But it wouldn't never do to free 'em and leave 'em here. I don't know anybody, hardly, in favor of that. Make 'em free and leave 'em here and they'd steal every thing we made. Nobody couldn't live here then."[6] When travelers left the major roads of the alluvial plains and river bottoms, this attitude became more prevalent—even in areas where relations among blacks and whites were intimate and fairly amicable (that is, "individual Negroes were all right, but not blacks, in general").

Small slaveowners were another matter. On their plantations, race relations were clearly old-fashioned, a case of master and servant. Paradoxically, it is precisely in the economically less advantaged areas of the South—uplands, Piedmont, and pine barrens, characterized by poor soil conditions and remoteness from adequate transportation facilities—where a residue of colonial patriarchalism flourished. This was not coincidental, because as both contributors to agricultural journals and travelers recognized, real paternalism depended on variables—an owner who knew his slaves individually and lived (and possibly worked) among them—that were not present on most large and commercialized plantations: "God pity the man who owns more than he can intimately know," a small planter remarked in the Southern Cultivator.[7] *A larger planter who lived at home wrote:*

For the management of plantation Servants, I have adopted a

6. Cited in James McPherson, "Slavery and Race," *Perspectives*, 3 (1969): 470–471.

7. "Treatment of Slaves—Mr. Guerry," *Southern Cultivator*, 18 (August 1860): 258.

*system, which works so entirely to my satisfaction, that I have
determined to send it to you. . . .*

*The fundamental principles upon which the system is based, are
simply these: that all living on the plantation, whether colored or
not, are members of the same family, and to be treated as such—
that they all have their respective duties to perform, and that the
happiness and prosperity of all will be in proportion to the fidelity
with which each member discharges his part.*[8]

*This was true paternalism, the expectation of mutual duties and re-
sponsibilities, the view that the plantation was a community, a family—
and a resident owner. It was not practiced by many of the largest
planters, who owned most of the slaves and largely controlled the political and economic life of the antebellum South. Paternalism, instead,
was the way of life of the smaller planters (fewer than ten prime hands
on about 500 acres), who were much more numerous in a society in
which nonslaveholders constituted more than half of the white population.*

*One of the major themes in Olmsted's trenchant observations of life-
styles in the antebellum era was his recognition of the rather significant
differences in the treatment of slaves and in the texture of white-black
relations on large and small units. Turning his horse away from the rich
Mississippi bottom lands above Natchez, he pursued an inland route
toward Tuscaloosa, Alabama. "The country grew less fertile, and the
plantations smaller," and soon he was in the households of a different
kind of slaveowning white.*

59. A Patriarch Who Could Not "Systematize"

Source: A Small Planter, "Management of Negroes," *De Bow's
Review,* 11 (October 1851): 370–371.

My hours of labor, commencing with pitching my crop, is from
daylight until 12 M.; all hands then come in and remain until 2
o'clock, P.M., then back to the field until dark. Some time in May
we prolong the rest three hours; and if a very hot day, even four
hours. Breakfast is eaten in the field, half an hour being given; or
they eat and go to work without being driven in and out—all
stopping when my driver is ready.

I give all females half of every Saturday to wash and clean up, my
cook washing for young men and boys through the week. The
cabins are scoured once a week, swept out every day, and beds

8. "Foby," "Management of Servants," ibid., 11 (August 1853): 226.

made up at noon in summer, by daylight in winter. In the winter, breakfast is eaten before going to work, and dinner is carried to the hands.

I do not punish often, but I seldom let an offence pass, making a lumping settlement, and then correct for the servant's remembrance. I find it better to whip very little. . . .

I have a fiddle in my quarters, and though some of my good old brethren in the church would think hard of me, yet I allow dancing; ay, I buy the fiddle and encourage it, by giving the boys occasionally a big supper.

I have no overseer, and do not manage so scientifically as those who are able to lay down rules; yet I endeavour to manage so that myself, family and negroes may take pleasure and delight in our relations.

It is not possible in my usual crude way to give my whole plans, but enough is probably said. I permit no night-work, except feeding stock and weighing cotton. No work of any kind at noon, unless to clean out cabins, and bathe the children when nursing, not even washing their clothes.

I require every servant to be present each Sabbath morning and Sabbath evening at family prayers. In the evening the master or sometimes a visitor, if a professor, expounds the chapter read. Thus my servants hear 100 to 200 chapters read each year anyhow. One of my servants, a professor, is sometimes called on to close our exercises with prayer.

Owning but few slaves, I am probably able to do a better part by them than if there were one or two hundred. But I think I could do better if I had enough to permit me to systematize better.

60. Olmsted Visits a Small Planter

Source: Frederick Law Olmsted, A Journey in the Back Country (New York, 1860, 1863), pp. 158, 160–162, 170–171, 173–174, 176, 197–198, 200–204.

I have considered the condition and prospects of the white race in the South a much more important subject, and one, at this time, much more in want of exposition than that of the African. But the great difference in the mode of life of the slaves when living on large plantations, and when living on farms or in town establishments, or on such small plantations that they are intimately associated with white families, has seemed to me to have been so much overlooked by writers, that I have departed widely from the narrative with which this volume commenced, and drawn from my traveling notes of a previous year, to more fully display it.

Continuing the horseback journey commenced in the rich cotton-bearing soils which border the Mississippi River, I turned eastward, not far above Natchez, and pursued an indirect route towards Tuscaloosa in Alabama. The country grew less fertile, and the plantations smaller. The number of whites (not of negroes) living upon plantations of the class chiefly described thus far in this volume (and in two instances, at length, in my first volume), is, of course, small. The more common sort of plantations and the common middle-class planter can hardly be seen by a tourist in any other way than that I now pursued, traveling in the interior, away from the rivers and the ordinary lines of communication, and independently of public conveyances. . . .

The majority of the interior plantations which came under my observation belong to resident planters, and are from four hundred to one thousand acres in extent, the average being perhaps six hundred acres. The number of negroes on each varies from ten to forty, more frequently being between twenty and thirty. Where there are fewer than ten negroes, the owners are frequently seen holding a plow among them; where there are over twenty, a white overseer is usually employed, the owner perhaps directing, but seldom personally superintending, the field labor. . . .

. . . In respect to the enjoyment of material comforts, and the exercise of taste in the arrangement of their houses and grounds, the condition of these planters, while it is superior to that of the Texans, is far below that of northern farmers of one quarter their wealth. But an acquaintance with their style of living can only be obtained from details, and these I shall again give by extracts from my journal, showing how I chanced to be entertained night after night, premising that I took no little pains to select the most comfortable quarters in the neighborhood which I reached at the close of the day. To avoid repetition, I will merely say with regard to diet, that bacon, corn-bread and coffee invariably appeared at every meal; but, besides this, either at breakfast or supper, a fried fowl, "biscuit" of wheat flour, with butter were added—the biscuit invariably made heavy, doughy and indigestible with shortening (fat), and brought to table in relays, to be eaten as hot as possible with melting butter. Molasses usually, honey frequently, and, as a rare exception, potatoes and green peas were added to the board. Whiskey was seldom offered me, and only once any other beverage except the abominable preparation which passes for coffee.

Until I reached the softly rounded hills, with occasional small prairies, through which flows the Tombigbee, in the eastern part of the State, the scenery was monotonous and somber. The predominating foliage of that of the black-oak, black-jack, and pine, except in the intervale lands, where the profuse and bright-colored vegetation common to the latitude is generally met with in great variety. . . .

A little after sunset I came to an unusually promising plantation, the dwelling being within a large inclosure, in which there was a well-kept southern sward shaded by fine trees. The house, of the usual form, was painted white, and the large number of neat out-buildings seemed to indicate opulence, and, I thought, unusual good taste in its owner. . . .

My horse stood in the yard till quite dark, the negroes not coming in from the cotton-field. I proposed twice to take him to the stable, but was told not to—the niggers would come up soon and attend to him. Just as we were called to supper, the negroes began to make their appearance, getting over a fence with their hoes, and the master called to one to put the horse in the stable, and to "take good care of him." "I want him to have all the corn he'll eat," said I. "Yes, sir--feed him well; do you hear, there?"

The house was meagerly furnished within, not nearly as well as the most common New England farm-house. I saw no books and no decorations. The interior wood-work was unpainted.

At supper there were three negro girls in attendance—two children of twelve or fourteen years of age, and an older one, but in a few moments they all disappeared. The mistress called aloud several times, and at length the oldest came, bringing in hot biscuit.

"Where's Suke and Bet?"

"In the kitchen, missus."

"Tell them both to come to me, right off."

A few minutes afterwards, one of the girls slunk in and stood behind me, at the furthest point from her mistress. Presently she was discovered.

"You, Bet, are you there? Come here! come here to me! close to me! (*Slap, slap, slap.*) Now, why don't you stay in here? (*Slap, slap, slap,* on the side of the head.*) I know! you want to be out in the kitchen with them Indians! (*Slap, slap, slap.*) Now see if you can stay here." (*Slap!*) The other girl didn't come in at all, and was forgotten.

As soon as supper was over my hostess exclaimed, "Now, you Bet, stop crying there, and do you go right straight home; mind you run every step of the way, and if you stop one minute in the kitchen you'd better look out. Begone!" During the time I was in the house she was incessantly scolding the servants, in a manner very disagreeable to me to hear, though they seemed to regard it very little.

The Indians, I learned, lived some miles away, and were hired to hoe cotton. I inquired their wages. "Well, it costs me about four bits (fifty cents) a day" (including food, probably). They worked well for a few days at a time; were better at picking than at hoeing. "They don't pick so much in a day as niggers, but do it better." The women said they were good for nothing, and her husband had no business to plant so much cotton that he couldn't tend it with his own slave hands. . . .

. . . Almost immediately afterwards he charged me a dollar for my entertainment, which I paid, notwithstanding the value of the tent was several times that amount. Hospitality to travelers is so entirely a matter of business with the common planters.

I passed the hoe-gang at work in the cotton-field, the overseer lounging among them carrying a whip; there were ten or twelve of them; none looked up at me. Within ten minutes I passed five who were plowing, with no overseer or driver in sight, and every one stopped their plows to gaze at me.

The next day, I passed a number of small Indian farms, very badly cultivated—the corn nearly concealed by weeds. The soil became poorer than before, and the cabins of poor people more frequent. . . . The next house, at which I arrived, was one of the commonest sort of cabins. I had passed twenty like it during the day, and I thought I would take the opportunity to get an interior knowledge of them. The fact that a horse and wagon were kept, and that a considerable area of land in the rear of the cabin was planted with cotton, showed that the family were by no means of the lowest class, yet, as they were not able even to hire a slave, they may be considered to represent very favorably, I believe, the condition of the poor whites of the plantation districts. The whites of the county, I observe, by the census, are three to one of the slaves; in the nearest adjoining county, the proportion is reversed; and within a few miles the soil was richer, and large plantations occurred.

It was raining, and nearly nine o'clock. The door of the cabin was open, and I rode up and conversed with the occupant as he stood within. He said that he was not in the habit of taking travelers, and his wife was about sick, but if I was a mind to put up with common fare, he didn't care. . . .

The house was all comprised in a single room, twenty-eight by twenty-five feet in area, and open to the roof above. There was a large fireplace at one end and a door on each side—no windows at all. Two bedsteads, a spinning-wheel, a packing-case, which served as a bureau, a cupboard, made of rough-hewn slabs, two or three deer-skin seated chairs, a Connecticut clock, and a large poster of Jayne's patent medicines, constituted all the visible furniture either useful or ornamental in purpose. A little girl immediately, without having had any directions to do so, got a frying-pan and a chunk of bacon from the cupboard, and cutting slices from the latter, set it frying for my supper. The woman of the house sat sulkily in a chair tilted back and leaning against the logs, spitting occasionally at the fire, but took no notice of me, barely nodding when I saluted her. A baby lay crying on the floor. I quieted it and amused it with my watch till the little girl, having made "coffee" and put a piece of corn-bread on the table with the bacon, took charge of it. . . .

At breakfast occurred the following conversation:

"Are there many niggers in New York?"

"Very few."

"How do you get your work done?"

"There are many Irish and German people constantly coming there who are glad to get work to do."

"Oh, and you have them for slaves?"

"They want money and are willing to work for it. A great many American-born work for wages, too."

"What do you have to pay?"

"Ten or twelve dollars a month."

"There was a heap of Irishmen to work on the railroad; they was paid a dollar a day; there was a good many Americans, too, but mostly they had little carts and mules, and hauled dirt and sich like. They was paid twenty-five or thirty dollars a month and found."

"What did they find them?"

"Oh, blanket and shoes, I expect; they put up kind o'tents like for 'em to sleep in all together."

"What food did they find them?"

"Oh, common food; bacon and meal."

"What do they generally give the niggers on the plantations here?"

"A peck of meal and three pound of bacon is what they call 'lowance, in general, I believe. It takes a heap o'meat on a big plantation. I was on one of William R. King's plantation over in Alabamy, where there was about fifty niggers, one Sunday last summer, and I see 'em weighin' outen the meat. Tell you, it took a powerful heap on it. They had an old nigger to weigh it out, and he warn't no ways partickler about the weight. He just took and chopped it off, middlins, in chunks, and he'd throw 'em into the scales, and if a piece weighted a pound or two over he wouldn't mind it; he never took none back. Ain't niggers all-fired sassy at the North?"

"No, not particularly."

"Ain't they all free there? I hearn so."

"Yes."

"Well, how do they get along when they's free?"

"I never have seen a great many, to know their circumstances very well. Right about where I live they seem to me to live quite comfortably; more so than the niggers on these big plantations do, I should think."

"O! They have a mighty hard time on the big plantations. I'd ruther be dead than to be a nigger on one of these big plantations."

"Why, I thought they were pretty well taken care of on them."

The man and his wife both looked at me as if surprised, and smiled.

"Why, they are well fed, are they not?"

"Oh, but they work 'em so hard. My God, sir, in pickin' time on these big plantations they start 'em to work 'fore light, and they don't give 'em time to eat."

"I supposed they generally gave them an hour or two at noon."

"No, sir; they just carry a piece of bread and meat in their pockets and they eat it when they can, standin' up. They have a hard life on't, that's a fact. I reckon you can get along about as well withouten slaves as with'em, can't you, in New York?"

"In New York there is not nearly so large a proportion of very rich men as here. There are very few people who farm over three hundred acres, and the greater number—nineteen out of twenty, I suppose—work themselves with the hands they employ. Yes, I think it's better than it is here, for all concerned, a great deal. Folks that can't afford to buy niggers get along a great deal better in the free States, I think; and I guess that those who could afford to have niggers get along better without them."

"I no doubt that's so. I wish there warn't no niggers here. They are a great cuss to this country, I expect. But 't wouldn't do to free 'em; that wouldn't do no how!"

"Are there many people here who think slavery a curse to the country?"

"Oh, yes, a great many. I reckon the majority would be right glad if we could get rid of the niggers. But it wouldn't never do to free 'em and leave 'em here. I don't know anybody, hardly, in favor of that. Make 'em free and leave 'em here and they'd steal every thing we made. Nobody couldn't live here then."

These views of slavery seem to be universal among people of this class. They were repeated to me at least a dozen times.

Antebellum Paternalism in Microcosm

HOUSEHOLD SLAVERY *changed least over time. Between the colonial and antebellum eras, its elements remained the same—a restrictive, intimate setting for the inescapably intense relations among blacks and whites that reduced slavery to its essentials. "A relentless reciprocity binds the colonized to the colonizer—his product and his faith." This is a process, Sartre argues, in which the master cannot make his slave an object without himself becoming a dehumanized creature. In slave society households, where the inherent contradictions of slavery were most apparent, it was sometimes difficult to distinguish the hunter and the hunted, the dancer and the dance:*

> *A petrified ideology devotes itself to regarding human beings as talking beasts. But it does so in vain, for the colonizers must recognize them first, even to give them the harshest or most insulting of orders. And since the colonizers cannot constantly supervise the colonized, the colonizers must resolve to trust them. No one can treat a man like a dog without first regarding him as a man. The impossible dehumanization of the oppressed, on the other side of the coin, becomes the alienation of the oppressor. It is the oppressor himself who restores, with the slightest gesture, the humanity he seeks to destroy; and, since he denies humanity in others, he regards it everywhere as his enemy. To handle this, the colonizer must assume the opaque rigidity and imperviousness of stone. In short, he must dehumanize himself, as well.*[9]

61. "He Denies Humanity in Others. . . . To Handle This, the Colonizer Must Assume the Opaque Rigidity and Imperviousness of Stone"

Source: T. D. Jones to Eliza, Princess Anne, Somerset County, Maryland, September 7, 1860, Butler (Thomas and Family) Papers, Louisiana State University Department of Archives and Manuscripts.

Princess Anne Somerset Co. Md
Septr. 7th. 1860

Eliza,

About two months ago Sandy handed me a letter directed to Mr. Levin Waters from you, requesting me to let you hear from your daughter Jennie; and expressing the hope that I will let her go to live with you. I read your letter to her. She seemed glad to hear from you, & her countenance lightened up with [a] Smile at the names of Aunt Liza & Tillie Anne (as she calls you and her Sister). But she says she does not want to go away from her Master. She is a sprightly lively active girl: & has injoyed good health, except that she has suffered for some time from three very severe boils—one on the top of her head, one over her left ear & one on

9. Jean-Paul Sartre, Introduction to Albert Memmi, *The Colonizer and the Colonized* (Boston, 1965), pp. xxvii–xxviii.

the side of her neck, the last just ruptured. She is very fond of me &
is a considerable annoyance to me for I cannot keep her off my
heels in the street, & viewing her in the light of a little orphan I
cannot spurn her carresses. Sandy & Sally are as well as usual:
Charlotte has had a severe and dangerous attack of brain fever, but
is now able to perform her duties, her child Sarah is well. As to
letting Jennie go to live with you I can hardly make up my mind
what to say. I would be reluctant to part with her. She is petted as
you used to be, she is a watchful little Spy as you used to be. She
has a good disposition, is neither cross, obstinate nor mischievous:
she is very useful for her services in the house, for going on
errands, and for nursing: & I should miss her very much. Nevertheless I know how to estimate the claims of a Mother and to appreci-
ate the affection of a Mother for her child. A request has been
made of me thro' Mr. Henry Morris to let Jennie go to you, but I
have not yet come to a decision.

However I profess to be a christian & have the happy and com-
forting assurance that I am, by the grace of God, what I profess to
be. I am governed by christian principles which impose upon me
the obligation to love mercy deal justly and walk humbly. Mercy
will open a listening ear to your request, justice will prompt me to
do what is right, and humility constrains me to condescend to answer the communication of her who, although formerly my servant, is not, on that account excluded from the consideration of
human sympathy, altho' you make no inquiry after my welfare,
were you restrained by indignation or malice because I parted with
you? I think you will acknowledge that I was to you a kind &
forbearing master & that you were an ungrateful Servant, & I think
you feel assured that if you had conducted yourself faithfully, no
offer would have tempted me to part with you. Your tender &
affectionate services to your afflicted former Mistress, created in
me an attachment for you, that nothing but your ingratitude &
faithlessness could have broken. But situated as I was after the
death of dear beloved and still lamented wife, the only alternative
presented to me was to quit house keeping or part with you—a painful one. Up to the period of this sad event you were as fine a Servant
as I ever knew. I wish you well. I am glad you have a good home &
hope you will try to deserve it. Let me advise you as your former
Master—as one who takes an interest in your welbeing in this

world, and still greater interest for welbeing in the eternal world & above as the one who stood sponsor for you in baptism, to repent of your misdeeds, to cease to do evil & learn to do well, to live up to the precepts of the gospel, & by the faith once delivered to the Saints, & daily pray to God, thro' Jesus Christ, for his good spirit to help your infirmities & to lead you in the way everlasting. Serve your heavenly Master & your present owner faithfully, and be assured that I greatly regret the occasion that resulted in the separation of you from your child. Those to whom you sent your love return their's to you. With unfeigned benevolence & charity

Your former owner
T. D. JONES

62. "IT IS THE OPPRESSOR HIMSELF WHO RESTORES . . . THE HUMANITY HE SEEKS TO DESTROY"

DAVID GAVIN's *reflections on the death of "my Man Friday" could have been written by Landon Carter for Jack Lubbar or Nassau. Gavin by his own admission was archaic; and Friday, an ancient slave, was his window on the past, and a link between the planter and his grandparents and family history. For Gavin, Friday was a way of escape into an unrecoverable past from a present in which he and other patriarchs (and matriarchs such as Rachel O'Connor) were so out of step.*

SOURCE: David Gavin Diary, Southern Historical Collection, University of North Carolina Archives.

Sat. May 31, 1856. Times are sadly different now to what they were when I was a boy . . . people worked for a liveing then, those who did not have property to support them, now many live on credit, or by some other swindling process. I remember in 1818 my father moved from this place to the old Belton place, now Estate of Wm Murray's, before that my mother spun, wove cloth, cooked and occasionally went to cow pen to milk the cows, father plowed and drove the waggon, made shoes and did other work. My mother always seed to her cooking and did a good deal of it, has her spinning and weaveing all done for the whole plantation white and black, no cloth or negro shoes were bought whilst father and mother lived, father made his own negro shoes and mother the clothes, few persons were in debt then except for property bought, and people were generally cautious of going in debt, and when in, tried to get out, now the object seems to be to get in and shirk round getting out as long as possible, and imprisonment for debt being now abolished and the homestead law allowing a bankrupt to retain a nice property, there is every inducement for the dishonest to swindle all they can, and temptations for the honest (if any) to forsake its paths. . . .

Monday June 23, 1856. At Indian Field church yesterday. . . . Men, manner and things change wonderfully in this changeable world. When I was a boy twenty-five years ago it was a great thing to have made a trip to Mississippi, it took 20 days, then it became more common and took 16 days, and I came once in fourteen from the Eastern boundary. Now men and women esteem it a small matter, they take the R. Road & stage and perform the trip in 2 or 3 days, it is too tedious and slow on horseback or with a carriage. But 25 or 30 years ago few persons in this section of country were in debt and when a man contracted a debt he generally made arrangements to pay it, now the general rule is if he makes any arrangements about it, it is to avoid its payment. Negroes were then $175 & 200.00 per head by the plantation or number, men $4 & 500.00 women $3 & 400.00, now plantations or gangs are from four to six hundred dollars, men from 8 to $1100.00 & women from $6 to 800.00, cotton about the same then as now, from 8 to 11 cts per lb. I believe however, that more is made to the hand for now there is little spinning done, most persons depending on buying their clothes and meat, those times 25 or 30 years it was rare for a farmer to buy either his clothes, shoes or bacon, all were made at home. Negro men then hired out for from $3 to six dollars per month now from ten to fifteen dollars per month. Our pine lands then sold for from ten to twenty five cents per acre now from one to three dollars per acre. People then went to church on foot, on horseback or in a waggon, now it is on horseback, in a buggy or carriage, with a waiting boy or boys.

July 4, 1856. To-day is the annaversary of American independence the 80th. 1776, I have no doubt in many parts there will be pretensions of great rejoiceings, but I cannot really rejoice for a fredom which allows every bankrupt, swindler, thief and scoundrel, traitor and seller of his vote to be placed on an equality with myself, which allows men to openly talk, plan and threaten to take away my property, threaten and abuse my person and even destroy my property with impunity. The Northern abolitionists are threatening and planning to take away or destroy the value of our slave property, and the demon democracy, by its leveling principles, universal suffrage, and numerous popular elections, homestead laws, and bribery are sapping the foundation of the rights of property in every thing.

August 29, 1856. My old man Friday is alive yet, he has dropsy in the chest, his testicle bag is swollen very much and has been larger than now, Dr. D. W. Moorer thinks it is wind and not water that causes it to sweell, he is ruptured. . . . I am giveing him cream of tartar and burnt coperas morning & night, with twelve pills per day made of flag & button snake root equal quantities with a little salt petre, with molasses or honey and enough of soft pine gum to make them stick, and a diet drink made of the inside bark of the root of Elder, at first I gave him a tea of the root of the mountain rosemary, but the elder seems to act better. . . .

Sat. Sept. 13, 1856. My old man Friday died this morning before day of dropsy in the chest . . . he has been so bad that he could not help himself, Mike nursed him night and day assisted by Big Jim and his daughter Mary. I have had him in possession since February 1843, he carried my keys and attended to feeding the horses and attending to my cattle, hogs and stock generall as long as he was able, and a great manager of hogs he was, and could remember more about the stock than I could; only yesterday he was directing Mike that the young hogs must be spayed next week, and had thread carried to him to see if there was enough of the right kind. After he was unable to do any thing much but ride after the hogs he noticed the yard and the little negroes and would remind me of many little matters to be attended to. He served my Grandfather and grandmother Gavin, my father not haveing come into possession of him because he died in 1838 before his mother who died in 1842. His (Friday's) mother was my grandmother Gavin's cook and died in Perry Co. Miss. 1843 or 4. He seemed like a connecting link between me and grand-father and grand-

mother Gavin, for he could talk to me and tell me of the actings
and doing of them and others of the olden time, about the connections of the family, their names and where they lived and moved to
or from. He says he was large enough to open the gate for people in
the Revolutionary war, was at the defeat of Gen. Sumpter (at
Fishing creek) during the revolution, that his master had to run,
and his mother Chloe got an old woman to claim herself and children to keep the tories and Brittish from takeing them. By these
circumstances, I suppose he was over eighty years old considerably.
He was older than my father and if he had lived until now he would
have been about 77 years old. He has lived a good number of years
more than I expect, but even that is short or appears a short time,
but few attain four score years, yet he must have been over. He
told me after dinner yesterday he could not live through the night.

63. "THE COLONIZERS MUST RESOLVE TO TRUST THEM"

RACHEL O'CONNOR *was an exceptional person, a strong, resourceful, and
admirable woman who lived in a time and place where male dominance
was the norm—rampant and unchallenged. Her letters describe a lonely,
middle-aged existence as a widow on a small cotton plantation in West
Feliciana Parish, Louisiana. Rachel mistrusted men—particularly white
men—deeply and bitterly. Her only contacts with whites were with the
overseers (most of whom she mistrusted because they chased the slave
women) and her brother (who owned the plantation), whom she
adored—and feared (realizing in her woman's heart that she knew so
much more about her plantation and what she was doing that he
thought she did).*

    *So Rachel's life was her slaves. In other ways she was more represen-
tative of the small planters of her time—she was deeply religious and a
matriarch to all her slaves, as well as to her nieces and nephews:
"Death must come & we know not the time," she wrote a niece in 1839.
"Obedience to Parents is the only promise in the ten Commandments of
a long life, and if a Parent ever experiences anything Heavenly on earth
it is from Dutiful children." Throughout her correspondence she talks
about "her little favorite," Isaac; but her maternal and protective views
of this child and the other blacks were true to the values of her age. Her
Christian piety was tempered by a cold, mercenary regard for the profits
and losses of slave births: "There is a fine chance of little negroes
coming on (should a blessing continue to attend them). They may
greatly assist in a few years." Another time she said of Isaac: "My little
favorite boy is worth a large amount. He can work in the garden
(some) already and his little innocent talk is my greatest company."[10]*

In April, 1836, Rachel reported on the health, care and feeding of the pregnant women, mothers, and their slave infants:

> Two [children] has been born here since I came home from your House. They are fine babies, one was a daughter of Pless's who is now a grandmother and Patience a great grandmother. I have sixteen little ones, the oldest six years old the 6 of July last, all fine healthy little children. My greatest favorite is to all appearance healthy, but so lean and thin in flesh that I get uneasy about him very often. Bridget the Woman that had her child the 21 of February last while I was with you will soon have another. She has four children the oldest only six years old July. She has had a dreadful rising on the thumb of her right hand.[11]

Like the colonial patriarchs before her, Rachel maintained a vigilant guard over her slaves' domestic lives. She was particularly incensed by black women who slept with their overseers. "I am glad to hear of your house girls behaving well," she wrote in 1834. "I have no doubt of their being right in judging mean low white men being their chief cause of their disobedience. It is all ways the case where they are, they cause more punishments to be inflicted, amongst the poor ignorant slaves, than all else they comit." When Leven, an overseer for three years, died, she again released her loneliness and frustration in real and imagined anxieties about the white men who oppressed her as well as her slaves: "I have lost poor Leven, one of the most faithful black Men, who ever lived, he was truth and honesty, and without a fault, that I ever discovered. He has overseed the plantation nearly three years and done much better than any white Man ever done here, and I lived a quiet life."[12]

SOURCE: Letters of Rachel O'Connor to David Weeks (her brother), Mary C. Weeks (her sister-in-law), and Mrs. A. F. Conrad, January 11, 1830–July 30, 1836, Bayou Sarah–St. Francisville, West Feliciana Parish, La., Louisiana State University Department of Archives and Manuscripts.

To Mary C. Conrad, January 11, 1830

My health has become so good that I have all most forgotten my age. I can attend to my affairs with ease [illegible] . . . to do some

10. Rachel O'Connor to Francis Weeks, January 9, 1839; to A. F. Conrad, March 18, 1836.

11. Rachel O'Connor to Mary Weeks, April 5, 1836.

12. Rachel O'Connor to Mary Weeks, July 6, 1834; September 4, 1840.

good for a while. You write so loving and kind to me that my very Heart overflows with gratitude and I will assure you that the confidence you place in me shall not be abused and promise to take the same care that I ever have done, and render a just account of every amt. to yourself & your Brother the greatest earthly wish that I now entertain is to afford you satisfaction. I have sixteen little negro children a raising the oldest of the sixteen a little turned of six years old all very healthy children excepting my little favorite *Isaac* he is subject to a cough but seldom sick enough to lay up. The poor little fellow is laying at my feet sound asleep. I wish I did not love him as I do but it is so and I cannot help it.

To Her Brother, April 10, 1830

The work of the plantation goes on very smoothly nothing amiss since you were over, nearly done planting cotton seed & corn. Mr. Patrick the overseer has a very sore throat and looks bad, but continues very attentive to his business, I sincerely hope he may raise a good crop, the negroes are all well, and the teams in fine order. I should indeed be very glad to go over to see your lovely family, and hope that the time may come that I can be spared without feeling as much uneasiness as at present if I should leave home there is several small children, two of them sucking babies and Hariet will soon have her young one, if no misfortune should befall her. Henny & Sarah, theirs, in five or six mon[ths] more, which will require my attention for some time If I should live, and I feel a greater desire to take care of them since I know they are yours, than I have done for seven years past.

To Her Brother, August 26, 1832

Mr Mulkey [the new overseer] behaves verry well and manages with much ease, I believe no white person troubles the quarter now, I am verry particular to deliver your orders as soon as they come, and so far he has done his duty in every respect, and I yet think him a smart man on a plantation, he has about twenty thousand weight of cotton picked, and the gin runing for the start, he has got up a part of the little wild mares and broke them to the gin. He is careful of the horses and all the stock . . . I have bought three

barrels of Lime to have the negro Houses whitewashed, as all the
people near here are going to try to keep the Cholera away, I have
all the milk churned everry morning to have it sweet for them,
which is said to be best for them to eat.

To Her Brother, October 23, 1833

. . . Mulkey is gathering the corn, it holds out better than I
expected when I wrote last I had raised a hope he would behave
better but I now think it very doubtful he is a shameless being,
nearly as bad as Patrick in the same way if it was not for that he
could oversee very well but as it is he has too many ladies to please
he appears to have a desire of saying something about another year
but I have given him no opportunity, neither will I urge him in the
least you may Judge of his conduct when you come.

A man by the name of Germany, who is said to be a good sober
industrious man applied to me for an overseers birth, I told him I
would write to you and that he would have to wait for your answer.
He oversees for Mr Bowman last year and he behaved very well
which I had often hear'd them both say before he left there today I
talked to Mr & Mrs Bowman particularly about Germany. They
both spoke highly of him, as a very sober industrious good man he
has a wife but no children, no negroes. His Father and family lives
three miles from Lewis Davis, and said to be industrious people.
Mr Bowman said there would be no danger of Germany behaving
as overseers commonly did amongst the negroes, that he was too
fond of his wife to behave in that way.

To Her Brother, October 31, 1833

. . . Mulkey behaves very well in every respect, excepting one,
and in that I must say he is worse than Patrick ever was, while he
oversee here, but I dont say anything to him about it, now I wish to
part in peace. Ma[rgare]t Downs has engaged him for next year to
oversee seventeen hands and gives the same that he gets here so
Mulkey says I hope they may do well he is a smart overseer but a
dirty beast after all.

To Her Brother, November 20, 1833

I have written once since I received your last, but I did not mention the behavior of the negro boys that I sent to Mr. Conrad. I had not made their new coats for them this fall, their last winter ones were quite good and the warning so short that I had no time to prepare clothes for them, as I should like to have done, but done as well as I could and started them the next morning after hearing of it at 12 o'clock the day previous. After they were gone I became very uneasy about there being at the sugar works without their new coats. I concluded to make each of that five, a good warm blanket coat, and send them down by Arthur which I done. Arthur returned home the next day with a letter from Mr Conrad saying that Harry, Eben & Littleton had left him and undertaken to make their home which by some means were taken and lodged in jail at Batton Rouge where he found them and took them back again to his plantation, where he says they behaved very well since.

I cannot help thinking that Mulkey gave them bad advice, or they never would have thought of acting so, them boys are too young, to undertake the likes, unless encouraged by some person. Dave, he loves I expect he advised him to behave well, and Frank being only eighteen years of age, he concluded to remain with Dave, the other three Mulkey had a particular spite at. Eben caught him and Eliza together, and told Mrs Mulkey of it which caused a great fuss, but as he was guilty he could not whip Eben unless I said so which I was very clear of doing. She and Eben were to go together as man & wife, but now I dont expect he will take her. The next day, the young madamn was confined to her room where I found her & whipped her myself and then cut her curls off and then started her to the field, where she has been ever since without grunting once. Mulkey knew all that I done and what it was for but never mentioned it to me. He now enjoys the company of his Ladies undisturbed, and from what I can hear he rejoiced on hearing the boys had to be whipped. If I did not think his talking to them had been the cause of their acting as they have of course I could blame none but themselves but as it is I hate the wretch on earth.

To Her Brother, December 6, 1833

In the first instance Harry & Frank came home [from Conrad's] on the first of this month. Frank looked so much worsted, that I was sorry for him. Harry did not look so bad. They told me that they left Eben sick, which alarmed me and I fixed Arthur immediately, and started him down to see about him and to bring him home by some means or other. I also wrote to Mr. Conrad to let Dave & Littleton come at the same time. Without the smallest idea of giving offence, or being refused. He ordered Arthur home without either saying, or writing an answer to my letter. So I do not know whether he ever intends to let me hear from the boys again, or not. They may be Dead by this time, a number Died on that plantation, with the cholera, or something else, very lately. The overseer and Driver are the cruelest beings I ever heard of. If the boys are a live, I wish you would send them home.

To Her Sister-in-Law, April 5, 1836

I wish Patty & Louisa great luck with there little ones, the latter is really smart, her other babe is only a year old. Two has been born here since I came home from your House. They are fine babies one was a daughter of Pless's who is now a grand mother and Patience a great grand mother. I have sixteen little ones, the oldest six years old the 6 of July last, all fine healthy little children. My greatest favourite is to all appearance healthy, but so lean and thin in flesh that I get uneasy about him very often. Bridget the woman that had her child the 21 of February last while I was with you will soon have another. She has four children the oldest only six years old July.

To Mrs. A. F. Conrad, July 30, 1836

The appearance of a renewal of old & grevious afflictions has almost distracted me never did I feel more humbled than I do at the present moment. God is my witness that I wish to act right since the arrival of your letter I have walked the garden with up lifted hands in fervent Prayer to my God laying my situation before him who knows all things and on my knees with my face to the floor asked his assistance. Praying to be directed the way that is right & now my Dearly beloved friend I must ask yourself & my sister to consider my unfortunate disposition which my Dearly beloved Brother was well aware of & could have informed you that to separate me from this plantation & the slaves on it would cause the remainder of my days to pass off in deep sorrow. If I could only be as many others in the world are I would willingly sign anything you would think proper but as it is and to change the affair from what it was in the commencement would be in a manner consenting to my own misery & wretchedness. . . . I am alone in the World, My Mothers children are all gone before me. . . . You will no doubt, find yourself disgusted with the acknowledgment I make of the attachment I feel towards those negroes on this place: but I do not see that I could do otherwise, after the care that I have taken to raise them and the blessings the Lord of Heaven & Earth bestowed in causing them to prosper under my care.

64. Poor Whites

ABOARD A SHIP *with a party of emigrants moving their families and possessions into the newer areas of the Southwest, Olmsted confronted poor white Americans, who in their own vernacular expressed eloquently and tragically the dilemma that would not be resolved by anything less than war: It wasn't right to keep Negroes as slaves, but if they were free, "they'd all think themselves just as good as we."*

SOURCE: Frederick Law Olmsted, *The Seaboard Slave States in the Years 1853–1854*, 2 vols. (1856; New York, 1904), 2:216, 217–219.

On the forecastle-deck there was a party of emigrants, moving with wagons. There were three men, a father and his two sons, or sons-in-law, with their families, including a dozen or more women and children. They had two wagons, covered with calico and bedticks, supported by hoops, in which they carried their furniture and stores, and in which they also slept at night, the women in one, and the men in the other. They had six horses, two mules, and two pair of cattle with them. I asked the old man why he had taken his cattle along with him, when he was going so far by sea, and found that he had informed himself accurately of what it would cost him to hire or buy cattle at Galveston. . . .

. . . They should try to find some heavy-timbered land, good land, and go to clearing; didn't calculate to make any crops the first year—didn't calculate on it, though perhaps they might if they had good luck. They had come from an eastern county of Alabama. Had sold out his farm for two dollars an acre; best land in the district was worth four; land was naturally kind of thin, and now't was pretty much all worn out there. He had moved first from North Carolina, with his father. They never made anything to sell but cotton; made corn for their own use. Never had any negroes; reckoned he'd done better or about as well as if he had them; reckoned a little better on the whole. No, he should not work negroes in Texas. "Niggers is so kerless, and want so much lookin' after; they is so monstrous lazy; they won't do no work, you know, less you are clus to 'em all the time, and I don't feel like it. I couldn't, at my time of life, begin a'using the lash; and you know they do have to take that, all on 'em—and a heap on't, sometimes."

"I don't know much about it; they don't have slaves where I live."

"Then you come from a Free State; well, they've talked some of makin' Alabamy a Free State."

"I didn't know that."

"Oh, yes, there was a good deal of talk one time, as if they was goin' to do it right off. Oh, yes; there was two or three of the States this way, one time, come pretty nigh freein' the niggers—lettin' 'em all go free."

"And what do you think of it?"

"Well, I'll tell you what I think on it; I'd like it if we could get rid on 'em to yonst. I wouldn't like to hev 'em freed, if they was gwine to hang 'round. They ought to get some country, and put 'em war they could be by themselves. It wouldn't do no good to free 'em, and let 'em hang round, because they is so monstrous lazy; if they hadn't got nobody to take keer on 'em, you see they wouldn't do nothin' but juss nat'rally laze round, and steal, and pilfer, and no man couldn't live, you see, war they was—if they was free, no man couldn't live. And then, I've two objections; that's one on 'em—no man couldn't live—and this ere's the other: Now suppose they was free, you see they'd all think themselves just as good as we; of course they would, if they was free. Now, just suppose you had a family of children, how would you like to hev a niggar feelin' just as good as a white man? how'd you like to hev a niggar steppin' up to your darter? Of course you would n't, and that's the reason I would n't like to hev 'em free; but I tell you, I don't think its right to hev 'em slaves so; that's the fac—taant right to keep 'em as they is."

C. Slaves Among Themselves

THE SOURCES *for blacks and whites outside their plantation routines present a different reality. The documents on the large and well-organized plantations (the memoranda to overseers and articles in agricultural journals) are set-pieces—portraits of actors posed in conventional roles and settings. But the records on slaves among their own people and on their own time are snapshots—vivid though fleeting glimpses of whites and blacks in unguarded moments. The accounts of resistance (from the day-to-day variety to the rebellions and conspiracies of Denmark Vesey and Nat Turner) are especially noteworthy as views of a slave culture that whites scarcely understood.*

The following documents help correct an inescapable conclusion of interpretations of American Negro slavery limited to the preceding evidence on plantation life from the whites' point of view—namely, that for most slaves the plantation must have been an all-encompassing experience. The sources, originating in black families, music, religion, day-to-day resistance, and insurrection, indicate that slaves had a family life of their own; that much of their community and culture was untouched by white values; and that some of their activities were beyond the control of even the most diligent and well-organized planter.

Family Life

A THOROUGH *investigation of slave family life is long overdue. There are intriguing views in documentary evidence. In the colonial period tobacco planters of the Chesapeake Bay often intervened in their slaves' domestic squabbles, purchased a mate and settled the new partners together, and occasionally placed a black youngster in a special task at his parent's request. In the Revolutionary era some enlightened masters advertised plantations for sale in newspapers, and mentioned that slaves would remain in families, or would not be removed from the plantation for any reason. In the same period most of the wealthy South Carolina planters, and a sizeable number of the moderately well-to-do, listed slaves in families in probate records (wills and estate inventories).*

After the abolition of the African slave trade in 1808, and the end of a reliable outside source of new laborers, whites realized they had to rely on the natural increase of their own slaves. By improving the slaves' material conditions and maintaining stable households, they sought to raise the birth rate. The interstate slave trade to the lower South, an important source of wealth for the upper South, made whites more supportive of black family life. Whether the end of the trade and slave raising also encouraged the use of studs as well as a more conventional family life of husbands and fathers is still not well known. The planters' insistence on a semblance of family was also a part of the "Management of Negroes" movement that produced the other signs of a more methodical regard for labor practices—hospitals, chapels, and nurseries. Presumably slaves in families were contented workers who were not so inclined to run off or rebel. Owners associated orderly domestic relations for slaves with well-run plantations:

> No rule that I have stated is of more importance than that relating to negroes marrying out of the plantation. It seems to me . . . it is utterly impossible to have any method, or regularity where the men and women are permitted to take wives and husbands indiscriminately off the plantation. Negroes are very much disposed to pursue a course of this kind. . . . The inconveniences that at once strikes one as arising out of such a practice are these. . . .
>
> Secondly—Wherever their wives live, there they consider their homes. . . .
>
> Thirdly—It creates a feeling of independence, from being, of right, out of the control of their master for a time.
>
> Fourthly—They are repeatedly exposed to temptations from meeting and associating with negroes from different directions, and with various habits and views. . . .
>
> Sixthly—When a man and his wife belong to different persons, they are liable to be separated from each other, as well as their children, either by the caprice of either of the parties, or where there is a sale of property. This keeps up an unsettled state of things, and gives rise to repeated new connexions.[13]

Family life also protected some slaves psychologically. But for others, the love between a man and woman intensified their tragedy:

Mobile [Alabama], May 20, 1854

Dear Sir

I hope you will make some arrangement with Goodman to keep Jackson and his wife together. They seem to be much attached to

---

13. *The Southern Cultivator,* 4 (March 1846): 44.

*each other. I left Jack at 8 O Clock sobbing most cruely. If I could
have purchased another negro of the same value I should have sent
him in the place of Jack. I must for the future decline attending to
business of this sort for besides the trouble of getting them together
(I was all the evening at it) the notereity of this matter, the painful
separation, Etc., Etc., is by no means pleasant.*

Respectively your,
W. H. Trone

Mobile, October 11, 1854

Dear Sir
    *Your boy Jackson has one of my women for a wife and I am
sending her with some others to my plantation. She seems to be a
good deal distressed about her husband. If you will sell the Boy at
a fair price I will purchase him. Please let me hear from you.*

Yours respectly,
D. W. Goodman[14]

The historiography of slave family life is on the threshold of a dramatic breakthrough as a new generation of social historians, using demographic techniques and data processing machines, raises questions that
were once considered impossible to ask. Rus Menard (with Lois Carr),
a historian for the St. Mary's City Commission in Maryland, is working
on comparisons of the birth rates of native African and American-born
slave women, in order to determine more precisely when the slave
population in the Chesapeake Bay area began increasing naturally. He
argues that African women, who did not arrive until they were in their
mid-twenties, gave birth to only a child or two. But once their American-
born daughters began bearing children at a significantly earlier age than
their mothers (from about age sixteen), slave family size (hence tillable
land and planter wealth) increased dramatically. Allan Kulikoff, who is
completing a model study of Prince Georges County, Maryland (much
of which is now the suburbs, parking lots, and shopping centers of
greater Washington, D.C.), in the late seventeenth century, has used
several hundred estate inventories to determine on what kinds of plantations, and to what extent, slave children had companions of their own
age to grow up with. And Barry Higman, in one of the best local studies
of slavery to date,[15] has correlated the origin, age, and sex of Jamaican
slaves with type of crop (sugar, ginger, cocoa, coffee), weather, eleva-
tion (gradations of mountain or plain), location, and scale of operation

14. William Phineas Browne Papers, Alabama State Department of
Archives and History.
15. "Slave Population and Economy in Jamaica at the Time of Emancipation" (Ph.D. diss., Department of History, University of the West Indies,
1970).

in order to evaluate with unusual clarity slave birth and death rates and family size.

In 1835 a sizeable number of North Carolina slaves accompanied their owners, who were resettling in Alabama. Separated from their mates and children who were temporarily left behind, they asked their mistress to include the following notes at the end of her letters. The second document, about a separation caused by the Civil War, is a letter from a black man to his wife.

65. "I Have a Great Many Messages"

SOURCE: Sarah Sparkman and slave letters, October–November, 1835, Brownrigg Papers, Southern Historical Collection, University of North Carolina Archives.

Sarah Sparkman to Her Sister,
Near Enfield, October 20, 1835

We are thus far on our journey to the far West Island. Camping out [is] much better than I expected. . . . The Negroes are all in high Spirits, they run and Play like children along the Road. It is remarked by every one that they never saw so many without being chained, and all looked so cheerful and happy last night. They were Fidling to night, Singing Hymns, we travel from 15 to 20 Miles a day, and they set up as late as if they were at Home. Sometimes the Negroes a Mile before us they stop at every Will Spring they find so many. 91 Negroes, and only 4 Whites—we are stared at—such a caravan.

Sarah Sparkman to Her Brother,
General Richard T. Brownrigg, Wythe, November 4, 1835

The Servants request me to send Many Messages to all their Friends and Relations, and your Dave requested me to Write a Letter to his Wife which I will do on the other page, and you can read it to her. You will see what a medly I have written for the Negroes. I hope you will read it to their Friends they say it is the very words they want to say to them you would be glad to see them so contented, and I hope they may continue so. We are encamped near a Meeting House, it is raining very fast. . . .

My Dear Wife

I write these few Lines to inform you of my health which is much better than it has been. I can walk all day and have a good appetite. We get fine Cabbage and good Water and great many Apples and I have seen great Sights. The Mountains and a great Many Towns, Rocks, Rivers, if I only knew my Master was Well and had you with [me?], I should be quite happy to get My Master to say something for you and in his Letter for it would comfort Me to hear from you all. Our Fellow Servants are in good Health and Spirits and all desire their Love to you and accept of my Love and good Wishes for [you, illegible] and my Children and Relations and Friends. May the Lord Bless you My Dear Wife and May we meet again is the Prayer of your Husband, Dave Brownrigg

This is for My Wife Amy, to Let her know that Myself and Children are well and I was Might Glad to hear from our Home but was sorry to hear that Master kept Sick. We have good time, all well and Hearty and all desire their Love to you and all our Friends. I hope to see you and the Children in the Spring. The Children and Polly are well also The Baby grows a little they all send a heap of Love to you and the Children

your Husband Author HOLLEY

My Dear Husband Hardy

I wish to let you know that I think of you often and wish to see you very bad. I have good health and the Children are [looking well?] but feel tired a little, but I see so many sights and have so many good [illegible] I wish you all had some of them. I hope yet to see you. Maria join[s]˙ me in Love to you and all of [our] Friends

your Loving Wife, ROSE

My Dear Wife Anis

I know you would be glad to hear from me and the Boys, we get along very well. The Boys obey me very well. I feel very anxious about you, but hope to hear you are doing well. I long to see you all in the Spring. We get on very fast in our journey and expect to reach our Home in four Weeks. All joine me in love to you and all our Friends.

your affectionate Husband, SANDY

MY DEAR MAMY CHERRY

I miss you very much but we girls talk and laugh and see so many Sights that I am very well satisfied. I was glad to hear from you all last Night, and I hope it will not be long before we all meet. Give my Love to my Granny and other Friends.

your affectionate Daugher, MARRY

MY DEAR MAMY AND SISTER

I was Mighty glad to hear last Night and Master was better and Sister had her Baby. Our Relations are all well that are with us and send a heep of love to her and the Children. Uncle Jacob say[s] tell his Wife he is Well and give his love to her and the Children

your affectionate Daugher, GRACE

Anis gives her Love to her Children and She is very well and all the Children keep well, they are all Satisfied

Sarah Sparkman to Her Sister, Mary W. Brownrigg, Mississippi, January 4, 1836

I have a great many Messages from the Servants they are better satisfied than at first. Anis says she never will be so untill you all come out. She desires her love to her children, says they are all well, and to her love to Phillis. Tome is well now and the Baby Violet has two teeth. India says please to let her know how her Mother and children are in fact they have so much to say about *all* give their love to all their Friends and their best service to Master, and Mistress. Cousin Mary and the children. They have a great deal of liberty in this State, Negro preaching and visiting more than with us.

66. "I TAK MY PEN IN HAND"

SOURCE: D. Walters to Sary ann, February 2, 1863, Terry (William, and Family) Papers, Louisiana State University Department of Archives and Manuscripts.

State of Luseaney, port h[udson]
feby the 2, 1863. Dear wife, i tak my pen in hand to let you no that
my health is inprove a lite. I hope that when this [these] few
line[s] come to hand tha [they] will find you all in Joy good halth.
We have teen [ten] yonk [Yanks] that dace [deserted?] frum the
yonk army, an come to ours. I wante you to give R.B. Sanders
fift[y] dolars to pay Jane [R]ush 41 dolars and you gite the nout
[note?] and take good cair of hite [it], and by 5 buchels of corn,
gite Col sanders to tent [attend] to all thise for you and gite hime
tent to payen yor taxes [i]f he pleses. I want you gite bob to red yor
letear an rite for you, I want you to rite to me soon and bob to rite
soon, I want you to gite all your thing home and take good cair of
them ef Mr. Winters will lete you have land to tend, you must
make all you cane. Gite, bob to shoe you how to due it [to plow?].
I want you to send me sum papear and invlope, the first chance you
gite an sum waf ears [?]. I must bring letear to close, excuse my bad
riten. N'oth more at present, but remai[n] yor efect[ionate] husban
on tel death. I want you to rite and tell bob i want you to rite soon.

D. WALTERS to
Sary Ann

Leisure

THE DESCRIPTIONS of the reactions of the Sparkman family slaves during
the trek to Alabama are remarkably similar in tone to the following
documents describing the leisure-time activities of slaves that took place
(with a strong African accent) in New York City and half a continent
away in a rural Louisiana parish. In both instances, the whites simply
recorded what they saw without attempting to either explain or comprehend a scene that suddenly unfolded before them. But the novelist
James Fenimore Cooper did mention that the American-born blacks of
New York City openly admired the music and dancing of the Africans
who were participating in the Dutch Pinkster Festival.

Dr. Samuel Cartwright (who hypothesized that Negroes who ran
away were afflicted with the disease "Drapemania") once led a group of
slaves into a swamp to escape an epidemic, and witnessed what may
have been a customary scene in the field hands' quarters.

67. "THEY ENCAMPED IN THE OPEN AIR AND BUILT FIRES"

SOURCE: Dr. Samuel A. Cartwright, "Remarks on Dysentery Among
Negroes," *The New Orleans Medical and Surgical Journal*, 11
(September 1854): 148–149.

On a large sugar plantation on the coast, belonging to Capt. Wm J. Minor, where the cholera appeared about two years ago, a removal of the negroes from one set of houses to another set (one of which had been built for the purpose) was twice tried without arresting the progress of the disease at all. At length, after forty had died, being called on to visit the plantation, and invested with full power to do as I pleased, I took about three hundred negroes sick and well, a mile or two back into a dry, open place in the swamp, where there was no house to be seen, or any preparation begun for building any. The overseer refused to obey until I recorded this fact in the plantation book, with an additional statement over my own signature, that a cloud was coming up, and in all probability there would be rain. Having made the record, I headed the line of march, and, sure enough, the rain came up and all got wet. They encamped in the open air and built fires, although the weather was warm, and some booths were directed to be made over the sick to protect them from the sun and the rain. The ashy-colored, dry skin conjurers, or prophets, who had alarmed their fellow-servants with the prophecies that the cholera was to kill them all, and who had gained, by various tricks and artifices, much influence over their superstitious minds, were by my orders, at twilight stripped, and greased with fat bacon, in presence of the whole camp—a camp without tents or covering of any kind, except some bushes and boards over the sick from the carts that conveyed them to the camp. After being greased, the grease was well slapped in with broadleather straps, marking time with the *tam tam*, a wild African dance that was going on in the centre of the camp among all those, who had the physical strength to participate in it. This procedure drove the cholera out of the heads of all who had been conjured into the belief that they were to die with the disease; because it broke the charm of the conjurers by converting them, under the greasing and slapping process, into subjects for ridicule and laughter, instead of fear and veneration.

68. "THE PINKSTER FESTIVAL"

SOURCE: James Fenimore Cooper, *Satanstoe* (New York, 1893), pp. 66–67, 72.

After showing Jason the City Hall, Trinity Church, and the City Tavern, we went out of town, taking the direction of a large common that the king's officers had long used for a parade ground, and which has since been called the Park, though it would be difficult to say why, since it is barely a paddock in size, and certainly has never been used to keep any animals wilder than the boys of the town. A park, I suppose, it will one day become, though it has little at present that comports with my ideas of such a thing. On this common, then, was the Pinkster ground, which was now quite full of people, as well as of animation.

There was nothing new in a Pinkster frolic, either to Dirck or to myself; though Jason gazed at the whole procedure with wonder. He was born within seventy miles of that very spot, but had not the smallest notion before, of such a holiday as Pinkster. There are few blacks in Connecticut, I believe; and those that are there, are so ground down in the Puritan mill, that they are neither fish, flesh, nor red-herring, as we say of a nondescript. No man ever heard of a festival in New England that had not some immediate connection with the saints, or with politics.

Jason was at first confounded with the noises, dances, music, and games that were going on. By this time, nine tenths of the blacks of the city, and of the whole country within thirty or forty miles, indeed, were collected in thousands in those fields, beating banjoes, singing African songs, drinking, and worst of all, laughing in a way that seemed to set their very hearts rattling within their ribs. Everything wore the aspect of good humor, though it was good-humor in its broadest and coarsest forms. Every sort of common game was in requisition, while drinking was far from being neglected. Still, not a man was drunk. A drunken negro, indeed, is by no means a common thing. The features that distinguish a Pinkster frolic from the usual scenes at fairs, and other merrymakings, however, were of African origin. It is true, there are not now, nor were there then, many blacks among us of African origin; but the traditions and usages of their original country were so far preserved as to produce a marked difference between this festival, and one of European origin. Among other things, some were making music, by beating on skins drawn over the ends of hollow logs, while others were dancing to it, in a manner to show that they felt infinite delight. This, in particular, was said to be a usage of their African progenitors.

Hundreds of whites were walking through the fields, amused spectators. Among these last were a great many children of the better class, who had come to look at the enjoyment of those who attended them, in their own ordinary amusements. Many a sable nurse did I see that day, chaperoning her young master, or young mistress, or both together, through the various groups; demanding of all, and receiving from all, the respect that one of these classes was accustomed to pay to the other. . . .

A party of native Africans kept us for half an hour. The scene seemed to have revived their early associations, and they were carried away with their own representation of semi-savage sports. The American-born blacks gazed at this group with intense interest also, regarding them as so many ambassadors from the land of their ancestors, to enlighten them in usages and superstitious lore, that were more peculiarly suited to their race. The last even endeavored to imitate the acts of the first, and, though the attempt was often ludicrous, it never failed on the score of intention and gravity. Nothing was done in the way of caricature, but much in the way of respect and affection.

Religion

TALLA BENA PLANTATION, *Vicksburg, Mississippi, 1850:*

> *This is Saterday night, & I hear the feedle going in the Quarter. We have two parties here among the Negroes. One a dancing party and the other a Praying party. The dancers have it tonight & the other party will hold forth tomorrow. They are very selfish and never attend each others meeting.*[16]

The "Praying" slaves of Talla Bena plantation who refused to dance may have been influenced by the repressive moralism that characterized Protestant fundamentalism in the early nineteenth century. But even the Baptist and Methodist church services slaves so joyously embraced and made their own were often "uninhibited frolics" according to white observers.

16. H. W. Payner to General Harding, Talla Bena, Mississippi, March 22, 1850, Harding-Jackson Papers, Southern Historical Collection, University of North Carolina Archives.

But to continue to argue, as some scholars have, that black Christians were only the excessively demonstrative imitators of a white religion that justified slavery with such sermons as "Servants Obey Your Masters" is to perpetuate old misunderstandings and to overlook the distinctive nature of black evangelism that infused white religious forms and practices.

Africans were a spiritual people. And remnants of their West African communal celebrations of ancient ancestors and other spirits were diffused in America and reinterpreted in various forms through the acculturative process. Two vital elements in the worship of old gods remained intact: the tribal dancers' shamanistic trances or possession states, and a susceptibility to visions. In colonial South Carolina, where African carry-overs were always more visible and resistant to change than elsewhere, a minister for the Society for the Propagation of the Gospel (the missionary arm of the English Anglican Church) reported in January, 1724:

> I find that our Negro Pagans have a notion of God; and of a Devil & dismal apprehensions of Apparations; of a God that disposes absolutely of all things; for asking one day a Negro-Pagan woman how she hapen'd to be made a slave, reply'd that God wou'd have it so & she could not help it. I heard another saying the same thing on the account of the death of her husband: and of a Devil who leads them to do mischief & betrays them, whereby they are found out by their Masters & punished.[17]

Viewing the competing Protestant missionaries through a West African cultural ambiance, slaves in the eighteenth century avoided the passive, arcane Anglican ritual and demonstrated a strong preference for denominations with services that made them participants and then transformed them into shouting, swaying, and ecstatic worshipers. Another S.P.G. minister reported from the Sea Islands in December, 1743: "There is no great progress made as yet in Instructing of Negroes. There are some, I fear, that are taught rather Enthusiasms, than Religion, who pretend to see visions, and receive Revelations from Heaven, & to be Conver[ted] by an Instantaneious Impulse of the Spirit. These are among Mr. Whitefields followers." Evidently George Whitefield's Methodism, Anglicanism with soul, tapped into West African ways of making the universe intelligible.

From the blending of African and American spirituality in the colonial period came two major alternatives or courses for slave evange-

17. Francis Varnad to the secretary of the Society for the Propagation of the Gospel, January 13, 1724, Society for the Propagation of the Gospel manuscripts relating to South Carolina (Library of Congress transcripts), Reel 2, South Carolina State Archives microfilm.

lism: *accommodation* or *rebellion*. While the former may often have been the case, as black Christianity worked as a safety valve to dissipate potentially revolutionary energy into religious ecstasy (and a passive acceptance of things as they were), it could, in the proper setting, produce a style of insurrectionary leadership that historically has appeared among tribal, agricultural peoples in colonial situations. The prophet and conjurer Nat Turner is an outstanding example of the way in which a charismatic leader with millennial visions can generate rebellion among traditional and conservative people.

The Afro-American evangelism that could branch one way and create a Nat Turner, or in another direction to produce countless thousands of nameless and obedient black Protestants, resurfaced many times after Emancipation. Its epicenter seemed to be the rice-coast Sea Islands, the ancestral home of the Gullah people. In the early 1930s Lydia Parrish (the author of Slave Songs of the Georgia Sea Islands) helped organize a large musical festival (Bessie Smith and the Sea Island Singers came out of this society). On a memorable night, Parrish reported, a Negro from Broadfield made the "sign of Judgment" with uplifted arm, and led sixty swaying singers in the shout "Can't Hide." The musicians began to move quietly, as in a trance, and it was soon evident, from a peculiar heart-clutching quality in the rhythm, that they were "possessed" by it. Song followed song, and the spell was not broken. Some in the audience wept, others applauded, but the Negroes appeared unaware of their surroundings. Several middle-aged Southerners said it was the first time they had seen the Negroes "get happy."[18]

69. "My Soul Is So Happy! Glory!"

Source: Henry E. Simmons (a Union soldier) to his wife, Suffolk County, Virginia, June 6–7, 1863, Henry E. Simmons Diary, Southern Historical Collection, University of North Carolina Archives.

I am tired of *visiting* I want to be at *home*. I am a Congregationalist & one all over, and tho I can get to other churches still none seems so much like home to me as the dear old Beuef Ch[urch]. . . . The Contrabands [ex-slaves] have a church about a mile from here & I want to go there. Their meeting commences at 10 in the morning & holds all day without stopping. You know we have a con-

18. Lydia Parrish, *Slave Songs of the Georgia Sea Islands* (New York, 1943), pp. 17–18.

traband from the rebel army with us & a good fellow he is too. I will stop a little while till I feel a little more in a writing fit.

I love you darling just as well as you can wish to be loved. I have just come from "Union Town" the contraband camp where I have been attending their church. Such a meeting. I never saw in all my life. I wish I could let you see it. The church was made of split logs & no floor & board seats and there were about 300 negroes in and a number of "moaners" were down on the ground and were crying suiging [sic] and praying. They would pray & then sing one man said "Now Lord didn't you say when one or two were call'd together in your name you'd come & be wid'em? Now we want you to come just as you said you would," another prayed "De good Lord take dese ere mourners & shake em ober hell but don't luff'em go." One man jumped up and began to yell "Glory! glory!!" and round he began to go saying "My Soul is so happy! Glory!" He Kept it up as much as an hour and a couple of Negro women began to do almost the same things. I will if I see you tell you more of this. The old minister began to preach and in 15 minutes he gave us a better sermon than the chaplain this morning did in an hour.

70. "Sobbing and Inarticulate Exclamations"

Source: Sarah A. Gayle Journal, 1829–1835, Special Collections, University of Alabama.

2d May 1833.   We were undecided what Church to attend this morning, but, finally, as I knew there were excellent preachers at the Methodist Church, I went there, and in consideration of the heat and crowd, suggested to Mr. Gayle he had better take the children and go to the Episcopal Church. He did, and I went near the pulpit, to a seat Mrs. Dyer offered, and enjoyed the breeze and the preaching for near an hour. At length, Dr. Cannon commenced the plan which was always my objection to him—viz—the attempt by any and every means, to operate on the feelings of his audience, so as to cause them to shout and weep, and make great out-cries. In this he succeeded today, I saw the gradual preparation making amongst the ministers, for that purpose, and contemptible indeed did it appear to me. My good feelings vanished, and distrust and scorn of the little arts employed, took their place. A negro in the gallery raised the yell, to which a dozen in a moment responded, sobbing and inarticulate exclamations, and then a general chorus of shouts and cries followed, and I rose to leave the confusion, which, in spite of my disapprobation, was rapidly sending the blood upon my heart, and taking the sight from my eyes. I expected Dr. Cannon to speak to me, or of me, when I came out. It is his custom, but if he had, I should have told him the truth. I regret, very sincerely regret, having gone.

71. "Oh, Yes!" "That's It, That's It!"

Source: Frederick Law Olmsted, *A Journey to the Back Country* (New York, 1860, 1863), pp. 188–189, 190.

The preacher was nearly black with close wooly hair. His figure was slight, he seemed to be about thirty years of age and the expression of his face indicated a refined and delicately sensitive nature. His eye was very fine, bright, deep and clear; his voice and manner generally quiet and impressive. The text was, "I have fought the good fight, I have kept the faith; henceforth there is laid up for me a crown of glory"; and the sermon was an appropriate and generally correct explanation of the customs of the Olympic games and a proper and often eloquent application of the figure to the christian course of life. Much of the language was highly metaphorical; the figures long, strange and complicated, yet sometimes, however, beautiful. Words were frequently misplaced, and their meaning evidently misapprehended, while the grammar and pronounciation were sometimes such as to make the idea intended to be conveyed by the speaker incomprehensible to me. . . .

As soon as I had taken my seat, my attention was attracted to an old negro near me, whom I supposed for some time to be suffering under some nervous complaint; he trembled, his teeth chattered, and his face, at intervals, was convulsed. He soon began to respond aloud to the sentiments of the preacher, in such words as these: "Oh, yes!" "That's it, that's it!" "Yes, yes—glory—yes!" and similar expressions could be heard from all parts of the house whenever the speaker's voice was unusually solemn, or his language and manner eloquent or excited.

Sometimes the outcries and responses were not confined to ejac-
ulations of this kind, but shouts, and groans, terrific shrieks, and
indescribable expressions of ecstacy—of pleasure or agony—and
even stamping, jumping, and clapping of hands, were added. . . . I
was once surprised to find my own muscles all stretched, as if ready
for a struggle—my face glowing, and my feet stamping—having
been infected unconsciously, as men often are, with instinctive bod-
ily sympathy with the excitement of the crowd.

D. The Insurrectionists:
Denmark Vesey and Nat Turner

DENMARK VESEY AND NAT TURNER, *leaders of the largest nineteenth-
century rebellions, were far removed from the realities of slavery
portrayed in the preceding documents on large-scale plantation organization and management. Both men were the products of essentially non-
plantation areas, which were themselves strikingly different from each
other, and so created distinctive styles of insurrectionary leadership.*

*Denmark Vesey was born in Africa sometime during the third quar-
ter of the eighteenth century. For twenty years he sailed with his master
in the Atlantic and the Caribbean, before they settled in Charleston,
South Carolina. In 1800 he purchased his freedom with a winning lottery
ticket, practiced carpentry, bought real estate, and raised a large family.
By 1820 he was organizing an insurrection that produced evidence on
leadership tactics, recruitment procedures, and objectives that in feeling
was remarkably like the documents for Gabriel Prosser's rebellion in
Richmond, Virginia, twenty-two years earlier.*

*Both conspiracies, drawing upon the resources of the major cities of
Virginia and South Carolina, never proceeded from planning to action.
In Charleston, Vesey's lieutenants, like the Prosser brothers and Jack
Bowler, were exceptional slaves—ship's carpenters, harness makers,
and such "trusted" house servants as the Governor's waitingman!
Vesey's consciousness-raising sessions (like the Gabriel conspirators'
interminable discussions of military ranking, arms, and who was to be
spared or killed) seemed an end in themselves; and both leaders came
to be enmeshed in ambitious strategies that were, in retrospect, too
grandiose. Vesey planned to take the entire city, which had a long
history of contact with the West Indies, and eventually sail to Haiti. For
more than a quarter of a century, black sailors and refugees from that
Negro republic (itself the product of a large and successful slave upris-*

ing against France) had frightened Charleston whites, and inspired the city's blacks.

But in important ways Denmark Vesey was a far more astute and effective leader than Gabriel Prosser: he recognized the slaves' cultural differences and their spirituality, and sought to connect black evangelism to revolution. Gabriel and his men, on the other hand, were too much like their owners, the deists and agnostics, who led the revolution in Virginia against Great Britain. While thousands of Tidewater slaves were captivated by an awesome fundamentalist revival (the southern Great Awakening), Gabriel could only explain the rebellion in secular and political terms. But the Charleston conspirators preached revolution in the meetings of the local African Methodist Episcopal Church; and Vesey used the Bible to teach slaves his unvarying theme: "You are in God's eyes equal to your masters; will you fight for that principle?"

Vesey also appreciated the significant acculturative differences between leaders and rank-and-file, which proved so divisive in the Prosser rebellion. Although an African, he was thoroughly assimilated, and so was Monday Gell, a leader and an Ibo who operated a harness shop in Meeting Street. Gabriel ignored George Smith's proposal to incorporate African ways by consulting the witches and wizards at the Pipeing Tree in King William County, but Vesey sent Gullah Jack, an Angola Negro and roustabout on the Charleston docks, among the Sea Islands blacks to incite rebellion. While Vesey used biblical stories and classical fables to convert reluctant city Negroes, Gullah Jack distributed mystical concoctions of parched corn and ground nuts to rice-field Africans in the countryside. Vesey collected money for shot and shell; Gullah Jack placed crabs' claws in the mouths of slaves to protect them from the white man's guns. In the meantime, the conspirators talked and talked and changed the time of attacks at least once. Finally they were discovered.

Nat Turner was a lon , in a Virginia county (Southampton) that was a social and economic backwater; and, in his insurrection—the first of its size and scope to progress beyond a planning stage since the Stono River uprising a century earlier—there were no meetings or recruitment. This was not a r ~ilion of talented city Negroes: tax records for his victims in the neighborhood of Cross Keys and Jerusalem (present-day Courtland) indicate that most whites paid yearly levies of a dollar or two on a few runty cattle, four or five slaves, and a few hundred acres of scratch—sparse—land, good for corn, hogs, tobacco, and little else. Only one artisan joined; when condemned, the court appraised him at $650, or nearly twice the value of Turner, and each of the other cornfield blacks.

Nat Turner, a brooding, self-absorbed man, was a wise and gifted leader. He was also too engaged in a wondrous and deeply introspective search for his own identity and mission in the world of slavery, too knowledgeable about the lack of revolutionary fervor among field blacks, to allow his holy war against whites to bog down in administrative detail and stifling, self-justifying rhetoric.

Like Vesey, Turner from his earliest days had been told he was special. But Vesey's unusual self-esteem and confidence were partially attributable to a chance encounter with a captain and white crew of slavers, while Nat Turner's strong ego was the product of the slave cabins. In his marvelous confession, he also mentions his father, who was a fugitive. As a young man, the son emulated his father, but returned voluntarily (much to the consternation of the other slaves) to become a religious ascetic. Fasting and praying, he waited for the supernatural signs that would release what he was storing, charging, and protecting. Turner (like Gabriel, who also could have run away with a large chance of success) was moved by larger ideals and principles. He too had come to identify his freedom with the destruction of whites and the liberation of all blacks.

But unlike the urban Negro conspirators, Prosser and Vesey, Nat Turner was sufficiently zealous, gifted, and believable to persuade a few blacks that his own resolution of slavery was theirs. Through poetic visions of black angels defeating white ones in the sky, warnings about Negro conjurers, and shrewd stories dramatized by number progressions and drops of blood on corn leaves, this immensely complex man convinced his followers that slavery was a social, not a personal, issue.

Turner's religious quest for self-discovery took years of preparation; his plan for rebellion and recruitment of only six slaves (which quickly grew to fifty or sixty well-armed horsemen) took a few weeks. Sunday night, August 22, he joined his men for roast pig around a small fire in deep woods; early the next morning they struck first "at home," the Joseph Travis place, and within the next forty-odd hours killed sixty-one whites—men, women, and children.

Turner's choice of victims is instructive. They were the small paternalistic slaveowners, the "real patriarchs," like Rachel O'Connor and David Gavin. One victim, Nathaniel Francis, for example, was the only man in the tax district who allowed free Negroes to live on his land. In his fictionalized account of the rebellion, the novelist William Styron created a revealing scene in which Nat, copying a map for his march, was surprised by a kindly, mercenary old woman who had hired him. The scene is psychologically accurate and bears an uncanny resemblance to the household and outlook of Rachel O'Connor.

> *Strange that, after a fashion, the woman's manner toward me had been ingratiating, even queerly tender, with a faint tongue-lick of unctuousness, benevolent, in a roundabout way downright maternal. Nuzzling around my black ass. In my heart of hearts I bore her no ill will. Yet she had never once removed herself from the realm of ledgers, accounts, tallies, receipts, balance sheets, purse strings,*

profits, pelf—as if the being to whom she was talking and around whom she had spun such a cocoon of fantasy had not been a creature with lips and fingernails and eyebrows and tonsils but some miraculous wheelbarrow. I gazed at the complacent oblong of her face, white as tallow. Suddenly I thought of the document beneath my shirt and again the hatred swept over me. I was seized with awe, and a realization: Truly that white flesh will soon be dead.[19]

Conspiracy in Charleston, South Carolina, 1822

DENMARK VESEY: THREE VIEWS OF HIS STYLE OF LEADERSHIP

72. "HE WAS ALWAYS LOOKED UP TO WITH AWE AND RESPECT"

SOURCE: James Hamilton, Jr., *An Account of the Late Intended Insurrection Among a Portion of the Blacks of this City.* (Charleston, S.C., 1822), pp. 17–18n.

As Denmark Vesey has occupied so large a place in the conspiracy, a brief notice of him will, perhaps, be not devoid of interest. The following anecdote will show how near he was to the chance of being distinguished in the bloody events of San Domingo. During the revolutionary war, captain Vesey, now an old resident of this city, commanded a ship that traded between St. Thomas' and Cape Francois (San Domingo). He was engaged in supplying the French of that island with slaves. In the year 1781, he took on board, at St. Thomas's, 390 slaves and sailed for the Cape; on the passage, he and his officers were struck with the beauty, alertness, and intelligence of a boy about 14 years of age, whom they made a pet of, by taking him into the cabin, changing his apparel, and calling him, by way of distinction, *Telemaque* (which appellation has since, by gradual corruption, among the negroes, been changed to Denmark, or sometimes Telmak). On the arrival, however, of the ship at the Cape, captain Vesey, having no use for the boy, sold him among his other slaves, and returned to St. Thomas's. On his next voyage to the Cape, he was surprised to learn from his consignee that Telemaque would be returned on his hands, as the

19. William Styron, *The Confessions of Nat Turner* (New York, 1967), pp. 327–328.

planter, who had purchased him, represented him unsound, and subject to epileptick fits. According to the custom of trade in that place, the boy was placed in the hands of the king's physician, who decided that he was unsound, and captain Vesey was compelled to take him back, of which he had no occasion to repent, as Denmark proved, for 20 years, a most faithful slave. In 1800, Denmark drew a prize of $1500 in the East Bay street lottery, with which he purchased his freedom from his master, at six hundred dollars, much less than his real value. From that period to the day of his apprehension, he has been working as a carpenter in this city, distinguished for great strength and activity. Among his colour he was always looked up to with awe and respect. His temper was impetuous and domineering in the extreme, qualifying him for the despotick rule, of which he was ambitious.

73. "His Favorite Texts"

Source: Lionel H. Kennedy and Thomas Parker, *An Official Report of the Trials of Sundry Negroes, Charged with an Attempt to Raise an Insurrection in the State of South-Carolina* (Charleston, S.C., 1822), pp. 17–20.

At the head of this conspiracy stood Denmark Vesey. For several years before he disclosed his intentions to any one, he appears to have been constantly and assiduously engaged in endeavouring to embitter the minds of the colored population against the white. He rendered himself perfectly familiar with all those parts of the Scriptures, which he thought he could pervert to his purpose; and would readily quote them, to prove that slavery was contrary to the laws of God; that slaves were bound to attempt their emancipation, however shocking and bloody might be the consequences, and that such efforts would not only be pleasing to the Almighty, but were absolutely enjoined, and their success. . . . His favorite texts were Zechariah Chapter 14th, verses 1, 2, and 3, and Joshua, Chapter 4th, verse 21; and in all his conversations he identified their situation with that of the Israelites.

Even whilst walking through the streets in company with another, he was not idle; for if his companion bowed to a white person he would rebuke him, and observe that all men were born equal, and that he was surprised that any one would degrade himself by such conduct; that he would never cringe to the whites, nor ought any one who had the feelings of a man. When answered, We are slaves, he would sarcastically and indignantly reply, "you deserve to remain slaves"; and if he were further asked, What can we do, he would remark, "Go and buy a spelling book and read the fable of Hercules and the Waggoner"; which he would then repeat, and apply it to their situation. He also sought every opportunity of entering into conversation with white persons when they could be overheard by negroes nearby especially in grog-shops; during which conversation he would artfully introduce some bold remark on slavery; and sometimes, when from the character he was conversing with he found he might be still bolder, he would go so far, that had not his declarations in such situation been clearly proved, they would scarcely have been credited. He continued this course, until sometime after the commencement of the last winter; by which time he had not only obtained incredible influence amongst persons of color, but many feared him more than their owners, and one of them declared, even more than his God.

74. "You May As Well Join Us"

SOURCE: Confessions of Bacchus, the slave of Mr. Hammet, William and Benjamin Hammet Papers, Duke University Library Archives.

They went together to Denmark Vesey's house near Bennets Mills that they were rec[eive]d by Denmark when they went into his yard at his house door, and the gate locked upon them. That Denmark after ascertaining it was Perault and another man (as Perault said to D) he went with them into the house. In a large room I seen ten or dozen men, a table in the midst of the room and a large book open on it, probably the Bible. Denmark asked me who I belonged to and my name, Perault immediately answered "Bacchus belonging to Mr. Hammet," Denmark asked me which Hammet, I said Mr. Benjamin Hammet, the gentleman who put old Lorenzo Dow in jail; and is an officer in Capt. Martendale's company. Perault says to me, "Bacchus I have some particular thing to say to you"; I asked what it was he said "that they were going to have war and fight the white people" and that I must join them: I said "Perault, I am sorry you brought me into this business and you better let it alone," and I considered some time; at last Perault say, *"Bacchus you need not fret, you may as well join us,"* Denmark then said *"any person who didn't join us must be treated as an enemy, and put to death,"* and I said if that is the case, well I will join you. We all three then went into the large room, and there I seen Rolla Bennet, Monday Gell, Charles Drayton, and Smart Anderson and another who I believe is Denmark Vesey's son. They had had the large Book open and something like a letter in it, which *believe come from some free Country off, may be St. Domingo*; and Denmark's son says to Monday shewing him something on the letter, "look here Monday see how they are making fun of we," *meaning the* people off in the free country. That Denmark, said "Friends we have a friend who is to go into the Country to raise the country negroes to come down, all who can, *must* put in money to raise a sum *to pay his master wages while he is gone,"* that they all put in, and I and Perault put in Seven pence. Denmark then said they must all swear, *that they all held up their right hand and swore,* and said after Denmark: "We *will not tell on one another, we will not tell any body, We will not tell if taken by the Whites, nor will we tell if we are to be put to death,"* that under the sanctity of this Oath he never told his master: This was the first meeting.

At the next meeting, I was asked by Denmark *if I could get any arms*, I told him may be *an old sword*; and he said no matter *any arms* I can get arms and powder, I said my *master has pistols, but I am afraid to take them, and* Perault said never mind We *will satisfy your master,** on that subject. He also stated how he was carried to Vesey's by [Pera]ult, How Vesey sat him a long side of him, and when he found he [illegible] to join him He asked him seven queries such as *"Did His master u[se] him well—Yes he believed so. Did He eat the same as his master, Yes sometimes not always as well as his master. Did his master not sleep on a soft bed, Yes. Did he Bacchus sleep on as soft a Bed as his master.* No. Who made his

---

* no doubt by a murdering argument, as a small Hatchet, with a long handle is in possession of the master; a very artful and deadly weapon it is. The horseman's sword was considered of little value and lay in the Back store.

master. God, *Who made you,* God. *And then arn't you as good as your master if God made him and you, arn't you as free,* Yes. *Then why don't you join and fight your master.* Does your master use you well, Yes I believe so. *Does he whip you when you do wrong,* Yes sometimes. *Then why don't [yo]u as you are as free as your master, turn about and fight for yourself.*

Denmark read at the meeting different chapters from the Old Testament, but most generally read the whole of the 21 chapter Exodus and spoke and exorted from the 16 Verse the words "and he that stealith man." He read frequently in a book about the complexion of people and said it was the climate of Africa made him Black but were not inferior to Whites on that account.

VESEY'S LIEUTENANTS

75. "Confidential Servants" and "Slaves of Great Value"

Source: Kennedy and Parker, *An Official Report of the Trials of Sundry Negroes, Charged with an Attempt to Raise an Insurrection in the State of South-Carolina* (Charleston, S.C., 1822), pp. 23–24, 41–44.

Vesey perceiving that so far everything had answered his most sanguine expectations, himself in possession of vast influence over his own colour, and their minds poisoned and embittered against the white population, began about Christmas 1821 to probe those whom he had selected as leaders; and found as he expected a ready acquiescence in his measures by all of them except *Monday Gell,* who wavered for some time before he joined. In the selection of his leaders, Vesey shewed great penetration and sound judgement. *Rolla* was plausible, and possessed uncommon self-possession; bold and ardent, he was not to be deterred from his purpose by danger. *Ned's* appearance indicated, that he was a man of firm nerves, and desperate courage. *Peter* was intrepid and resolute, true to his engagements, and cautious in observing secrecy where it was necessary; he was not to be daunted nor impeded by difficulties, and though confident of success, was careful in providing against any obstacles which might arise, and intent upon discovering every means which might be in their power if thought of before hand. *Gullah Jack* was regarded as a Sorcerer, and as such feared by the natives of Africa, who believe in witchcraft. He was not only considered invulnerable, but that he could make others so by his charms; and that he could and certainly would provide all his followers with arms. He was artful, cruel, bloody; his disposition in short was diabolical. His influence amongst the Africans was inconceivable. Monday was firm, resolute, discreet and intelligent. With these men as his principal officers, amongst whom Peter and Monday was certainly the most active, Vesey began to seduce others at the commencement of the present year. . . .

It is difficult to conceive what motive he [Vesey] had to enter into such a plot, unless it was the one mentioned by one of the witnesses, who said that Vesey had several children who were slaves, and that he said on one occasion he wished to see them free; Rolla was the confidential servant of his master; so much so, that when his master's public duties required his absence from his family, they were left under the protection of that slave; yet that very man undertook to head a party, whose first act was to be, the murder of that master, who had reposed such confidence in him, and had treated him with great kindness. Ned was also a confidential servant, and his general good conduct was commendable. . . . Peter was a slave of great value, and for his colour, a first rate ship carpenter. He possessed the confidence of his master, in a remarkable degree, and had been treated with indulgence, liberality, and kindness. . . . Monday enjoyed all the substantial comforts of a free man; [he was] much indulged and trusted by his master; his time and a large portion of the profits of his labour were at his own disposal. He even kept his master's *arms* and sometimes his money. He is a most excellent harness-maker, and kept his shop in Meeting-street. Monday is an *Ebo*, and is now in the prime of life, having been in the country 15 or 20 years.

THE CONSPIRATORS ARE TRIED AND CONDEMNED

76. "DIE SILENT"

SOURCE: Lionel H. Kennedy and Thomas Parker, *An Official Report of the Trials of Sundry Negroes, Charged with an Attempt to Raise an Insurrection in the State of South-Carolina* (Charleston, S.C., 1822), pp. 44–46.

The conduct and behavior of Vesey and his five leaders during their trial and imprisonment, may be interesting to many. When Vesey was tried, he folded his arms and seemed to pay great attention to the testimony given against him, but with his eyes fixed on the floor. In this situation he remained immoveable, until the witnesses had been examined by the Court and cross-examined by his counsel; when he requested to be allowed to examine the witnesses himself. He at first questioned them in the dictatorial, despotic manner, in which he was probably accustomed to address them; but this not producing the desired effect he questioned them with affected surprise and concern for bearing false testimony against him; still failing in his purpose, he then examined them strictly as to dates, but could not make them contradict themselves. The evidence being closed, he addressed the Court at considerable length, in which his principal endeavour was to impress them with the idea that as his situation in life had been such that he could have had no inducement to join in such an attempt, the charges against him must be false; and he attributed it to the greatest hatred which he alledged the blacks had against him; but his allegations were unsupported by proof. When he received his sentence, the tears trickled down his cheeks; and it is not improbable if he had been placed in a separate cell, he might have made important discoveries; but confined as four of the convicts were in one room, they mutually supported each other; and died obedient to the stern and emphatic injunction of their comrade [Peter Poyas], "Do not open your lips. Die Silent, as you shall see me do."

Rolla, when arraigned, affected not to understand the charge against him, and when it was at his request further explained to him, assumed with wonderful adroitness, astonishment and surprise. He was remarkable throughout his trial, for great presence and composure of mind. When he was informed he was convicted and was advised to prepare for death, though he had previously confessed his guilt, he appeared perfectly confounded; but exhibited no signs of fear. In Ned's behavior there was nothing remarkable; but his countenance was stern and immoveable, even whilst he was receiving the sentence of death; from his looks it was impossible to discover or conjecture what were his feelings. Not so with Peter, for in his countenance was strongly marked disappointed ambition, revenge, indignation, and an anxiety to know how far the discoveries had extended, and the same emotions were exhibited in his conduct. He did not appear to fear personal consequences, for his whole behavior indicated the reverse; but exhibited an evident anxiety for the success of their plan, in which his whole soul was embarked. His countenance and behavior were the same when he received his sentence, and his only words were on retiring, "I suppose you'll let me see my wife and family before I die?" and that not in a supplicating tone. When he was asked a day or two after, if it was possible he could wish to see his master and family murdered who had treated him so kindly! he only replied to the question by a smile.

Rebellion in Southampton County, Virginia, 1831

77. An Overview

Source: Extracts from the letters of the senior editor, *Richmond Constitutional Whig*, August 29 and September 3, 1831.

On the route from Petersburg, we found the whole country thoroughly alarmed; every man armed, the dwellings all deserted by the white inhabitants, and the farms most generally left in possession of the blacks. On our arrival in this village, we found Com. Elliot and Col. Worth with 250 U. States troops, from the neighbourhood of Old Point, and a considerable militia force . . .

Jerusalem [now Courtland] was never so crowded from its foundation; for besides the considerable military force assembled here, the ladies from the adjacent country, to the number of 3 or 400, have sought refuge from the appalling dangers by which they were surrounded.

. . . Rumors had infinitely exaggerated the first, swelling the numbers of the negroes to a thousand or 1200 . . . but it was hardly in the power of rumor itself, to exaggerate the atrocities which have been perpetrated by the insurgents: whole families, father, mother, daughters, sons, sucking babes, and school children, butchered, thrown into heaps, and left to be devoured by hogs and dogs, or to putrify on the spot. At Mr. Levi Waller's, his wife and ten children were murdered and piled in one bleeding heap on his floor. . . . The killed, as far as ascertained, amount to sixty-two . . .

a large proportion of these were women and children. It is not believed that outrages were offered to the females. . . .

Mrs. Vaughan's was among the last houses attacked. A Venerable negro woman described the scene which she had witnessed with great emphasis. It was near noon, and her mistress had been making some preparation in the porch for dinner, when happening to look towards the road, she descried a dust and wondered what it could mean. In a second, the negroes mounted and armed, rushed into view, and making an exclamation indicative of her horror and agony, Mrs. Vaughan ran into the house. The negroes dismounted and ran around the house, pointing their guns at the doors and windows. Mrs. Vaughan appeared at a window, and begged for her life, inviting them to take everything she had. The prayer was answered by one of them firing at her, which was instantly followed by another and a fatal shot. In the meantime, Mrs. Vaughan, who was upstairs, and unapprised of the terrible advent until she heard the noise of the attack, rushed down and begging for life, was shot as she ran a few steps from the door. A son of Mrs. Vaughan, about 15, was at the still house, when hearing a gun, and conjecturing, it is supposed, that his brother had come from Jerusalem, approached the house, and was shot as he got over the fence. . . . In a most lively and picturesque manner, did the old negress describe the horrors of the scene; the blacks riding up with imprecations, the looks of her mistress, white as a sheet, her prayers for her life, and the action of the scoundrels environing the house and pointing their guns at the doors and windows, ready to fire as occasion offered. When the work was done, they called for drink and food, and becoming nice, damned the brandy as vile stuff. . . .

It is with pain we speak of another feature of the Southampton Rebellion; for we have been most unwilling to have our sympathies for the sufferers, diminished or affected by their misconduct. We allude to the slaughter of many blacks, without trial, and under circumstances of great barbarity. How many have thus been put to death (generally by decapitation or shooting) reports vary; probably however some five and twenty and from that to 40; possibly a yet larger number. To the great honor of General Eppes, he used every precaution in his power . . . to put a stop to the disgraceful procedure.

We met with an individual of intelligence, who stated that he himself had killed between 10 and 15. He justified himself on the ground of the barbarities committed on the whites; and that he thought himself right, is certain from the fact of his having narrowly escaped losing his own life in an attempt to save a negro woman whom he thought innocent, but who was shot by the multitude in despite of his exertions. . . .

Now however, we individually feel compelled to offer an apology for the people of Southampton, while we deplore that human nature urged them to such extremities. Let the fact not be doubted by those whom it most concerns, that another such insurrection will be the signal for the extirpation of the whole black population in the quarter of the State where it occurs.

THREE VIEWS OF NAT TURNER: AS A "RUNAWAY," A RELIGIOUS FANATIC, AND A REVOLUTIONARY

78. "Bright Complexion . . . Broad Shouldered"

Source: W. C. Parker to the Governor, Jerusalem, Southampton County, September 14, 1831, Executive Papers, September 1831, Virginia State Archives.

Sir, Understanding you are anxious to have a description of Nat the contriver and leader of the late insurrection in this County, I have been at some pains to procure an accurate one. It has been supervised and corrected by persons acquainted with him from his infancy.

He is between 30 & 25 years old—5 feet six or 8 inches high. Weighs between 150 & 160 rather bright complexion but not a mulatto, broad shouldered, large, flat nose, large eyes, broad flat feet rather knock kneed, walk[s] brisk and active, hair on the top of the head very thin, no beard except on the upper lip and the tip of the chin, a scar on one of his temples produced by the nick of a knife, also one on the back of his neck, by a bit[e], a large knot on one of the bones of his right arm near the wrist produced by a blow.

79. "THE WORK OF FANATICISM"

SOURCE: *Richmond Constitutional Whig*, September 26, 1831.

Our insurrection, general, or not, was the work of fanaticism—
General Nat was no preacher, but in his immediate neighbourhood, he had acquired the character of a prophet; like a Roman
Sybil, he traced his divination in characters of blood, on leaves
alone in the woods; he would arrange them in some conspicuous
place, have a dream telling him of the circumstance; and then send
some ignorant black to bring them to him; to whom he would
interpret their meaning. Thus, by means of this nature, he acquired
an immense influence over such persons as he took into his confidence. He likewise, pretended, to have conversations with the Holy
Spirit; and was assured by it, that he was invulnerable. . . . 'Tis
true, that Nat has for some time, thought closely on this subject—
for I have in my possession, some papers given up by his wife,
under the lash—they are filled with hieroglyphical characters, conveying no definite meaning. The characters on the oldest paper,
apparently appear to have been traced with blood; and on each
paper, a crucifix and sun, is distinctly visible; with the figures
6,000, 30,000, 80,000 etc. There is likewise a piece of paper, of a
later date, which all agree, is a list of his men; if so, they were short
of twenty. I have been credibly informed, that something like three
years ago, Nat received a whipping from his master, for saying that
the blacks ought to be free, and that they would be free one day or
other. Nat in person, is not remarkable, his nose is flat, his stature
is rather small, and hair very thick, without any peculiarity of
expression. As a proof of his shrewdness, he had acquired a great
influence over his neighbourhood acquaintance, without being noticed by the whites—pretends to be acquainted with the art of
making gunpowder, and likewise that of making paper. . . .

80. "CHILDHOOD CIRCUMSTANCES"

SOURCE: *The Confessions of Nat Turner . . . As fully and voluntarily made to Thomas R. Gray* (Baltimore, 1831).

SIR,—You have asked me to give a history of the motives which
induced me to undertake the late insurrection, as you call it—To

do so I must go back to the days of my infancy, and even before I was born. I was thirty-one years of age the 2d of October last, and born the property of Benj. Turner, of this county. In my childhood a circumstance occurred which made an indelible impression on my mind, and laid the ground work of that enthusiasm, which has terminated so fatally to many, both white and black, and for which I am about to atone at the gallows. It is here necessary to relate this circumstance—trifling as it may seem, it was the commencement of that belief which has grown with time, and even now, sir, in this dungeon, helpless and forsaken as I am, I cannot divest myself of. Being at play with other children, when three or four years old, I was telling them something, which my mother overhearing, said it had happened before I was born—I stuck to my story, however, and related some things which went, in her opinion, to confirm it—others being called on were greatly astonished, knowing that these things had happened, and caused them to say in my hearing, I surely would be a prophet, as the Lord had shewn me things that had happened before my birth. And my father and mother strengthened me in this my first impression, saying in my presence, I was intended for some great purpose. . . . My grandmother, who was very religious, and to whom I was much attached—my master, who belonged to the church, and other religious persons who visited the house, and whom I often saw at prayers, noticing the singularity of my manners, I suppose, and my uncommon intelligence for a child, remarked I had too much sense to be raised, and if I was, I would never be of any service to any one as a slave—To a mind like mine, restless, inquisitive and observant of everything that was passing, it is easy to suppose that religion was the subject to which it would be directed, and although this subject principally occupied my thoughts—there was nothing that I saw or heard of to which my attention was not directed. . . . When I got large enough to go to work, while employed, I was reflecting on many things that would present themselves to my imagination, and whenever an opportunity occurred of looking at a book, when the school children were getting their lessons, I would find many things that the fertility of my own imagination had depicted to me before; all my time, not devoted to my master's service, was spent either in prayer, or in making experiments in casting different things in moulds made of earth, in attempting to make paper, gun-powder, and many other experiments, that although I could not perfect, yet convinced me of its practicability, if I had the means. I was not addicted to stealing in my youth, nor have ever been—Yet such was the confidence of the negroes in the neighborhood, even at this early period of my life, in my superior judgment, that they would often carry me with them when they were going on any roguery, to plan for them. Growing up among them, with this confidence in my superior judgment, and when this, in their opinions, was perfected by Divine inspiration, from the circumstances already alluded to in my infancy, and which belief was ever afterwards zealously inculcated by the austerity of my life and manners, which became the subject of remark by white and black.—Having soon discovered to be great, I must appear so, and therefore studiously avoided mixing in society, and wrapped myself in mystery, devoting my time to fasting and prayer. . . . As I was praying one day at my plough, the spirit spoke to me, saying "Seek ye the kingdom of Heaven and all things shall be added unto you." Question—what do you mean by the Spirit. Ans[wer]. The Spirit that spoke to the prophets in former days—and I was greatly astonished, and for two years prayed continually, whenever my duty would permit—and then again I had the same revelation, which fully confirmed me in the impression that I was ordained for some great purpose in the hands of the Almighty. Several years rolled round, in which many events occurred to strengthen me in this my belief. . . . Now finding I had arrived to man's estate, and was a slave, and these revelations being made known to me, I began to direct my attention to this great object, to fulfil the purpose for which, by this time, I felt assured I was intended. Knowing the influence I had obtained over the minds of my fellow servants (not by the means of conjuring and such like tricks—for to them I always spoke of such things with contempt) but by the communion of the Spirit whose revelations I often communicated to them, and they believed and said my wisdom came from God. I now began to prepare them for my purpose, by telling them something was about to happen that would terminate in fulfilling the great promise that had been made to me . . . about this time I had a vision—and I saw white spirits and black spirits engaged in battle, and the sun was darkened—the thunder rolled in the Heavens, and blood flowed in streams—and I heard a voice saying, "Such is your luck, such you are called to see, and let it come rough or smooth, you must surely bare it." I now withdrew myself as much as my situation would permit, from the intercourse of my fellow servants, for the avowed purpose of serving the Spirit more fully. . . . And I wondered greatly at these miracles, and prayed to be informed of a certainty of the meaning thereof—and shortly afterwards, while laboring in the field, I discovered drops of blood on the corn as though it were dew from heaven—and I communicated it to many, both white and black, in the neighborhood—and I then found on the leaves in the woods hieroglyphic characters, and numbers, with the forms of men in different attitudes, portrayed in blood, and representing the figures I had seen before in the heavens. And now the Holy Ghost had revealed itself to me, and made plain the miracles it had shown me . . . it was plain to me that the Saviour was about to lay down the yoke he had borne for the sins of men, and the great day of judgment was at hand. . . . And on the 12th of May, 1828, I heard a loud noise in the heavens, and the Spirit instantly appeared to me and said the Serpent was loosened, and Christ had laid down the yoke he had borne for the sins of men, and that I should take it on and fight against the Serpent, for the time was fast approaching when the first should be last and the last should be first. Ques[tion]: Do you not find yourself mistaken now? Ans[wer]: Was not Christ crucified? And by signs in the heavens that it would make known to me when I should commence the great work—and until the first sign appeared, I should conceal it from the knowledge of men—And on the appearance of the sign (the eclipse of the sun last February) I should arise and prepare myself, and slay my enemies with their own weapons. And immediately on the sign appearing in the heavens, the seal was removed from my lips. . . .

. . . On Saturday evening, the 20th of August, it was agreed between Henry, Hark and myself, to prepare a dinner the next day for the men who we expected, and then to concert a plan, as we had not yet determined on any. . . . it was quickly agreed we should commence at home (Mr. J. Travis') on that night, and until we had armed and equipped ourselves and gathered sufficient force, neither age nor sex was to be spared (which was invariably adhered to).

81. THE TRIALS OF NELSON, LUCY, AND NAT TURNER

SOURCE: Minutes of the Southampton County Court, Virginia State Archives microfilm. Published by permission of the Clerk of the Southampton County Circuit Court.

At a Court of Oyer and Terminer. 3rd day of September 1831, for the trial of . . . Nelson, the property of Jacob Williams, charged with insurrection. . . .

Caswell Worrell, also a Witness, being sworn says that he overlooks for Jacob Williams the owner of the prisoner. That on Thursday preceeding the Monday on which the insurrection broke out the prisoner told the witness that they might look out and take care of themselves, that something would happen before long, that anybody of his practice could tell these things. That on Monday August 22nd he came in the morning by Jacob Williams's where the prisoner resided and found him from home. . . . Went to the new ground where the rest of the negroes were at work, that at about one hour after the prisoner came to the new ground dressed in his best clothes. Complained that he was too Sick to work, put on his old clothes which he had with him and desired Witness to go to the house with him which he did and returned just before the insurgents arrived and believes the prisoner wished to decoy witnesses home that he might be killed.

Cynthia a Slave being charged and Sworn as a Witness States— that on Monday the 22nd of August last the prisoner came home early in the morning seemingly very sick. Went to his house, dressed himself very clean, while the negroes were in the yard. Came into the kitchen, asked for some meat, took his Misstresses meat out of the pot, Cut a piece off, said "Cynthia you do not know me, I do not know when you will see me again." Steped over the dead bodies without any manifestation of grief.

Stephen a Slave being sworn and charged Says he and Mr Edmond Drewry went to Jacob Williams's on Monday the 22nd August last for corn while consulting about who should go for a corn measure. Mr. Drewry said, "Lord who is that coming" immediately the negroes rode up killed Mr. Drewry, Mr William's wife and children, told Nelson to go with them, he seemed unwilling to go but insisted upon dressing before he went was forced to go with them lagged behind when he was guarded, went to Mrs Vaughans but did not participate in the murder. That the prisoner drank with them and had his tickler filled by his own request.

The Court after hearing the testimony and from all the circumstances of the case are unanimously of opinion that the prisoner is guilty.

At a Court held for Southampton at the Courthouse the 19*th* day of September 1831.

Lucy a negro Woman slave late the property of John I. Barrow, who stands charged with conspiring to rebel and make insurrection was this day set to the bar in custody of the Jailor of this County. . . .

Mary T. Barrow, a Witness for the Commonwealth, being sworn says that on the 22nd of Aug. last when the insurgents came to the house of her late husband (John T. Barrow), and were entering the yard, and she the witness was making her escape, the prisoner, a girl about 20 years of age, Seized and held her about one minute and until another negro took her away, that she does not know certainly what her intentions were, but thought it was to detain her.

Bird, a negro slave being charged and Sworn, as a Witness for the Commonwealth says that he found several Weeks after the murder of Mr. Barrow, four pieces of money in a bag of feathers and covered with a handkerchief, that the room was occupied by the prisoner and another (Moses, since hung).

Moses, a Slave, was Sworn and charged as a Witness for the Commonwealth, & says that after the murder was committed, he saw the prisoner in Company with the insurgents at the door.

Robert T Musgrave being Sworn as a Witness for the Commonwealth says that after his examining the prisoner she stated that she had fled thro the kitchen and concealed herself in the cornfield.

The Court after hearing the testimony and from all the circumstances of the Case are unanimously of opinion that the prisoner is guilty in manner and form as in the information . . . And the Court value the said Slave Lucy to the sum of two hundred and Seventy five dollars.

At a Court of Oyer and Terminer Summoned and held for the County of Southampton on Saturday the fifth day of November

1831 for the trial of Nat alias Nat Turner, a negro man Slave late the property of Putnam Moore an infant charged with conspiring to rebel and making insurrection.

Present, Jeremiah Cobb, Samuel B. Hines, James D. Massenburg, James W. Parker, Robert Goodwin, James Trezvant, & Orvis A. Brown Gent. Carr Bowers, Thomas Preston & Richd. A. Urquardt. For reasons appearing to the Court it is ordered that the Sheriff summon a Sufficient additional guard to repel any attempt that may be made to rescue Nat alias Nat Turner from the custody of the Sheriff.

The Prisoner Nat alias Nat Turner was sent to the Bar in Custody of the Jailor of this County, and William C. Parker is by the Court assigned Counsel for the prisoner in his defence, and Merewether B. Broadnax, Attorney for the Commonwealth, filed an Information against the prisoner, who upon his arraignment pleaded not guilty. . . .

James Trezvant being Sworn said that Mr James W. Parker and himself were the Justices before whom the prisoner was examined previous to his commitment. That the prisoner at the time was in confinement but no threats or promises were held out to him to make any disclosures. That he admitted that he was one of the insurgents engaged in the late insurrection and the chief among them. That he gave to his Master & Mistress Mr. Travis & his Wife the first blow before they were dispatched, that he killed Miss Peggy Whitehead. That he was with the insurgents from their first movement to their dispersion on the Tuesday morning after the insurrection took place. That he gave a long account of the motives which led him finally to commence the bloody scene which took place. That he pretended to have had intimations by signs & omens from God that he should embark in the desperate attempt. That his comrades and even he was impressed with a belief that he could by the imposition of his hands cure diseases, that he related a particular instance in which it was believed that he had in that manner affected a cure upon one of his comrades, and that he went on to detail a medley of incoherent and confused opinions about his communications with God, his command over the clouds &c &c which he had been entertaining as far back as 1826.

The Court after hearing the testimony and from all the circumstances of the case are unanimously of opinion that the prisoner is guilty in manner and form as in the Information against him alledged and it being demanded of him if any thing for himself he had or knew to say why the Court to judgment and execution against him of and upon the premises should not proceede, he said he had nothing but what he had before said. Therefore it is considered by the Court that he be taken hence to the Jail from whence he was taken therein to remain until Friday the 11th day of November instant on which day between the hours of ten O'Clock in the forenoon and four o'Clock in the afternoon he is to be taken by the Sheriff to the usual place of execution and then and there be hanged by the neck until he be dead. And the Court value the said Slave to the Sum of three hundred and seventy five dollars.

Ordered that William C. Parker be allowed the Sum of ten dollars as a fee for defending Nat alias Nat Turner late the property of Putnam Moore an infant.

JER COBB

E. Murderous Plots and Outbreaks by Plantation Whites and Blacks

THE SOUTHAMPTON INSURRECTION *was the only sizeable, organized nineteenth-century rebellion. After 1831 resistance seemed to be more fitful, violent, and deadly, and occurred chiefly on smaller plantations. Documents in this section describe rather aimless violence among field hands and overseers; they reveal relations between blacks and whites, and among blacks themselves, that conflict sharply with an influential argument that the "typical plantation slave" was the archetypal "Sambo":*

docile but irresponsible, loyal but lazy, humble but chronically given to lying and stealing; his behavior was full of infantile silliness and his talk inflated with childish exaggeration. His relationship with his master was one of utter dependence and childlike attachment: it was indeed this childlike quality that was the very key to his being.[20]

A view of plantations as monolithic "closed institutions" that made slaves creatures who had lost their identity and become their Sambo

20. Stanley Elkins, *Slavery: A Problem in American Institutional and Intellectual Life* (Chicago, 1959), p. 63.

roles cannot be properly evaluated until much more is known about the correlations between slave behavior and plantation size, structure, and degree of routinization. (Perhaps it may be shown that some of the largest planters in the late antebellum era were able to stifle even the most inward-directed, day-to-day styles of resistance by creating routines and structures that made slaves Samboes.) Meanwhile the Sambo stereotype has gained a wide and uncritical audience. In explaining his novel The Confessions of Nat Turner, *William Styron gives an example of how pervasive variations of the stereotype have become—underlining the importance of reassessing that view in light of documentary research:*

> *the many millions of other slaves [other than Nat Turner] reduced to the status of children, illiterate, tranquilized, totally defenseless, ciphers and ants who could only accept their existence or be damned, and be damned away, like the victims of a concentration camp.*[21]

82. "He Did Not Care a Dam for Any White Man"

SOURCE: Robert Ruffin Barrow Books, 1857–1858, Southern Historical Collection, University of North Carolina Archives.

Saturday, 25 July 1857. Saturday morning abot 5 oclock while geting out the ploughes I ordered John Smith to Hury up more or I would take the responsibility of helping him to do so with the Cow hide. Whereupon he gave me to understand he did not care a dam for any white man and would not do any more untill his master Mr Barrow came home. I then caled several of the boys to help me & in so doing he bit som of them which let him loose again when he caught me by the arm tore my coat and made a grab for my throat. I threw him from me & caught up a padle which I struck Him with twice and had I of Killed him I should not of felt eney Conscientious Scruples in the matter.

GEORGE P. BUCKNALL

83. "I Am Not Going to Be Whipped by Anybody"

SOURCE: Deposition of Albert Foster, overseer, before the Coroner's Inquest (July 5, 1857), Concordia Parish Inquest Case File,

21. William Styron, *New York Review of Books*, 1 (September 26, 1963): 18–19.

1857, Louisiana State University Department of Archives and Manuscripts.

Driver Bill came to me. Sam "had become unmanageable was destroying cotton." Ordered S. to be whipped, later swore he would not be whipped. Bill sd. he would get the overseer. Samuel swore, he might get who he choose, and followed the driver, threatening to cut him to pieces with his hoe.

I went to the field along with the Driver, and found Samuel working, probably one hundred yards from the rest of the hands, he came to the end of the row as soon as I rode up. I asked him what was the matter, he said there was nothing, only the Driver had an ill will at him. I told him to wait till the driver got up as I always wished to hear both parties, as soon as Bill got up, I asked him what was the matter, he Bill immediately told me the same as he had done at the house. I then asked Samuel if he had refused to get down for punishment when the driver ordered him, he answered at once, Yes, by God, I did and I am not going to be whipped by anybody, either black or white. I told him to stop, as I allowed no negro to talk in that way, and that he knew that. I then ordered him to throw down his hoe, and to get down, he swore God damn him if he would I repeated the order, and he again swore he would not. I moved my horse nearer to him when he turned and ran off. I kept my horse standing and called to the rest of the hands to catch that boy, not one of them paid the least attention to me, but kept on at their work. I then started after Samuel, myself, and overtook him and turned him. I ordered him to throw down the hoe and stand, he swore, God damn him if he would, and again ran off. I ran at him again and again turned him and repeated my order and got the same answer he started again and I after, got him again within 4 or 5 yards when he whielded round, with his hoe raised in both hands and struck at me with his full force my horse swerved aside and passed him his hoe descending I think within one or two feet of my head, pulled my horse up, and drew my pistol. Samuel was then standing with his hoe raised. I fired across my Bridle arm when he fell.

GEO. W. GORDAN
Justice of the Peace.

84. "You Boys Are a Cowardly, Chicken-Hearted Set"

THIS DOCUMENT, *a letter from an embittered older man defending his son (?), Aleck, describes an event that seemed momentarily to turn inside-out a quiet and wealthy Louisiana community. For convenience the principals in a conspiracy among whites and slaves—one that ended in the murder of two overseers on adjoining plantations—are listed: Duncan B. Skinner and McBride, overseers and victims; John McAllin, a white man charged with complicity in the murder of the overseers by Henderson, a slave carriage driver and valet, Reuben, a slave driver, and Anderson, another slave. Darcas was McAllin's black mistress for more than fifteen years.*

SOURCE: A. K. Farrar to H. W. Drake, Esqr., Farrar (Alexander K., and Family) Papers, Louisiana State University Department of Archives and Manuscripts.

Kensington, Louisiana, September 5, 1857

DEAR SIR:

Yours of the 24th August, relating to John McAllin, and requesting a full history of his case, came to hand by the last mail, and now I proceed to reply: The Overseer of Mrs. Sharp, Duncan B. Skinner, was found dead in the woods. A coroner's inquest was held, and a verdict from the jury that he came to his death by a fall from his horse. His brother Jesse Skinner was not satisfied with the verdict, and called upon the neighbors to assist him in an investigation. Caution was observed to prevent the design from becoming public. Mrs Sharp was not apprised of the intention until the morning of the investigation. Her overseer went to the field, brought all the Negroes to the house, and placed them upon a line before the company assembled. He permitted no conversation among them, nor was there any permitted during the investigation. Several of the men were handcuffed and tied to trees, sufficiently far apart to prevent the hearing of conversation. The cook of Mr Skinner was taken aside and told that something bad had happened upon the place, that it could not happen without her knowing it, and that she had better tell all about it.

We then examined a number of the other negroes, their confessions all agreed, and corroborated with each other, as well as the statements of Jane and Reuben. Henderson was sent for, and tied off from the others. At first he denied knowing anything had been done on the place that was wrong. His conversation and looks however clearly indicated his guilt. Reuben had previously told us that in the struggle, Skinner had caught Henderson by the throat, and that the mark or print of his finger nails were still to be seen. We examined and the scars were plainly imprinted upon his throat. Several of those who composed the coroner's jury were present, and they as well as the whole crowd assembled, expressed themselves as being fully satisfied that Reuben, Henderson and Anderson had murdered Skinner, and that nearly every negro on the plantation knew something about it. . . .

Reuben said that he had a 20 dollar gold piece belonging to Skinner and that he had given it to Darcas to take care of. Darcas being a house servant we went over to the house, and demanded her to give up the money Reuben had given her to keep. She took us upstairs, over the hospital, and got a 20 dollar gold piece, saying that it was the money Reuben gave her, and that she knew of no other money. Henderson still denied knowing of anything wrong, or that he had any money belonging to any one. . . .

Upon being whipped he [Henderson] made a full confession agreeing precisely with what the others had stated. He also told of his throwing the powder and shot flask of Skinner in the horse pond, and took us to the place, and after some searching we found them both. Upon being asked where his portion of the money was, he said that it was in Mr. McAllin's trunk, that he had given it to Darcas to put there and she said that she had done so. . . .

We asked what made them think of hiding their money in McAllin's trunk, and why they called his name, which led to the following disclosure, to wit: Darcas was, and had been, the "Sweetheart" of McAllin, for some 15 years or more. That she told them [the Negroes] that McAllin said he was trying to marry their mistress, and that for some time past he had not been making such good headway, and it was on account of Skinner. That it seemed like Mrs. Sharp had more confidence in Skinner than any body else. That she went by every thing he said, and the only chance he [McAllin] had, was for the Negroes to put Skinner out of the way. That if they would do that, he [McAllin] could then marry their mistress, and then there should be no overseer, and they (the negroes) should have better times. . . .

Henderson, the carriage driver, states that he went up stairs one night to get McAllin's boots to black, that McAllin was standing by a window looking out towards the quarter, listening to a noise there, occasioned by Skinner's whipping some Negroes. That he said, Hen there is quite a fuss in the quarter tonight, and that he [Henderson] replied yes, but it is no uncommon thing here. To which McAllin replied, well if I was you boys, I would get rid of that man. How, asked Henderson? Why: I would put him out of the way. After some further talk Henderson went downstairs with the boots, and in the morning when he returned with them, McAllin rose up in his bed, and said, Hen how long did that fuss last last night, in the quarter? I don't know sir. It is such a common thing here, I didn't pay much attention to it. Well: says McAllin, you boys are a cowardly, chicken-hearted set, or you would not stand that man's whipping and beating you so. You would put him out of the way. If you were to do so, then I could marry the widow, and there would be no overseer, and you would all have better times. The Negroes on being asked if they understood what McAllin meant by putting out of the way, replied, Why killing him of course. Henderson further states that this conversation was held the last time McAllin was at the place before the death of Skinner. That he [Henderson] went out among the Negroes and they formed the plan to kill Skinner. He further states that when McAllin returned after Skinner's death, that Darcas bore all the messages, which were as above stated. . . .

A few days after the investigation at Mrs. Sharp's, a number of us met at Mr. Foules's. He had got the sheriff to send his three men, who murdered McBride [Foules's overseer] out to his house in order that they might produce something that would corroborate their confessions. They made full confessions, produced the watch, hat, shoes, clubs, etc. From their statements we learned that they knew that the Sharp negroes had murdered their overseer, and as the "white folks" couldn't find it out, they were induced to make a similar experiment. A few days after this, we met at the Magnolia Plantation, the Estate of Stephen C. Smith. The negroes had no knowledge of our coming. They were drawn up and put upon a line, and no conversation permitted among them. They were also examined separate and apart from each other, and confessed to having harbored Anderson—how he had told them all about the murder of Skinner, and how he said he didn't care much if it was found out, that he had no peace of his mind since Skinner was killed—he "harryragged him so." Anderson had previously made the same statement to us. Reuben in his confession stated, that he had made up his mind, that if the "white folks" ever got after him about the murder, that he intended to tell all about it as he had no peace of mind, since it was done, and had not had any good sleep since. They confessed to having seen Henderson also, and that he had told them all about the murder. In short confirmed every thing that Mrs. Sharp's negroes had said about McAllin's wanting to marry their mistress, and his wanting the negroes to put Skinner out of the way. . . .

McBride was an entire stranger in our community. No one knew him before he came to oversee for Mr. Foules, and after that, he was not known off of the place by but few. McAllin *did know him*. And we think that he must have had some conversation with Darcas concerning him. . . . Hetty [one of Foules's Negroes] heard John say about a week or less before the murder that he would kill him or have satisfaction in some way for his [the overseer's] abuse to him [John]. Heard Ruben say while he was driver that if Mc-Bryde served him as he done other negroes on the place that he [Reuben] would put him out of the way, either by killing or poisoning or in some way—on the evening of the murder she [Hetty] was coming along through the field on the Natchez road, she heard hollering in the direction of the place of the murder, but thought it was a boy after the mules. . . .

The reports which are in circulation and which are well authenticated, are in themselves sufficient to convict McAllin of lying, and of guilt as to complicity in the murder. It is reported that he says that he was about to marry Mrs. Sharp, and the community here being a rich, proud and haughty one, they wanted to drive him off, because he was a poor mechanic and they did not want to see him elevated along side of them. Another one is that he and Skinner were friends, that the plot was to kill him as well as Skinner, that Aleck Farrar wanted them both out of the way, because they prevented him from getting certain property from Mrs. Sharp

—leaving the inference that Aleck Farrar produced the murder, and wanted to have him murdered also. Again that Aleck Farrar wanted to drive him out of the country because he knew that he [McAllin] knew that he [Farrar] cheated Mrs. Sharp out of some property. And also that if the Negroes were instigated to commit the murder, they were instigated to do it by Aleck Farrar, through a negro of his, who traveled back and forth between his places. . . . I have lived to but very little purpose in this life, if in the community in which I am known, it is even rendered necessary for me to deny such vile and infamous charges—I have now hurriedly sketched down the principal portion of the testimony in this case, there is however much more connected with it, if I were to enter into the [illegible] and detail of it all, quite a volume would be required.

Yours respectfully,
A. K. FARRAR

85. THE SPARTANBURG, SOUTH CAROLINA, SLAVE TRIALS

IN THE BACK–COUNTRY MOUNTAINS of South Carolina, the Spartanburg District Court tried more than 300 slaves between 1835 and 1865. The transcripts of these trials, along with subpoenas for witnesses and jury members, were recently rediscovered in the Spartanburg County Courthouse. They are one of the most complete records of slave resistance and, like the Farrar account, provide unusual views of the private lives of slaves and non-slaveowning whites.

In sharp contrast to the large commercialized plantations, most of the farms in the Spartanburg area were small, and farmers owned only a very few slaves each. But apparently these slaves were resourceful and daring people who resisted the system—and sometimes were arrested.

Of the more than 300 slaves brought to trial, over half were accused of stealing goods ranging from leather and scrap iron to other slaves. The following list, taken from one of the trials, suggests that an entire store was cleaned out.

State of South Carolina
Spartanburg District

To Wylie Arnold
Constable

Whereas Joseph McCosh of the District of York and State aforesaid, hath this day made Oath before me J. R. Ellis A Magistrate in and for the District aforesaid, that the following goods (vizt) Pieces of Crape for Dresses, velvet ribbend Black, sterl. Clasp for *reticule, Brass Clasps, plated table spoons, Bombazetty, Calicoes, Linens, stockings, ladies Blk Pombu and other articles of Merchandise and leather pocket Books, were in the night of the 24th July last . . . feloniously taken, stolen and carried away out of the Store House of him said Joseph McCosh.*

Slaves were also accused of assaults on whites and other slaves, exposing themselves to white women before inviting them to make love (punishments for this were surprisingly light), of drinking and selling liquor illegally, gambling, lying, forgery, poisoning, arson, insurrection, rape, and murder.

The trials were held before a magistrate and five freeholders of the District, who acted as a jury. Almost half of the slaves charged were acquitted; those found guilty were usually sentenced to be publicly whipped and sent home. Only in the most serious cases, such as murder, rape, or insurrection, were slaves executed (and the state indemnified the owner for his loss).

Slaves were allowed to testify in cases involving other slaves but not in any case involving a white. When called upon to remark on the character of a fellow black, or to account for the whereabouts of a friend or spouse at the time of a crime, slaves protected themselves and each other—"I never saw anything, never knew anything." These glimpses of slaves talking about themselves and their world give us clues about what they did when they were not working, and how they tried (often successfully) to control their own lives. Not all antebellum slaves were caught up in the machinery of commercial plantations, and the Spartanburg trials are a testimony to the strength and resistance of a proud back-country people.

SOURCE: *State of South Carolina* v. *Larkin, property of Thompson Robbs,* March 11, 1850, Spartanburg Slave Trials, South Carolina State Archives.

State of South Carolina
Spartanburg District
    I Andrew Bonner Esqu for this Dist. do certify that the testimony of Wm Westbrook Narcissa Martin & John Martin Jr taken before me in a case the state against Larkin a negro man belonging to Tompson Robbs of this District for stabbing the negro man Jason belonging to Capt John Martin of this District at Robert Martins on this instant is as follows— Wm Westbrook being sworn says he saw Jason come up to Larkin and said Larkin dont banter

me. Larkin said I dont banter you Jason. Jason then spoke & said, They say you have said you can whip me Larkin then said God-damn you if you will follow me to the end of the lane I can do it. Jason then said shuck your linen & turned about & drew his coat Larkin then started off. Jason then followed after him a few paces and he saw Larkin draw his knife. While walking from Jason, Jason said you have drawed your knife put it up or I will nock you in the head with a stick. Jason then picked up a stick & threw it down. Then took up a smaller one. Then walked up by the side of Larkin as he went on & took him by the hand. Larkin then shifted his knife in his left hand. Then he looked off. I then looked and saw Jason strike Larkin two blows on the head with a stick the stick broke in pieces knocking off Larkins Cap, and Larkin then struck back and stabed Jason in the right side. They instantly then engaged in a fight and Jason had the better of it.

This testimony is confirmed by all the witnesses & sworn to & subscribed before me March 3rd 1850

A. BONNER   Mag.   her
                                        NARCISSA ✕ MARTIN
                                                  mark
                                        WILLIAM WESTBROOKE
                                                  his
                                        JOHN   + MARTIN
                                                 mark

State of South Carolina
Spartanburg District

At a magistrates Court convened at the House of A Bonner Esq on the 11th day of March 1850 . . . for the purpose of investigating a charge preferd against Larkin a Slave the property of Thompson Robbs for the murder of Jason Slave the property of Capt John Martin Sen, At the House of Robert Martin in the State and Dis-trict above named on the 3rd inst by Stabing him in the right Side with a Pocket knife.

The Folowing Freeholders, being previously summond as Jurors, were in attendance To wit Gilbert Sarratt, P. P. Goforth, Wm G Clark, H. G. Gaffney Esqu. Doct T. G Gaffney, Capt. L. C.

Cooper, George Petty & Saul A. Camp. The folowing were chosen
by owner of Prisoner which formed the Court To wit

D.B.P. Moonnar   H. G. Gaffney, Esq. ⎤
   Mg   Doct T. G. Gaffney │
                               Capt. T. C. Cooper ⎬ Freeholders
                               Wm G. Clarke   │
                               Gilbert Sarratt   ⎦

The above Jurors being sworn the charge was read to prisoner
who plead Not Guilty. Whereupon the Folowing Evidence was
offerd in behalf of the State, To wit

Wm Westbrook Sworn

   The first that witness heard was Jason said to prisoner, Larkin
dont banter me . . . Prisoner said he did not. Jason then said that he
heard that Prisoner had said that he would whip him Prisoner said
God dam you if you go with me to the end of the lane I can whip
you Jason then said Shuck your Linnen and turned round and
pulled off his coat Larkin started towards the end of the lane Jason
folowing, some four or five paces behind Prisoner put his hand in
his Pocket and pulled out his knife Witness thinks It was open
when he pulled it out Jason picked up a stick about Six feet long,
and told prisoner to drop his knife or he would knock him in the
head. Prisoner made no reply as witness heard. Jason then droped
that stick and took up a small one about two foot long, then walked
up to the right side of Prisoner and caught hold of his right hand in
which he had the knife and said drop that knife prisoner then
Shifted the knife into his left hand. Witness then took his eyes off of
them for a moment when he again looked he saw Jason strike
prisoner two licks on the back of the head. Prisoner was in the act
of turning round and struck rather a back handed lick with his
knife and hit Jason about one inch below the ribs in his right side
he then made a lick at him on the other side but his knife went shut
in his hand Consequently he did not cut him they then Gatherd
prisoner still striking with his knife shut in his hand Jason proved
too hard for him. The knife was a common Pocket knife The above
hapend at Robert Martins in Spartanburg District on the 3d inst.
Witness and brother was sitting by the fence previous to the above

fight alluded to when prisoner came up and remarked that he had had a fight with Jason that morning prisoner then left and Jason came up and said that he had had a fight with Larkin

Cross examined by S. Bobo Attorney for Prisoner.

Jesse Hammet sworn. Witness some two or three hours after the fight examined the head of the prisoner and saw nor felt no marks of violence whatever was present when Jason died the day folowing the fight thinks there is no doubt but Jason Bled to death from the wound inflicted in his side by Prisoner

Cross Examined by Bobo.

Prisoner and Jason were both Puking when he got to the place some two or three hours after the fight.

James Amos sworn.

Witness says that sometime previous to the day of the fight that prisoner was at his Fathers, his Father said something to prisoner and he said he was going to behave himself. Mr Hoard then said something to him and he cussed him and said it was none of his business. Mr Hoard said something else and Prisoner tried to get out of the house to where Hoard was but was prevented.

Cross examined by Bobo.

Prisoner was drinking saw him down the road at a Wagon think he got Liquor of the Wagoner. Prisoner is quite peaceable when Sober.

William Westbrook recalled.

The stick that Jason struck prisoner with was about two foot long was a size larger than a corn cob. It broke into two or three pieces the second lick.

Here the evidence for the State Closed.

Defence:
Jacob Cantrell sworn. Witness went to Robert Martin's the morning of the fight as I left saw prisoner coming Witness went home and returned in about one hour found prisoner in the Store

house prisoner called for Liquor. Martin pourd some out in a mug and set it on the counter and said there is your Liquor then either the prisoner touched Martin or Martin touched Prisoner and they went out Martin came in directly with I think fifty cents in his hand. Prisoner folowed demanded his change of Martin and would not drink the Liquor. Martin told the Prisoner that he did not have his change. Witness went to Martin by request of Prisoner for the Change. Martin replied that that [sic] it would be all right directly. Martins son then went behind the counter to his father and got a knife & went out side of the house and gave it to Jason. Jason then came in and told prisoner that he was demanding change and he never had that much and to leave there prisoner said he would not go for he intended to have his change before he went Prisoner and Witness then went out of the house and spoke to Williams about it. Williams said he would see to it. Witness then left. The report of the neighborhood is that Jason kept a white woman, had children by her, she lived in the house with his Master.

Robert Scruggs Sworn. Witness says Jason's character was not very good, the report is that he keeps a white woman at home it is reported that she has a child by him, the Land that Robert Martin lives on is said to belong to Capt John Martin (which John Martin admitted in court). Witness some two or three years ago had a conversation with John Martin in regard to Jason's keeping this white woman. Martin remarked that he did not know how he could better himself for if he put her off he was afraid Jason would steal more from him for her than it cost to keep her there at home. Witness examined the wound on Jason his guts were out got them in Consider that the wound killed him.

Doct T G. Gaffney sworn. Witness considers that perhaps if there had been a skillfull Phisician at hand he might have been saved but from the description of the witnesses the wound was very dangerous.

Noah Williams Sworn. Proves nothing

Here the case was closed.

Mr Bobo adressed the Jury who returned and brought in the verdict. . . .

We find the boy Larkin guilty of manslaughter and say that he shall receive One hundred Lashes on his bare back forthwith.

D.B.P. MOONNAR (Magistrate)

> H. G. GAFFNEY
> WILLIAM G. CLARK
> GILBERT SARRATT
> L. C. COOPER
> T. G. GAFFNEY

} Free holders

Which sentence was put into execution by W. B. Godfrey

Const.

D.B.P. MOONNAR   mg

86. "HANGING CALMLY"

SOURCE: A. K. Farrar to W. B. Foule, December 6, 1857, Farrar (Alexander K., and Family) Papers, Louisiana State University Department of Archives and Manuscripts.

Commencement, Louisiana, December 6, 1857

DEAR SIR:

I intended to ride down to see you today but have not had time. I have now to start down to Woodville. I wanted to talk with you about the hanging of the Negroes. I think all that is necessary is to show the Negroes that there is no doubt about the hanging, in order to do away with any impression that may prevail among them that the "White folks send them off and don't hang them &c &c." If the Negroes are brought out in public to be hung and they get up and talk out that they are prepared to die—that they have got religion and are ready to go home to heaven &c &c—it will have a bad effect upon the other Negroes, hence I think to prevent unfavorable impressions that the best plan would be to hang them all privately and have them brought out in the Country and burried by the Negroes upon the spot where the murders were committed. If they could be hung publickly and not allowed to talk any, it would make no difference, but I am satisfied that impressions would be made of a bad tendency by their being allowed to talk. I have no particular wish about the matter only that the Negroes in our Country may not be impressed with the belief that hanging is not such a dreadful thing, in as much as they see those who are about to be hung, or [illegible] hanging calmly, and with evidence of their preparation of going home to heaven &c &c.

Yours truly,
A. K. FARRAR

IV
The Civil War Era
An Abolitionist and a Rice Planter
View the War in the
Carolina Low Country

WITH THE COMING *of the Civil War the planter's "system" fell apart before his eyes. In many areas slaves wandered about the countryside; crops were abandoned; and horses, stores, boats, and barns were looted and burned by armies of the Union and the Confederacy and by hungry, angry blacks.*

Few were spared; a letter published in the New York Tribune, June *10, 1865, read:*

> Good masters and bad masters, all alike shared the same fate—the sea of Revolution confounded good and evil, and in the chaotic turbulence, all suffer in degree. Born and raised amid the institution [of slavery] like a great many others, I believed it was necessary to our welfare, if not to our very existence.

Louis Manigault, a member of an old South Carolina Huguenot family, incorporated this letter by another rice planter into a personal narrative of the war, which he wrote in a ledger for Gowrie plantation, near Savannah, Georgia. Meanwhile, north and east on the Sea Islands, Arthur Sumner, a New England abolitionist and Port Royal schoolteacher, recorded his views of the war in the rice country, of General William T. Sherman's army, and the Gullah Negroes in letters to Northern friends.

87. "A CHANGE DISCERNED AMONGST THE NEGROES"

SOURCE: Gowrie Plantation Books, vol. 4, Manigault Papers, Southern Historical Collection, University of North Carolina Archives. Published by permission of James M. Clifton, who is preparing the Manigault Papers for publication.

The unrighteous and diabolical War now waging between our Confederate States and the United States is causing great distress amongst the Sea Coast Plantations, of South Carolina and Georgia. A brief Synopsis of the History of our Savannah River property for the past year will be interesting hereafter as showing how even in our secluded position we were not entirely exempt from the sufferings of the times. In May 1861 I left Savannah River, after having spent the entire winter with my family on Gowrie plantation. During the summer the regular plantation work continued without interruption, whilst we spent it quietly (our first) in our Charming residence, no 5 Gibbs Street, Charleston. All was quiet around our two Cities of Charleston and Savannah until the attack and fall of Port Royal early in November. Then at once was a Change discerned amongst the Negroes but especially amongst those in the vicinity of Beaufort. Some were Captured by the Yankees and as we are informed Compelled to work for them in erecting Batteries on Hilton Head Island and other places, whilst with the Masters and Overseers driven from the numerous plantations in that neighborhood great numbers of Negroes were running away, seeking to avoid work of every kind, besides stealing all they Could lay their hands upon. Already some murmuring was extending itself to the Savannah River plantations. We had no trouble with Negroes, but from Clear indications it was manifest that some of them were preparing to run away, using as a pretext their "fear of the Yankees." During the examination of the Settlements of Gowrie and East Hermitage plantations in November the Overseer found a quantity of plantation shot and powder which one Man (Ishmael) had been stealing during the summer, he at the same time Confessing it was his intention to go with the Yankees; since then however he is a Completely Changed individual. On Monday 11th November 1861 I left Charleston (alone) for Savannah; there having been no frost it was not prudent to venture upon the plantation and the Overseer (Mr Wm Capers) met me in Savannah. For one who has never witnessed the Cruel effects of War the mind Can hardly realize its saddening tendencies upon all Classes. The most self-possessed have their feelings worked upon, whilst deep and thoughtful expressions become stampt upon Countenances otherwise Calm and unruffled. History informs us that at the Close of the Revolutionary War, Men's minds were excited to such a degree

Concerning the fate of their Country that when peace was declared their emotions were so great as to deprive some of their reason "and one aged patriot in Philadelphia died." This feeling I now for the first time Can Comprehend. In Savannah quite a Panic had taken place, numerous families were hastening to seek shelter in the interior of Georgia whilst all business was at a stand. The same feeling existed in Charleston; Indeed had the Enemy known the weakness of our two Cities and the great Consternation spread throughout our entire Community in November 1861, they would surely have caused us far more injury than they did, whilst strange to say six months have since then elasped during which period we have very much fortified ourselves, whilst the Yankees have not as yet advanced upon either City. After a long Conversation with the Overseer, who soon Convinced me that all was not quite Correct upon the plantation, we determined I should remove Ten of the Men at once, selecting such as we deemed most likely would Cause trouble. Three of them had to be removed by force (attempting to run away they were Caught the same night & handcuffed) the remaining seven Came very willingly. This war has taught us the perfect·impossibility of placing the least Confidence in any Negro. In too numerous instances those we esteemed the most have been the first to desert us. House Servants, from their Constant Contact with the family become more Conversant with passing events and are often the first to have their minds polluted with evil thoughts. For my own part I am more than ever Convinced that the only suitable occupation for the Negro is to be a Laborer of the Earth, and to work as a field Hand upon a well disciplined plantation. It has now been proven also that those Planters who were the most indulgent to their Negroes when we were at peace, have since the Commencement of the war encountered the greatest trouble in the management of this Species of property.

With us upon Savannah River, my favorite Boat Hand, a Man who had rowed me to and from Savannah from my earliest recollections of Gowrie plantation (1839), one who had been kindly treated by my Father and family upon numerous occasions, a Man bought with Gowrie (1833), my Constant Companion when previous to my marriage I would be quite alone upon the plantation, and a Negro We all of us esteemed highly. Singular to say this Man "Hector" was the very first to murmur, and would have hastened to the embrace of his Northern Brethren, Could he have foreseen the least prospect of a successful escape. He was the first Negro I took with me from the plantation on to Charleston and is now (May, 1862) safe. Such is only One of the numerous instances of ingratitude evinced in the African Character.

1862, 20th Sept'r.   One of our Prime Hands ("Charles Lucas") absconded from the plantation. He had been in charge of our Stock, and having allowed eight of the choicest Hogs to depart from the plantation in some unaccountable manner, received his due punishment. His next step was to follow the animals which he had most probably killed himself, and sent to the retreat where he expected soon to follow. I will here remark that the half dozen fine cows which I had always kept upon the plantation were sold by me (for what was considered a high price at that time, 28 Cts. per lb.) to a Butcher in Savannah in the Spring of 1862. This was through fear of their being all stolen some night by our Negroes.

This so named "Charles Lucas" (from having once belonged to a Mr Lucas) is the second Negro thus far who has left the place; the first being a very notorious character, a Carpenter Known as "Jack Savage" (his former Master being a Mr Savage of Bryan County) who ran away from the Camp on the night of the 21st February 1862. After an absence of upwards of a year from the plantation, most of which time was passed in the dense Carolina Swamp near the McPherson plantation, in company with "Charles Lucas" and other runaway Negroes, "Jack Savage" returned of his own accord to us, 16th August 1863, looking half starved and wretched in the extreme. We always considered him a most dangerous character & bad example to the others. He was sold in Savannah (Sept'r 1863) for $1800, & left with his new Master for Columbus Ga. "Charles Lucas" was caught 7th August 1863. . . .

> Apart from religious considerations, although, by the loss of the cause and the institution, I have suffered like the rest, yet am I content; for the conduct of the Negro in the late crisis of our affairs has convinced me that we were all laboring under a delusion. Good masters and bad masters, all alike, shared the same fate—the sea of Revolution confounded good & evil; and, in the chaotic turbulence, all suffer in degree. Born and raised amid the institution, like a great many others, I believed it was necessary to our welfare, if not to our very existence. I believed that these people were content,

happy and attached to their masters. But events and reflection have caused me to change these opinions; for if they were necessary to our welfare, why were four fifths of the plantations of the Southern States dilapidated caricatures of that elegance and neatness which adorn the Country-seat of other people? If as a matter of profit they were so valuable, why was it that nine tenths of our planters were always in debt and at the mercy of their factors? If they were content, happy and attached to their masters, why did they desert him in the moment of his need and flock to an enemy whom they did not know; and thus left their, perhaps, really good masters whom they did know from infancy?

> The above correct Remarks are taken from a Letter published in the New York Tribune June 10th 1865 by Augustin L. Taveau of Charleston So. Ca.; a Gentleman Known to our family, & a Planter.

88. "A Sort of Oceanic Grandeur"; "We Lords and Ladies"

AS EARLY AS SPRING, 1862, *many Northern abolitionist societies sent missionaries to the South to aid, settle, and educate freedmen in areas conquered by the Union armies. One of the first regions to which they were sent as part of an "experiment" by the Federal Government was the land Louis Manigault wrote about—Port Royal and St. Helena Islands, along the South Carolina–Georgia seacoast.*

There the high-minded missionaries met the Gullah people, most African of all southern blacks. A semicolonial society was re-created. The Yankee teachers, settling comfortably into abandoned plantation and town houses, soon wrote home long letters about "curious" African customs, and problems with shiftless, "insubordinate" Negroes, whom they often called (regardless of age) their children or babies.

Although some of the emissaries were undoubtedly effective teachers and practiced what they had preached in New England, others, such as Arthur Sumner and Edward Philbrick, eventually became planters themselves and assumed some of the attitudes of that class. Sumner never made money at this venture (although Philbrick did), and re-turned to full-time teaching; but he retained in his private correspon-dence a definite regard for blacks as inferior. This crucial episode in American race relations is described in a superb book by Willie Lee Rose, Rehearsal for Reconstruction: The Port Royal Experiment (*New York, 1967*).

SOURCE: Typescripts of the Arthur Sumner Letters in the Penn School Papers, Southern Historical Collection, University of

North Carolina Archives. Published by permission of the Boston
Public Library.

Arthur Sumner to Nina Hartshorn, Port Royal, S.C., May 18, 1862

These negroes speak with an inarticulate jabber. The sounds roll
round in their great chops, and come pouring out through their
huge mouths, so that I find it easier to understand a foreign language than confused utterance. Their idioms, too, are funny. I told
Byron, a boy who waits upon me, that I was going to distribute
clothing on his place. "Talk *we* house?" said he:—meaning, "Are
you speaking of our house?" "Talk me get dinner," means, "do you
mean that I shall get dinner?" Byron came to me with a message
from his mother: "Ma says if you give her some trade"—imagine
such a sentence uttered as if it were a word of many syllables. Can
you make it out? Oh, dull girl! the meaning is clear. "Ma wants to
know if you will give her some *thread?*" More indistinct than their
speech is the identity of their faces. They are all black, and look
precisely alike. I cannot, owing to my feeble vision, distinguish
those with whom I am in constant companionship, except by some
peculiarity of voice, height, or bearing. With white people I depend
chiefly upon color, to identify those I know. But this mode is unavailing here, for their faces are like a round path of vacant space.
I could as easily distinguish one circle of perfect darkness from
another of the same size, as to separate Napoleon or General Jes-
sup from April or Jackson.

I am greatly interested in this people. They have the making of a
very interesting society. They are humble, docile, courteous, and,
for their advantages, intelligent. They are extremely eager to learn
to read. While I am writing, there have been a dozen men women
and children to my room, wishing me to do them a lesson.

To Joseph Clark, St. Helena Island, July 7, 1862

We had a glorious celebration of the Fourth. All the negroes on
this island were assembled, and marched in a melodious proces-
sion, bearing green branches, and singing "Roll, Jordan, Roll"
down through the beautiful shady road to the old Episcopal
Church. Around this picturesque building, in front of the platform

they gathered in a great crowd under the moss-grown oaks, while our majestic gridiron waved above them. General Saxton and one or two others made brief remarks. The heft of the festivities was music and dried herring.

Oh, I wish you and all my friends could have heard these Africans sing! I never listened to more impressive music than this. The singing was intrinsically good; the songs strange and beautiful; and their swaying to and fro with the melody, seemed to have a sort of oceanic grandeur in it.

After the darkies had devoured their "co-lation" of crackers, herring, and molasses, we lords and ladies rode down to Mr. Hooper's headquarters where we had a fine lunch all to ourselves —about twenty of us. Myself and another passed the evening. The negroes on the plantation, hearing us sing, were attracted in a crowd around the house, and bye and bye, thronged up onto the piazza (with permission) and held a "Shout," a strange, barbaric, central-African dance and song. I tell you what—if some of these Ethiopian minstrals should come down here and learn how to bring out a genuine Negro dance and song, it would be the best enterprise could be devised. One of these "Shouts" would be a fortune to them.

To Joseph Clark, St. Helena Island, May 21, 1863

My third class (including only those who come pretty regularly) numbers 38, with an average attendance of 30 scholars. Their ages are all the way from 8 to 16, but the average is about 10 years. Only 10 or 12 knew their letters when they first came to me; and but two or three could read at all. They have been reading out of Ellsworth's Progressive Primer for a month, and today they finished the 43 page. The book contains 58 pages of reading. Six or seven read without spelling, and three or four have to stand by me while I point out the letters with a pencil. The remainder read by spelling without assistance of mine. I give them nearly two hours a day (in the morning) devoted entirely to reading and spelling. Some of them are the prettiest little things you ever saw, with solemn little faces and eyes like stars. But this is a digression. . . .

Some four or five read now, quite fluently, out of the Second Reader, and with a pretty good delivery of the sense, but most of them still stumble a good deal over such words as "devoured, par-tial, although, carried, stripped, anxious, scattered, &c." In Arith-metic, they are learning the Multiplication Table, and can tell, from the card, the first three columns. They know by sight, the numbers as far as 100, when I write them on the board, and show, I think, a marvellous quickness at it.

This first class of mine are real jewels. I should like to have you see them. The girls are very particular about their dress. They come in their Sunday clothes, and look as trim and as pretty as if they were not black. When the girls of the second class were first transferred to the first, they came in looking rather dingy; but when they saw how very aristocratic the others looked, they were aghast; and the next day they appeared in great style.

I am unable to discover any difference in ability, between the blacks and mulattoes; although perhaps it would be interesting to build up a theory on the subject.

To Joseph Clark, St. Helena Island, June 15, 1863

Joseph, I am ill. I am only slightly ill. Just enough to cause me to keep quiet for a few days, without obliging me to give up my school. But the moment I am shelved, everything in and about the house goes wrong. Gates are left open; so that the horses get out and the cows get in, where they should not. Saddles, ropes, curry combs and brushes, tubs, boots, chickens, pigs, carriages, horses and boys, are left where they have no business and where they get spoiled. The truth is these negroes are absolutely selfish. A mean lot, I think. Industrious enough; capable of independence; plucky enough, among themselves; but selfish, ungrateful, deceitful, hypo-critical, and licentious. Of course I don't mean to speak so of the whole race. But I can say that of those whom I have met. This opinion is no sudden change in my feelings. I think much better of them than I did before I came down here; and as to their capacity, my estimate rather increases than diminishes. But I have lost that liking for them which I had during my first acquaintance with them. When an anti-slavery man first mingles with these people, he is delighted; for he sees only the outside. They are habitually courteous and respectful—he is charmed with that and with their apparent humility. They tell the story of their wrongs and former sufferings; they talk religion most devoutly—he is touched. Then he writes beautiful articles for the Northern papers, in which the Negro is dressed out in a white garment of sanctity, with a halo—all stuff!

These people are what Slavery has made them. I don't blame them; but there they are. I am only astonished that they should be fit to live after such generations of mere animal life. A higher race would have lost all moral sense; would have come out of the system with all the negroes' vices and many more. The negro is temperate, both in eating and drinking; prone to forgive injuries, or as you may say, not vindicative; fairly inclined to industry; *not* very affectionate (so far as I have observed) not *deeply*, but only warmly, religious:—very much as the most ignorant and superstitious of the Roman Catholics are. Very likely my children are as vicious as their parents. But if they are, I shut my eyes to it—the little darlings. The little black tots. They are *some*, let me tell you.

To Joseph Clark, July 9, 1863

This teaching wears upon my throat. I shouldn't wonder if I should be forced to give it up next winter. I am permanently worse than I was six months ago. But my general health is very good indeed, and I continue to enjoy the life exceedingly. One of the teachers within two miles of us is a mulatto girl named Charlotte Forten. She is a very charming young lady of about 20 years, with uncommonly graceful manners, and a very agreeable voice. She is a superior person, in every way; and I see no reason why a fellow might not fall in love with her just as readily as if she belonged to the haughty race of Saxons. . . . Her uncle is a rich and talented mulatto named Robert Purvis, of Phildelphia—said to be a very handsome, gentlemanly, and cultivated man. Her father withdrew, many years ago, to London, where he cherishes the hatred to his country which any man of spirit must have, who has a crop of African blood in his veins. Miss Forten would go too; but she says it would be cowardly to desert the cause of her race. Imagine the deep wrath and scorn which such a high-bred lady must feel at the indignities to which she is subject at the North. . . .

So I will leave you this afternoon & ride over to my babies. I have about 20 babies, on the other side of the island, belonging to my first class. They are, mostly, about 15 or 18 years old, and three are grown up—45 years old. They are very nice babies, let me tell you. One of them, Martha Anne, about 12 years old, is the most bewitching little creature. I hug her as often as I think decorous, and if it were consistent with my dignity I should kiss her every day. There are two or three sweet little girls who are called by my scholars my "huggin' girls," because I always have 'em in my arms while they recite. I'm sorry to say they are rather dirty. If they were clean I should kiss 'em, although such a proceeding would excite the most unbounded astonishment throughout the plantations. I don't suppose these children ever received a caress or a word of tenderness since they were infants. The children are invariably spoken to in harsh and peremptory tones by all grown niggers, and are whipped unmercifully on the least offence. Yet they are very obedient to their parents, and certainly stand much more in awe of adult darkies than they do of us mild-eyed missionaries.

To Joseph Clark, February, 1865

The army has gone now: off to march and fight, and to conquer. The negro element again appears in Beaufort. While Sherman's men were there, they were cast into utter insignificance, and slunk out of sight. Sherman and his men were impatient of darkies, and annoyed to see them so pampered, petted, and spoiled, as they have been here. They hustled them out of the way, and the blacks were rather afraid of them.

I am afraid you think I am unfaithful to my anti-slavery principles, and forgetful of the old feelings which prompted my coming here. But this is not the case. I am exasperated (and so is every other white man in this place) at the mischievous indulgence shown to the negro. It is a common remark here, that "a white man can get no justice." This inhumane leniency is doing a great deal of harm, in many ways. It is teaching them to despise the laws, and to believe that Liberty means License. It is creating in the minds of the white people a very bitter feeling against the blacks, which, of course, is mutual. If Justice had been shown to both parties, from the beginning, there would, I believe, have been far less antagonism. There will always be, however, until the blacks are as intelligent and well-educated as the whites, a contempt felt by the latter, and dislike and distrust by the former. It is so here, and must be so everywhere. The negro has always been oppressed by the white man, and knows that even now he has it in his power, from his superior intelligence and requirements, to cheat him. Even the best of the young men sent down here by benevolent societies at the North, have failed to gain their confidence. They are stupid and ignorant, and therefore incapable of comprehending that a man who has it in his power to cheat them, should fail to do so. They would do it, and they judge others by their own standard of morality. Much of this distrust will be well-grounded. For, when the South is thrown open to immigration, hosts of unscrupulous men will come down and swindle the Negro as they used to swindle the Indian. The Black has got a long struggle before him, 'ere he will gain all his rights; but I would rather, for his own sake, see him oppressed for generations, than be spoiled and petted as he has been here. He would come out of the struggle more manly and self-reliant.

CODA

89. The Welsh Neck Baptist Church Minutes (South Carolina), 1738–1932

UNTIL RECENTLY *the Arthur Sumner letters concluded this documentary history. That decision made sense chronologically, and the letters were instructive about such important matters that seemed to sum up the experience of slavery as the deterministic character of roles, and the racist views of some of the very best white friends blacks had in Reconstruction America. (How easy it was for northern whites in the proper context to slip into planter roles and attitudes; and how readily exslaves became, at least in white eyes, dependent, tractable, or childishly unruly.)*

To end with the Sumner letters was to conclude on a depressing note. But what could be done about the racism of the truly sincere and dedicated young teachers of Port Royal? Blacks a few miles away facing a similar situation had an important solution—separation. After worshiping amicably with whites for a hundred years, the Negro members of a Baptist church (in the northeast South Carolina Piedmont) formed their own congregation in 1867. What they had to do in Reconstruction society was evidently impossible without their own church, leaders, and ritual.

In 1737 Welshmen from Pennsylvania settled on the Pee Dee River (opposite Society Hill) and formed the Welsh Neck Baptist Church. By the 1770s a sizeable portion of the membership was black, and for nearly two centuries the congregation was a tightly knit community (the church disbanded in the Depression of the 1930s). The record the congregation left is unbroken, 1738 to 1932, except for a four-year period during the Civil War. Following the war the members' first actions when getting back together were characteristic: they collected seventy-two dollars for a poor man, and disciplined members who had ostracized an impoverished war widow for boarding Union soldiers in her home.

The Welsh Neck Baptists were a warm, unassuming, honest people. One suspects they were much like Rachel O'Connor, David Gavin, and the "plain folk" Olmsted met in the poorer regions of the South. Their slaves came to church with them, and together (galleries were not built until the nineteenth century) they sang, shouted, cried, and sweated during moving, down-home services that lasted most of Sunday morning. Once a month after worship, blacks and whites reconvened in a small group and censored members for petty social transgressions (usually drunkenness, swearing, or fornication), and received others back into the church (usually drunks, profaners and fornicators) who had been expelled previously. In an admirable spirit of Christian fellowship and generosity, these Baptists dealt with issues unheard of in any other type of document on slavery.

The Welsh Neck Church Minutes plunge the reader back into the eighteenth century, slavery's formative period, and, in an account of the censure of a black brother who killed a witch, recall the importance of the African background. Insights on slave family life are provided by a profound soul-searching the congregation underwent in the 1820s regarding the slaves' "double [plural] marriages." Many blacks, separated by sales from their mates, asked to remarry and remain in the church. Although the Bible, the Baptist guide, prohibited remarriages while ex-partners lived, tradition and family ties proved to be stronger sanctions for social action by the small planters of Welsh Neck.

Church records have been passed over by many scholars. But ways they may illuminate the social history of common people are described by Loulie Owens, a historian and an archivist of Baptist Church Records:

Of all the churches in South Carolina, the Welsh Neck Church has kept the fullest record over the longest period of time. Beginning at its time of construction, clerks carefully set down the church's actions, it covenants, and confessions of faith. At intervals they recorded the rolls of members. In the early part of the 19th century, the book evidently became worn and a clerk painstakingly copied it into a new ledger. This copy is still owned by the church and has been shared with a number of collections through microfilm.

It is easy to know what these Welsh Baptists were like from such a record. They literally watched over one another's morals in typical Puritan spirit. . . .

The quality of tolerance and Christian graciousness of this congregation made it stand out from most of the pioneer churches. For two thirds of the 18th century, these churches served as courts to regulate local order and personal conduct. Colonial government was conducted from Charleston until 1769 when more accessible district courts were established. This situation encouraged a harsh attitude in most of the frontier churches.[1]

1. Loulie Owens, *Saints of Clay: The Shaping of South Carolina Baptists* (Columbia, S.C., 1971), pp. 29–30.

The minutes also demonstrate the ways frontier churches served as primary agencies of social control, and the importance of beliefs in holding together even the most improbable groups (religious communes today in Colorado and New Mexico are more cohesive and longer-lived than secular ones), as well as the usefulness of institutions in bringing about significant changes in attitudes and customs. But most important, the document is "unconscious evidence" about people during their unguarded moments, and another example of the interdependency, and varied roles, of whites and blacks in slavery. Once interdisciplinary methods are refined and applied to sources of this type, more satisfactory explanations of the personal dimension of slavery will be possible and, on that base, we may expect even deeper investigations of the Civil War and slavery's meaning for our society as a whole.

SOURCE: Minutes of the Welsh Neck Baptist Church (W.P.A. typescript), The South Caroliniana Library, University of South Carolina.

Oct. 6 [1759]. It was determined that any member who travel'd up & down river on Sabboth day "without an absolute necessity" would be censured.

Sept 5 [1779]. A great many of those baptized by Mr Winchester have been excommunicated, both white and black; but the greater number of blacks; many of the later upon examination appeared to be very ignorant of the nature of true religion.

Soon after Mr Winchester left Pee Dee, he fell into the error of universal restoration, which he first published in Philadelphia where after baptizing a great many, he was the means of dividing the Baptist Church in that City.

27th July [1779]. Thomas Ayer, Elizabeth Raburn and Bibby Bruce were baptized: As also Scipio, Sancho, Pompey, Dundee, Fanny, Cretia and Nancy (Servants of Col. McIntosh) and Boston and Mingo (servants of Thomas Evans), Robert and Priss (servants of Abel Wilds), Frank (servt. of William Ellerbe) Will (servt. of Col Kershaw) and Will (servant of John Wilds) and Ludlow (Sev^t of Estate of Hart) Jethro (servt of Job Edwards) Hampton (Sert of the widow Lide) and Sus (Servt of Charles Mason).

Feb^{ry} 3rd [1816]. Whereas we have many black members in our Church, who being servants, cannot perform the requisitions of the Church's Covenant, and Whereas a summary of duties is regarded important for them also—Resolved—That a suitable Covenant for the black members of the Church is necessary: And that brethren Dossey and McIver be requested to draught one; and present it to the next Conference, for adoption.

The Committee appointed to draught a Covenant for the black members of our Church reported by reading the Covenant:

Voted: That it be received as the Covenant of our black members; and that it be read and explained to them tomorrow by the Pastor.

April 6th [1816]. The Covenant above spoken of, was read and explained to the blacks and by them unanimously adopted. The Covenant together with the records relating to the blacks are kept in a book where their names have been recorded.

Feb 18 [1820]. Kitty, svt. of Mrs. Mary Winds, who had been for some time since forsaken by her husband, and who requested the privelege to take another, was so far regarded by the Church, as to appoint a committee to inquire into the cause of their separation and her general conduct. Her case was considered, and the Committee reported favorably of her character; and regarded her released from the man as husband; yet could not view her at liberty to take another husband, whilst the former was living; notwithstanding he had taken another wife. The report was adopted, and Kitty was advised to continue in her present state, while her husband remained alive. But she departed from this instruction, and took another husband, for which she was excluded.

Septr 3rd [1825]. . . . The Church attended to the Cases of several black members, who were reported by the black Deacon, Scipio, to be in disorder: & upon the report of a Committee, appointed to enquire into the facts; excluded the following persons, viz, *Molley*, servant of Alexr. Norwood, for a turbulent, quarrelsome temper, which has hurried her into acts of violences, of which there was satisfactory proof. All labour with her, had proved unavailing. She had also been guilty of Lying. *Bess.* Servant of Genl. Williams, for the crime of Adultery, & the Ordinary dissimulation to hide it. *Winney.* Servant of Alexander Sparks. She had been under censure, & had been laboured with in vain. She had withdrawn herself from the Church & expressed a wish to be cut off: Also *Mourning* the servant of James Ellerbe, for Adultery. The Pastor was requested to announce these acts of the Church, to the black members tomorrow, with such remarks, as prudence might suggest. Adjourned by Prayer as usual.

May 21st [1826].   After Divine Service, the Church was called to sit in Conference. . . .

The attention of the Church was now called to the consideration of a subject unparalleled in the Annals of this Church. The Pastor announced, that one of our black members, Jim, late the property of the Est. of McIntosh (Now Mr. Alexr. Norwood's) had been arrested by legal process: & tried for the murder of Rachel an aged Woman (the property of Alexr. J. McIntosh) also a member of this Church.

One of the brethren informed the church, that he had been Called on, & tho with much reluctance, had set as a member of the Magistrate's Court, that had tried the case. There was but little testimony introduced; but enough to satisfy the Court, that the accused was guilty, at least as an accessory to the Murder. After some enquiry into this unhappy affair by the Church it was thought expedient to Commit the investigation of it to a special Committee; & the following brethren were nominated by the Pastor, viz: Wilson, Kirven, Atkinson, Armstrong; & Bro. Campbell was afterwards added by request. The Church now adjourned, that the Committee might begin at once, with the investigation, & the black members were all requested to remain.

June 3d [1826]. The Church met. Sermon by the Pastor. After a short interval formed conference, & proceeded to business. . . . The Committee appointed to investigate the charges against Jim, were called upon, & they submitted the following facts, as the result of their enquiry into this distressing affair. They understood that *Shine*, the wife of Jim was implicated, & Sister McIntosh, being present was requested to relate certain facts which had come to her knowledge. She stated, that Shine was examined at different times, & at first denied that Jim her husband was at home, that night, & said he was not guilty. She afterwards manifested great distress, & confessed that Jim was at home (whose house was quite near the

house of the deceased) and told her, he intended to beat the old
woman. He should draw blood to prevent her from doing him any
more mischief, being as he long supposed a *Witch*. He went out of
his house; & afterwards returned & drank whiskey; He then went
out again. This testimony was fully corroborated by Dinah, servant
of Sister McIntosh. . . . *Marian* was first examined. She testified
that she knew her husband Plenty had threatened to Whip Rachel,
for having tricked or injured him; being as he believed a Witch. He
quarreled with her in April; & after that Jim, the accused, brought
a Grape Vine to her house; & she understood it was for Plenty to
beat the Old Woman with. The Vine was kept. She had however
persuaded her husband not to whip Rachel. The Witness farther
stated, that the night on which the murder was committed, Shine
came to her house, to borrow a frock. Witness asked what she
wanted with it, but she would not tell. Witness asked, if Jim had
come, & was told he had not come. Witness offered Shine a certain
frock; but she wanted a dark one; & obtained it; & took at the same
time the Grape Vine, that had been left by Jim. After it was
known, that Rachel was killed, Witness was [in] much distress; &
went to Shine to know, what she wanted with the frock. The suspicion now & not before arose in her mind, that it had been used to
disguise Jim; & he had killed Rachel. Shine would not own it; said
the frock was not injured, & wanted to return it to Witness. She
refused to take it, & would not look at it; but insisted to be told, if
the frock had been used by Jim. Shine would not tell her; until last
Monday; When she confessed to her, that the frock had been bor-
rowed for Jim; that he was present when Rachel was killed; but did
not kill her. Witness was asked, how she felt towards the deceased.
She acknowledged that sometimes thoughts of suspicion passed
through her wicked heart; but she did not encourage them; &
[s]ought an opportunity at a certain time to be friendly & live at
peace with her. She thought the deceased had slighted her. *Creassy*
was next examined, who stated, she knew the deceased was accused
of being a Witch. They had often talked together about it, & the
decd. lamented her case. She had tried to console her. They had
talked together the day before her death; & she then declared herself innocent of the Charge of Witch Craft. Witness also testified
that Shine had confessed to her, that Jim had killed Rachel. *Peter*

was last examined. He knew nothing, except what the foregoing witnesses had told him. The Morning after the murder, having fears about Jim, he went to him at the Blacksmith shop, where he worked; & asked him, if he had been over the river, the last night. He paused, then said he did not go over, had started; but forgot something and turned back. Peter was asked, if had lost fellowship, with Marian. He replied, he had. Here the examination of the Witnesses closed. This Report of the Committee was accepted; & they were requested to continue their enquiries, as there were fears, that other members, were in some way concerned in this Melancholy & dreadful affair.

The Church, upon this testimony, believed that there could not be a doubt of the Guilt of Jim, as principal; & his wife Shine, at least as accessory of the crime of Murder. It was considered proper, the Church, on this occasion, should express their disapprobation, in the strongest sense Whereupon it was unanimously agreed, that Jim & his wife be excluded from the Church; It was also considered that Marian, stood Charged with a high degree of guilt in this affair; & as the Church could not tolerate the least participation in this Awful Perpetration of Crime, She was also unanimously excluded & the Pastor was requested, on the next Sabbath to give such admonition & instruction to the black members of the Church as this Melancholy event seemed to require.

Lord's day 6th May [1827]. After Divine Service, the Church were called together, to attend to some cases of disorder amongst the black members. Sam, the property of Mr A. Sparks, had been guilty of disorderly conduct, in violently opposing the Marriage of Old Mingo, an Aged member of this Church, with Peggy. He had been laboured with [by] Scipio; & other members, but with no good effect. He was present & acknowledged, that he had been greatly out of temper & had done wrong: but as he afforded no evidence of repentance, he was laid under the censure of the Church. Some of the above disorder occurred at a funeral sermon preached by Scipio. After which he was invited to Marry Old Mingo, to Peggy the wife of the deceased. These circumstances, seemed to render it necessary, that the subject of our black members assembling for funerals, should be submitted to the Church, &

to have a decision of the whole body on the propriety of Funeral Sermons.

December 2 [*1828*].   There is no record of a regular Church Meeting in this month. On the fourth Lord's day, The Church were called together. . . . In the course of this month, a number of black persons were recommended & brought forward, by the Coloured brethren, who had examined them. They were examined by the Church & ten of the number, received for baptism. . . . During the examination of the black persons, the following question arose, *viz.* "If a person applies to a Church of Christ for admission to the Ordinances; & gives such testimony of faith & repentance, as in Ordinary cases would be thought satisfactory: but it is known, that while in a state of sin, this person had separated from one companion; & was living in the familiar intercourse of Husband & Wife with another; is the Church warranted by the Gospel, to receive such person into fellowship, while both companions are known to be living? This question gave rise to considerable discussion. The Church, being unprepared for a decision, postponed it, for further consideration, untill a future Meeting.

Dec 11 [*1828*].   At a subsequent meeting, appointed to consider the above question, The Church, after much serious deliberation & Prayer, still felt unable to come to a decision; & agreed, on adjournment, to consider the case, when apart; with earnest prayer.

January 2 [*1829*].   The Church met on the Saturday before the first Lord's day; & after a Discourse by the Pastor, formed conference. . . . The subject of intermarriage among the Coloured people, which had been postponed for several Meetings, was again considered; but no distinct conclusion could be formed. Upon Inquiry, it was found, that some of our coloured members had formed what may be termed double Marriages, since the public confession of Religion; such added to the difficulties in the case.

18th [*January 1829*].   After Divine Service, the Church Met, & granted letters of dismission to Jim, Dolly his Wife, & Dinah, the property of Messrs John & Edward Edwards, who had removed to the State of Mississippi. A letter was refused to Dicey, one of their number, had left a husband here, still living, & had taken another husband since her removal. During the inquiry at this meeting, it was ascertained that a number of the coloured members were implicated on the subject of Double Marriages, & some since they had become members of the Church. The following persons are in the state last mentined, viz, *Bristol* & *Betty* his wife now members. *Billy* & *Phillis*. Billy, not a member, when he left his first wife, now living, 20 years ago, & united with Phillis then a member. *Smart*, baptized when a Youth. Upon arriving at manhood took Lilly to Wife, A rude, Wicked girl then, & while she remained his Wife. They separated. She took another husband; & he another Wife, Henrietta, contrary to Stephen's advice, & in violation of the Covenant, which he acknowledges he remembers. Lilly and Henrietta have since been received into the Church. *Molly* & *Peter*. The latter a member when he took Molly to Wife, some twenty years ago, whose husband was then & still is living. *Caesar* (McDonald's) separated from a Wife more than 20 years ago; when a member; & afterwards took to Wife Patty Jackson, a Widow, who is now a member of this Church. *Tabby*, was removed from Virginia, where she had a husband. She United with the Church here, & afterwards took a husband, a wicked man, from whom she has also separated. *Sucky* is charged with having put away one husband, and taken another, since she became a member.

31st [*January 1829*]. Being the Saturday before the first Lord's day in February. The church met. The weather being wet & very inclement but few attended. After some religious exercises, formed Conference. Other brethren having come in, the Church again took up the subject of double Marriages. Some time was spent in its consideration but as yet no proper rule of action could be fixed on. They felt particularly embarrassed in regard to the old members, who had been recieved & held in fellowship by our Fathers in the Church; & it was agreed that the subject be again postponed to another meeting.

After Sermon by the Pastor, he requested the Church to remain together, When he submitted the following resolutions, which after much reflection he thought the only expedient, to relieve the Church of its present embarrasment & settle the question, which has caused so much difficulty & anxiety for the last two months, viz. "It has been found, upon examination, into the state of our coloured members, that some of them had long been living with a second Companion in the familiar intercourse of husband or Wife; after having separated from one or more that were still living & in the same neighborhood. In some of these instances they had a number of Children. The Church feel greatly embarrased, on account of this unhappy state of things & are still not perfectly satisfied as to what they ought to determine in relation to them. However after much Prayerful searching of the Holy Scriptures; & seeking to God for direction: *It is Resolved.* 1st that great deference is due to the memory of the Fathers of the Church; & we cherish such respect for their Opinions & Conduct, that we dare not, without the most express warrant from the Word of God, reverse what they had deliberately done. Therefore since the Church was given to us in this condition; & we lived Years together with the persons above alluded to in Christian Union; We think it now a less evil to retain them in fellowship, than to disown them for a wrong, that probably was not known by the Church at the time of their reception; & not viewed by themselves in a Scriptural point of light, as the most of them are bound servants; & have not been taught to read the Sacred Word. 2nd. But as we know that many of the younger members have been better instructed in the nature & perpetuity of the Marriage obligation; while we would neither reverse the doings of our Venerable Elijahs, nor dictate to posterity; We resolve for ourselves to instruct, reprove, & labour with any, who have knowingly departed from the Gospel rule; & their Covenant engagements & if possible correct the wrong; or exclude them from our connection.

3rd. That Servants, separated by their owners, & removed to too great a distance to visit each other, may be considered as virtually dead to each other; & therefore at liberty to take a second Companion, in the life time of the first; as the act of separation was not their own voluntary choice; but the will of those, who had legal control over them. These resolutions being read & considered were Unanimously adopted. In Conformity with the last resolution, a letter of dismission was granted to Dicey; Which had been refused, Lord's day, 18th of last month.

9 *May* [1829]. There being pleasing indications of a revival at Antioch; & the people manifesting a desire to have the word preached unto them; the Pastor attended on the 9th & the day following the Sabbath. The house being too small for the Congre-

gation, the exercises were under a grove. There was deep & solemn attention given to the Word. At the close of the other exercises exhortation, singing & prayer were continued for some time. There was great concern among the people, & many came forward, desire[in]g special prayer for them. A weekly prayer meeting had been held in this neighborhood for some time. It was not fixed, to be held, every Tuesday Afternoon at Antioch.

3 *July* [1829].   The Committee in the case of Bro. Armstrong made the following report: "That they had an interview with the individual accused. Your Committee brought before him, in plain terms, the reports they had heard; & the Charges that had been alleged; A part of which was admitted, & a part positively denied. He acknowledged, that he did on a certain Lord's day ride to Cheraw; & did transact Ordinary business; which he said he had no other time to do; And while there, did meet with & employ a certain free Woman of Colour, to nurse his infant child; & brought her with him, on the same day, to his house (& was seen on the way by two of the brethren) but denied in the most positive terms having had any illicit connexion with said Woman, as reported & suspected: But owned that he did not lodge in his own house at night & refused to give to your Committee a reason, for so strange & unusual a course of Conduct. They regret the entire failure to obtain relief to their minds, in this interview; & they feel constrained to say, there is too much ground to fear, that Bro Armstrong had lived for a time past, an inconsistent life for a Christian professor. That there is an entire Want of fellowship with the members of the Church there can be no doubt; And from the facts known to Your Committee there is a want of confidence in the Community at large." The Report was accepted.

21 Oct. [1832].   After Service, the Church attended to the case of *Cupid* (Mrs. McCullough's) He was charged with lying; & giving medicine of his own to a sick negro Woman, & visiting the plantation contrary to the Orders of the owners. He confessed the several charges against him and was excluded.

3 *July* [1836].   After Divine Service, *Richmond* (Dr. Smith's) was excluded for Adultery.
Phillis (His wife) placed under censure for intemperate & unbe-

coming language during the examination of her husband's case, & cited to appear before the Church. . . . The black Deacons were directed to a case of variance, between *Phillis* (Now under censure)· *Eliza* & *Nancy* (all of them Dr Smith's), And if necessary to call for the aid of Some of the White members. Hannah (Col. Williams) charged with disorderly conduct by Anson (Sister Wm.s) her husband, was placed under censure, & cited to appear the next Lord's day.

Aug. 7 [*1836*] *Lord's Day.*   After Divine Service by our Pastor, *Lassy* (Bro. Wilson's) appeared before the Church & acknowledged her fault. She had become reconciled to the person [with] whom she had quarrelled. Censure removed.

Sept. 3 [*1836*].   *Bob* (Bro. D. R. W. McIver's) was reported for disorderly conduct in the Village. He had gotten into a quarrel with a negro, & into a serious difficulty with a white man. . . .

Lord's Day 4th Sept. [*1836*].   After Service, attended to discipline with colored members. *Phillis* was present. The Black Deacons asked for aid in settling the difficulty between her, Nancy & Eliza. Brethren Campbell & Wilson were requested to assist them. *Prince* & *Lary* his wife (Bro. A.M. McIver's) were reported for disorderly conduct. *Lary* had been guilty of quarreling & using profane & vulgar language to another woman. She was placed under censure. *Prince* was charged with whipping his Wife, and another woman on the plantation, producing much disturbance, & contrary to his masters' orders. He was absent, tho' directed to attend: Brethren Wilson, Mahony, and A. M. McIver were appointed to examine into his case & require him to appear before the Church on the third Lord's day.

14 Jan [*1837*].   Letters of dismission were granted to Jemima Scott & Clara Burnett free persons of colour to join the Baptist Church, Charlotte No. Car.

3 Feb. [*1838*].   It was resolved that the Gallery be appropriated to the use of the Coloured people; & that the Pastor & Deacons be authorized to make the arrangements necessary for their occupying it.

Sat. April 30 [*1853*]. The Committee on the *Character* of the meetings of our *Colored members* in the Lecture Room was continued. . . . *Nancy* (Miss Julia Hawes) who had been received for baptism, has been forbidden by her mistress to be baptized, and has joined the Methodist Church, & the vote receiving her is hereby rescinded.

Aug. 6 [*1853*]. The *Committee* on the *Character* of the meetings of our *colored members* were not ready to report, & were continued.

Oct. 1st [*1853*]. The *Committee* on the *Character* of the *meetings* of our *Colored members*, also on granting Licenses to preach, made a report which was laid over until our next meeting.

Nov. 6th [*1859*]. 20 Colored persons were baptized.

Sat. Sept. 1 [*1860*]. It was resolved, instead of the usual afternoon services, that *service* will be *held for the Colored* people immediately after the Colored Sunday School exercises.

Saturday, May 12 [*1866*]. After a suspension of our regular Church Meetings for more than four years, the Church met after a sermon by Brother J. O. B. Dargan, and intered on business.

Lord's Day, Nov. 25th [*1867*]. A called meeting was held, at which a *Committee* of *Brethren* of the Colored, appeared on behalf of the Church, who announced that they had *organized* themselves into a Church, having *elected* a *Pastor* & *Deacons* and now ask that this Church sanction their act. Agreed to by the Church. They also ask for *letters* of *dismission* for *all members* of their *Color* who may apply for them.

Index